HMS TH

- Secrets and Scandal

- Aftermath of a Disaster

David Roberts

publication

Further copies of this book are available from:-
Middleview
New Road, GWESPYR
Flintshire. U.K
CH8 9LS
Tel : (44) 01745 886769
e-mail: info@AvidPublications.co.uk
Other publications from Avid / Middleview are detailed
at the rear of this book.

HMS. THETIS - Secrets and Scandal
- *Aftermath of a Disaster*
ISBN 978-0-9521020-0-7

Cover Illustrations:
Front: Flag draped coffins of *Thetis* victims at Maeshyfryd Cemetery,
Holyhead, 1939. The brick lined graves are in the foreground. Courtesy of Mrs.
Marjorie Beattie, daughter of Bill Watterson, Cammell Laird Ship Fitter,
lost on *Thetis.*
The crest of HMS *Thetis*, ironically it is showing the Goddess Thetis
rising from the waves.
Rear: *Thetis* after being raised, a wreck beached at Traeth Bychan, Anglesey.
Copy of Personal minute No.194 from Winston Churchill,
the First Sea Lord in 1939.
Frontispiece: The dedication of the *Thetis* monument and mass grave at
Maeshyfryd Cemetery, Holyhead, 1947. The Slabs of Welsh slate bearing the
names of all those lost can clearly be seen in the foreground.
Courtesy of Mrs. Barbara Haydock, granddaughter of Admiralty Overseer
W.H.Aslett, lost on *Thetis.*

Acknowledgements

I should like to gratefully acknowledge the following persons and organisations without whose kind help, support, advice and assistance this book would never have happened:-

Charles.E.T Warren and James Benson, for their research, in the middle 1950's, to start the ball rolling with '*The Admiralty Regrets*'. The files on *Thetis* were closed for thirty years after the event and they therefore had no access to them. I did, but without their core work to give me a foothold none of the following would have been possible.

Mr.Derek Arnold

Mr. Fred Lawless

The Public Record Office, Kew.

Imperial War Museum - Dept. of Sound Archives

Dr. Timothy Ashplant - Liverpool John Moores University

Commdr. Jeff Tall OBE RN Rt.. Royal Naval Submarine Museum

Mr. Nick Tall, Jeff Tall's son.

Mr. Jeremy Owens - Royal Naval Benevolent Trust

Trinity House

BBC Radio Merseyside

Jane Vidler, Asmita Kapadia - Barclays Bank, London

Mrs. Maureen Miller-Burgess Hill, Sussex

Mr. Patrick Strevens-Cranbrook, Kent

Mrs. Eluned French - Holyhead, Anglesey

Mr. Owen Aled Owen - Pentraeth, Anglesey

Mr. Miles Leadbetter- Clitheroe, Lancashire

Mrs. Shirley Grimsdale - Brighton, Sussex

The Bank of England Archives

Mr. Ray Gritt & Mr. Roger Stentiford of SOCA

(Submarine Old Comrades Association)

Mr. Alan Middleditch-General Accident Insurance Co.

Dr. John Dymond GP and Mrs Christine Dymond, Kew, London

Mr. Bill Evans

Mr. Ian Boumphrey

Mark & Adrian Rickards aka 'The Denim Brothers'

Ms. Sam Fear

Mr. Eric Coates

Mr. Don Hardisty

I should like to extend my particular gratitude to Mrs. Sue Elston who transcibed the many hours of taped interviews integral to this book.

The whole story of the aftermath of the *Thetis* disaster owes much to the relatives of those lost who were left behind. They provided me with their time, valuable documents and photographs. Often these were all that they had left. This is the first time that they have had the opportunity to tell their stories and I am very grateful that they told them to me. They are:-

Allen, Bill
Batten, Roy
Beattie (nee Watterson) Marjorie
Bleakley (nee Crombleholme) Edith
Craven, John
Daly, Cynthia (nee Allen)
Dillon-Shallard, Harry
Gaul (nee Summers) Agnes
Glenn, John
Gore-Brown (nee Glenn) Brenda
Homer, Hanley
Kipling, Robert
Levelle (formerly Summers) May
Moore (nee Robinson) Barbara
Newton (nee Beattie) Jean
Ryan, Paddy
Smithers, Edie
Wells, Peter
Willcox
Woods, Howard
Woods, Ian

One step at a time,
Polarity Hill,
If the bad guys don't get you,
Then the good guys will.

American-Indian singer / songwriter Buffy Saint-Marie:
from her song : 'The Big Ones Get Away'
- *Coincidence and Likely Stories.*

HMS THETIS

- *Secrets and Scandal*

- *Aftermath of a Disaster*

Contents:

For Denise and Luke

Introduction

If you have never heard of His Majesty's Submarine *Thetis* don't buy this book. I may be doing both myself and yourself a disservice by this guidance but it is important.

In order to fully comprehend the enormity of this tragedy you should first read *Thetis - The Admiralty Regrets - the disaster in Liverpool Bay*. Assuming that you **are** aware of the whole sad *Thetis* story, to discover the shocking secrets and scandals in the aftermath of this disaster then **this** book, *Thetis - Secrets and Scandal* is a must for you.

The last year of the last millennium saw the 60th anniversary of the disaster in Liverpool Bay with the loss of 99 men aboard HM Submarine *Thetis*.

I did not lose anyone in the *Thetis* disaster of 1939, nor was I even born. So why me? Why did I travel the length and breath of Britain to talk to relatives of those who died on *Thetis,* talking to witnesses of the event, and trying hard to open the closed doors of secrecy and scandal that the whole event was shrouded in?

I was born and bred in Birkenhead on Merseyside, where the port and docklands were once the biggest and busiest in the whole world. My father was a cranedriver at the Birkenhead shipyard of Cammell Laird for most of his working life, and also served in the Royal Navy as a Stoker during the Second World War. The eldest of six children, I gave my parents some financial concerns by passing the eleven plus examination and attending the local grammar school. I left school six months before my 16th birthday with a swimming certificate, it was for a breadth in the shallow end and I had one foot down! Much much later I was fortunate enough to acquire an academic education at the University of Liverpool and yet later at Liverpool John Moores University.

However back in the late 1960's it was no great surprise when I served my own mechanical engineering apprenticeship in Cammell Laird, thus changing from a boy to a man in a world of working men, steel and ships.

I also grew up hearing stories about the last war which almost exclusively concerned the world that I was a part of. Stories of men, ships and the sea. One such story was technically a peace-time event. In June 1939 His Majesty's

Submarine *Thetis* was lost in Liverpool Bay during her acceptance trials from Cammell Laird, taking 99 men with her. In its day this was the worst submarine disaster in the world and in 1999 it is still the worst submarine disaster in British history.

Only four men escaped from the stricken vessel. Two of them were naval officers, another a naval rating and the fourth a Cammell Laird chargehand fitter. *Thetis* was eventually salved and the bodies removed from her. She was refitted, then renamed and had a war as HMS *Thunderbolt*. Chillingly, *Thunderbolt* was sunk by the enemy with all hands in the Mediterranean Sea exactly four years and one day after she had been lost in Liverpool Bay.

Many of the men lost aboard *Thetis* were Cammell Laird men, ordinary working class tradesmen just doing their jobs.

World wars, not surprisingly, have a habit of eclipsing events such as this; and so it was against this background of war that the *Thetis* disaster was perhaps conveniently forgotten, only remembered in the folk lore of the shipyard and the town of Birkenhead.

I first heard the story from my own father and knew from his telling that it had been 'a bad business' and that, in his words, 'they could have got those poor buggers out'. Any Birkenhead man would confirm this when the subject of *Thetis* came up. There was no great detail there, just an impression that **'they'** had been let down by **'them'**, that the ordinary men on *Thetis* had been sacrificed and that the families left behind had been shoddily treated.

Word was, so the working men of the town had it, that **'they'** could have got **'them'** out of the submarine. That the navy, its officers and the Admiralty itself had wanted the submarine more than they had wanted the men; that there was a war looming and *Thetis* was a brand new and very expensive weapon of war, more important than the men inside it; that the men could have been saved but the submarine itself may have been lost; that 'somebody should have paid' and that the relatives 'only got buttons in compensation'.

The story lay dormant in my own life as a career, studies, marriage and family vied for my attention, time and effort. I had always had 'a soft spot' for Cammell Laird even though I left the yard after the completion of my apprenticeship. But my father saw out his working life there, through the rollercoaster of nationalisation, denationalisation, industrial unrest and threats of closure. I had always watched the fortunes of the yard. This was the place and these were the men that gave me my bedrock engineering training, this was where many of my opinions and values were embedded, this was where I became a man, and this was where I came from. The yard, like many others, eventually closed down in 1993.

With such a background it is a small step to writing about maritime affairs and where better to start than Cammell Laird? My first book on the subject was published in 1991[1], a second in 1993[2], and a commercial one hour film on the 150 year history of the shipyard in 1994[3]. In the same year I began regular broadcasting for BBC Radio Merseyside on maritime affairs, work that is still going on today.

In all of the above work *Thetis* is only briefly mentioned, a dark chapter in an otherwise famous history, a shadow over the yard's great achievements.

Then I found the book. The book about *Thetis*. It was in my local library, in a sorry state, and clearly marked on the frontispiece: -

'PLEASE TAKE CARE OF THIS BOOK, IT IS THE ONLY REMAINING COPY ON WIRRAL AND IS IN GREAT DEMAND'. DONATION

In 1939 the *Thetis* disaster literally stunned the nation. How could such a thing happen? It was made even more tragic by the pictures that flashed around the world showing the stern of the vessel actually sticking out of the water with a flotilla of small boats and powerful navel vessels clustered around her! Why didn't they get the men out?

Now I could know the whole story, and what a story it is. Written in the late 1950's by two former naval officers, *'The Admiralty Regrets'*[4] is the only and thus far definitive work on the specific subject of the loss of HMS *Thetis*. It is a shocking tale of mis-management and a catalogue of errors and delays, resulting in a tragedy that, in my father's words, 'should never have happened'.

The book in some respects was like my own family's involvement with shipbuilding and my own engineering apprenticeship at the shipyard, it formed the foundation for all that has been written here thus far and that which is to come. It goes back to my first and lasting love affair with the maritime history of Cammell Laird and Birkenhead's inextricable link with the shipyard, as well as the obvious history of Merseyside as a great port. Consequently there is a heavy reliance here upon the book as a primary reference and as a jumping off point to other areas of research.

The whole *Thetis* story still has tremendous resonance in popular Merseyside memory and after almost four years of broadcasting stories of the sea to BBC Radio Merseyside listeners, varying from the 20th century sinking of the *Laconia* to the exploits of the 17th century Captain William Kidd, I was so intrigued by the *Thetis* story that I considered it was time to retell the story for two reasons:

1)   A new generation had probably never heard the story

2)   I had not told many stories concerning submarines / submariners and here was such a tale with a highly local content.

I told the story of *Thetis* over a six-week period on BBC Radio Merseyside during September / October 1997 and the effect was spectacular. The station was besieged with telephone calls and demands for the book. It simply wasn't available. The only available copy was the one I had borrowed from the Birkenhead library, and even that had been 'a donation'!

With my publisher's hat on I tracked down the owners of the rights to the work and obtained the rights to reprint the title. '*Thetis - The Admiralty Regrets - the disaster in Liverpool Bay*'[5] was published in October 1997 and was received very well by the general public as well as maritime enthusiasts.

Simultaneous with my efforts, but unknown to me, a local writer, Fred Lawless, had been commissioned by the BBC to write a 75 minute-radio drama about the disaster. '*Close enough to touch*'[6] was broadcast nationally on Radio 4 on Saturday October 10th 1997 and subsequently rebroadcast on BBC Radio Merseyside on Tuesday November 4th 1997. The radio play only heightened interest in the subject, so much so that the whole of that afternoon's phone-in programme, with Radio Merseyside presenter Roger Phillips, was taken up by *Thetis* with Roger, Fred Lawless, Derek Arnold and myself responding to the callers.

Derek Arnold is the son of the only navy rating who survived *Thetis*, Leading Stoker Walter Arnold.
Walter Arnold died in 1974 and it took me a long time to find his son.
Giving a talk on the subject of Cammell Laird one evening to a meeting of a local association, *Thetis* was mentioned as usual and after the slide show a gentleman approached me saying he knew Arnold's son and used to work with him! It turned out that after all my phone calls and enquiring letters Derek Arnold lived some 800 yards from my home! Derek was also kind

enough to write a highly illuminating foreword to the reprinted *Thetis* book, from his own perspective and from his memories of what his father had told him.

The responses from callers to the Radio Merseyside station were widely divergent between angry, sad and disgusted, but at the same time informative and knowledgeable. One common thread ran through them all; bitterness and contempt for the way the whole affair had been handled. Many of these leads were to be followed up and will be referred to later in this book. Such was the volume of calls that the telephone operators could not always keep a record of caller's names and numbers, thus the following comment cannot be substantiated in any referenced manner. Nonetheless I clearly remember one caller in particular. He stayed in my mind and was the man who proved in many ways that times really did seem to have changed. I think he was 'Eddie from Aintree' and his opening gambit was:

'Didn't anyone kick-off about this at the time'?

To readers who may be unfamiliar with the expression, 'kicking-off' is a Merseyside phrase for 'aggressively questioning' a decision or a statement, or to start an argument which would probably lead to violence by 'kicking-off', or simply to hit somebody, thereby 'kicking-off' a fight! Nothing that could be said by the studio 'panel' could placate Eddie, not 'things were different in 1939' nor 'the war came along and *Thetis* was forgotten'. Eddie wanted someone or something to 'kick-off'. He was, as mentioned earlier, 'new' to the whole sorry episode of *Thetis* and he was angry in his own way. In my own non-violent way, I decided to try and get to the bottom of the whole sorry business once and for all, if for no one else, for those like Eddie.

I had my suspicions that the *Thetis* affair was not a clear-cut accident and the echoes of the shipyard folklore were still with me. After reading Warren & Benson's work I became convinced that this was the case; and that there had been clear and conscious decisions made on the basis of class, rank, finance and by government institutions (i.e. the British Admiralty, the Royal Navy and ultimately the British Government itself), which: -

a) contributed to the disaster itself;

b) managed the aftermath of the disaster in such a way as to deprive relatives and families of the victims of any substantial compensation, as well as being incredibly parsimonious, judgmental and hardhearted towards those same relatives, in particular those of 'non-officer class', working men both

- Aftermath of a disaster

naval and civilian lost on *Thetis*;

    c) used the war and the 'officer class' old boy's network to deliberately 'protect their own' and thus hamper any claims for compensation from relatives. (It was not possible to sue the crown until 1953, almost 15 years after the events in Liverpool Bay.)

    This book then is the story of a disaster and its immediate aftermath. It also records the memories of those who were bereaved by the events, how it affected their lives and even followed some of them to the grave.

    There are a number of threads and themes that run through the book. It is in part about my research as a writer, sometime broadcaster and historian, communicating with the public through the medium of radio, sometimes painful interviews with bereaved relatives through audio-tape and video film. It is also about dealing with the Royal Navy and the Admiralty, with the various benevolent societies and insurance companies that handled the *Thetis* disaster Fund, and finding my way into the archives of the Bank of England. It is about wearing different hats for different scenarios; researcher, writer, publisher, broadcaster. And at other times 'just a local man from Birkenhead'.

    It is about trying to prise information from large insurance companies and highly placed trustees of funds, and conversely sometimes attempting to cajole and persuade memories of long ago from those who were often still distressed by what happened to them - working class folk who 'didn't really know any better at the time'. [7]

    I have tried to make sure that future researchers of such matters do not fall foul of the same blind alleys and deliberate 'arm's length' attitudes of some parties which I encountered. In many ways it is also a detective story, how circuitous the route sometimes has to be to get to where you want to go, to get that final confirmation of a name, a date, or an amount of money. How to find your way around the Public Record Office in Kew, London, The Imperial War Museum Archives in London and 'The Old Lady of Threadneedle Street'- The Bank of England, and how fate often takes a hand, in this case in the form of a London based General Practitioner, Dr. John Dymond, and his wife, Christine Dymond, who runs a Bed & Breakfast business for students and researchers, close to the Public Record Office.

    I kept a log of every phone call, almost every listener who rang into the radio station and every letter I sent / received on the subject. This was vital. To those who may be embarking upon any similar quest I cannot overemphasise the value of what I call an 'event log'. It is hard with a subject of such breadth to remember people's names, who said what to whom and when, especially when dealing with government departments, civil servants and Royal Navy PR 'spin doctors'.

A strand of the book is an analytical one in trying to focus on how the disaster had different experiences and repercussions for the different people involved: officers, ratings, civilians and their relatives, throughout their own lives and until death.

Thetis was literally a microcosm of pre-war society. In a floating steel tube some 125 feet long and 15 feet in diameter were packed 103 men. Naval Commanders and Lieutenant Commanders, no fewer than ten of them, down through Petty Officers, Leading Seamen and Leading Stokers to Able Seamen and Stokers. The whole ranking and classification system of the Navy was there.[8] Civilians fell into a number of other categories: Civil Servants, Cammell Laird employees; managers and foremen, six of these; and workmen, Engine Fitters, Electricians, Caulkers and Ship Fitters; employees from other shipyards and machinery manufacturers; a Mersey River Pilot; and finally two employees of a Liverpool catering company, Liverpool City Caterers, on board to supply the 'bean feast'[9] that was part and parcel of the handover of any ship to the Royal Navy.

In the Royal Navy of the 1930's and the immediate war years the distinction between officers and men was particularly polarised. The divisions between fore and aft (for'ard being the home of the crew and aft reserved for officers) are neatly framed by Godfrey Winn in his (1944) *Home from the Sea*.

> I had up until now only caught glimpses and heard faint
> echoes of what life was really like for the lower deck, all the
> lower decks of the world. Nearly always communication
> between us was inevitably constrained by the presence of a
> liaison officer, who, however well meaning, was regarded as a
> spy from the other end of the ship…. after listening to a few
> yarns, he would conduct me aft again. For'ard and aft: only
> those who have sailed, not as passengers but as members of
> the crew, can precisely assess the immense distance from one
> end to the other, even in a small ship like a corvette.[10]

- Aftermath of a disaster

As Winn says ' all the lower decks of the world'. Class distinction was just as prevalent on Civvy Street. The Liverpool of the last year of peace was a disconsolate place.

> The Anglican bishop criticised the appearance of 80,000 unemployed as 'normal'. The unemployed themselves emphasised this when the N.U.W.M (National Union of Unemployed Workers) held a 'lie-down' demonstration in Lime Street. Their protest was a demonstration of modern times, halting traffic for fifteen minutes.[11]

Rank within the Navy paralleled class in society, and many of those left behind after *Thetis* provide testimony to these divisions. The disaster itself shook the nation and provoked an unprecedented wave of national sympathy. The press had a field day when the Admiralty had to survive a great deal of pressure and criticism. Coverage of the event was no less than all engulfing and this book also attempts to show that even this overwhelming publicity was unable to withstand the twin tides of impending war and lack of any interest from the establishment in what was apparently a mere unfortunately timed incident.

There was *'an apparent lack of sufficient concern at the top level in the Navy'*.[12] Yet even this wholesale coverage sometimes got it wrong and provided false hopes for those waiting.

The book also tries to understand and analyse the contemporary mechanisms of political, social and military control as they affected those involved in the *Thetis* disaster before, during and after her fateful sea trials. Legal and political control was vested firmly in the hands of the establishment. Until 1953, as pointed out earlier, it was not possible to sue the Crown; and the Admiralty, as agents of the Crown, were thus untouchable. Social control in this case was exerted through the military i.e. the Royal Navy. Those who survived to tell the tale clearly 'toed the line' or were practically gagged.[13]

Ironically it was the idiosyncratic system of 'dual control' on newly-built naval vessels which also gave rise to some confusion as events unfolded and further 'muddied the legal waters' in the aftermath of the disaster. *Thetis* was not *technically* a Royal Navy ship although she flew the white ensign. The purpose of a sea trial is just that, a trial to acquire formal acceptance of the ship by her buyers, in this case the Admiralty. The dive was to be carried out, according to the contract between Cammell Laird and the Admiralty, 'by naval officers and crew, but the contractors shall work the main and auxiliary machinery'.[14]

The Admiralty and the Royal Navy had such total control of the event itself, that to this day arguments rage about how other parties were prevented from rendering assistance as the Navy had to do things 'their way'.[15] This attitude persisted right through the official enquiry when yet further offers of information and materials were rejected.[16]

The Admiralty and the Royal Navy had total control of information until the worst had happened, and most damning of all, they, as a part of the 'establishment', had total and secret control over the 'official' aftermath in terms of the Official Secrets Act, internal confidential reports, public inquiries and the remit of same. The Admiralty had their thoughts focused elsewhere upon the looming world war and were reluctant to give any prominence to the events in an effort to protect themselves from adverse comment and censure, even going so far as to conceal material evidence from the public gaze.[17]

The control of finances is also considered in the book. After the disaster collections were made in every dance hall, football ground and cinema in the country. I have uncorroborated reports that every serving man in the China fleet at the time donated a days pay to the Disaster Fund. Early donations to the *Thetis* disaster fund (some times referred to as the *Thetis* Relief Fund and yet other times as the *Thetis* Memorial Fund) included those from Martins Bank, Higsons Brewery, Lewis' of Liverpool and the Liverpool Stock Exchange.[18] Reports vary but generally approx. £150,000 is a consensus figure of the amount that was raised for the fund. In 1939 when a tube of toothpaste cost 6d (approx. 2p), a *Daily Express* broadsheet newspaper 1d (approx. 0.4p) and a Kodak 'Brownie' camera was 5s 6d (approx. 27p),[19] such a sum was talking telephone numbers. Who administered it? Who got what? Where did it go?

In some respects it is this control, by appointed establishment worthies, that provides the most striking perspective upon social class and attitudes in the last years of peace between the wars. There is a persistent belief among the majority of those dependants whom I have spoken to that 'the money just got lost' and that 'we certainly could have used some help. But we never got it'![20] Those left behind, especially those of the working classes, were treated

- Aftermath of a disaster

in a manner that is quite literally incredible today.

A final objective of the book is to give a voice to those who have never been heard before; those loved ones left behind to cope with the stresses of living through a world war without husbands, sons, fathers or brothers. The relatives were dispersed over the whole country and have not been easy to find in some cases, but the search will continue for those not traced by the time you read this book. One big advantage however was the concentration in and around Birkenhead of the families of so many Cammell Laird men, who all had a harrowing tale to tell. Their stories and the stories of their loved ones are inserted here and there as the book goes along its way. To those not included here I can only apologise and hope that the book provides you some small comfort.

It must also be said, before what is to come, that it was not my intention to besmirch the reputations or legacies of those involved in the *Thetis* disaster. I have simply tried to get to the truth of the matter. It is time it was told. Those left behind deserve it. If this same truth is uncomfortable so be it. The responsibility for these events cannot be filed away any more.

Individual responsibility may be highlighted but it was the responsibility of those in authority to discover this publicly before my work. They did not, and if any disclosures here do not agree with the 'official' line then the work will have served its purpose.

His Majesty's submarine *Thetis*, outside of the town of Birkenhead, appears to carry a sense of anonymity with only a vague sense of some loss of life 'during the war'. Such is the all-encompassing power of world war that events chronologically close to it involving significant loss of life are claimed by it. *Thetis* apart I cite the appropriately titled *Forgotten Empress*,[21] a book by David Zeni, published in April 1998, as a further example of a chronologically close incident involving significant loss of life. The *Empress of Ireland* was a passenger vessel operated by the Canadian Pacific Railroad Company on a regular crossing between Liverpool and Quebec. On May 29th 1914, just one month before the precursor to world war one, the assassination of Archduke Ferdinand of Austria, the *Empress of Ireland* was involved in a collision in the St. Lawrence River, sinking very quickly. This resulted in more passengers losing their lives than had done so on the *Titanic*. Yet this vessel became 'an unrecognised stepchild in the family of maritime tragedies'.[22] [*Titanic, Empress of Ireland* and *Lusitania* were all lost within three years of each other].

If the *Empress of Ireland* was an 'unrecognised stepchild' then *Thetis* appeared to be born out of wedlock in 1939 and spirited away to hide those responsible from the shame and the stigma of accusing fingers.

As David Zeni attempted to reclaim the *Empress of Ireland* so this book is also an attempt to reclaim *Thetis*. My approach was in some respects not really knowing where it would lead me, one avenue opening up into another three, and making conscious decisions, decisions which I will try to share with the reader, about which route I might follow next, which may or may not bear fruit. It is about a subject and about a search. There are blind alleys, dead ducks and elements of providential intervention.

I have used archival material from the Imperial War Museum, the Royal Naval Submarine Museum at Gosport/Fort Blockhouse - still today the headquarters of RN Submarines, the Public Record Office and the Bank of England. I have garnered a great many of the surviving press reports in addition to transcripts of contemporary radio news broadcasts. I have interviewed or spoken to relatives of the deceased and survivors, some of the very few widows and numerous sons and daughters, brothers and one sister of those lost on *Thetis* as well as interviews with relatives of three of the key personnel involved in the disaster; the sons of Walter Arnold, Roy Glenn and Frederick Woods.

The aim of this book is not to retell the story of Warren & Benson but to try and look at the whole tragic event again and its aftermath in terms of class, power and control. With the benefit of 60 years hindsight, access to public records previously closed for 30 years, good fortune in making personal contacts and my own experiences of shipbuilding, it is an attempt to unravel the strands of the story that led from Liverpool Bay all around the country and the world.

One vital and important aspect of this book may appear to be missing. This pre-war tragedy concerned 103 men in a submarine and those above the surface who were also men.

Women do not, at first sight, play a part in the events. However this would be so far from the truth as to render this book unfair and misogynist.

Whenever I think of this disaster I imagine the women and loved ones shut outside Cammell Laird's gate at the bottom of Green Lane in Birkenhead, waiting for news that nobody was giving them, some of them there all night long. All they knew was that '*Thetis* had failed to surface'. They must surely have suffered as much as the men aboard the submarine.

Many of the interviews in this work are with women left behind, many daughters and two, obviously very rare, *Thetis* widows among them.

As is always the case when men die in such circumstances, it is the women left behind who have to cope, raise a family and live what is left of their own lives,

This whole book is for the men, women and children of *Thetis*. It is also for the rest of us, to make sure it never happens again.

Class: Officers, Men & Civilians

In the introduction to this book, particularly the subject of class and class divisions within a given period of time has been to the fore. What do they mean, 'class' and 'class divisions', and more specifically what did they mean in 1939? Eric Hobsbawm describes Britain as *'the country in which class divisions were... more simplified than elsewhere... most people working on the assumption that there are only two classes which count, namely the 'working class' and the 'middle class'.*[1] The fact that Britain is essentially a two-political-party democracy would tend to support this view; but in the wider aspect there seem to be many more sub-divisions both inter and intra class than this apparently clear divide would have us think.

In an attempt to parallel the class divisions of society and the class divisions of the Royal Navy more than Hobsbawm's two-tier simplification is required, and perhaps a more modern sociological explanation fits the bill. Ralf Dahrendorf's *On Britain*[2] does, I believe, provide the best analogy between the wider social classes and those within the Royal Navy:

> Class in Britain is like a layer cake in which clear distinctions can be drawn between the bottom of the cake, the jam in the middle, and the chocolate on top...there is the ancient line between the estates of 'those who work' and 'those who don't work' or, ... the 'working class' and the 'upper class', not to forget the 'middle class' between them that has done its work and arrived... there are other finer distinctions. These are regional and professional, sometimes denominational, but above all they draw lines between layers... There is a very old, an old, and a more recent upper class; there is an upper middle, a middle middle and a lower middle class; there is a skilled, semi-skilled and an unskilled working class - and this is only the beginning of such distinctions.[3]

The expressions *'class'* and *'class divisions'* have the same highly structured denominations as Dahrendorf's theory within the military, and yet

- Aftermath of a disaster

there are even more multiplicities of meanings particularly within the Royal Navy between the wars. Class in the Royal Navy is a clearly defined system of rank, power and authority. Seamen, telegraphists, cooks and stokers could be leading, first, second, or in the case of stokers even third & fourth class.

The men in the middle (Dahrendorf's jam), the Petty Officers or Warrant Officers were also classified, either Chief Petty officer or just Petty officer. Petty / Warrant Officers were exclusively drawn from 'the ranks' or the 'lower decks', that is the ratings, and would never become 'real' officers; they were N.C.Os, non-commissioned officers. All of these classes apply only to men, ratings, and non-officers. Thus the class divisions between officers and men were further sub-divided and arguably offered a system of tighter regimented control. Such class divisions did not apply to 'real' officers. Each Officer has a title, a clear marking of his place in the pecking order of seniority, Lieutenant, Lieutenant-Commander, Commander and so on. Yet even among the officer class there would come a point at which officers of the same rank need some method of establishing individual status and seniority and this was done on time served. Should two equal rank officers be introduced to each other the first question asked after the formal introductory pleasantries would be 'how much service do you have?'[4], the longer serving man thus establishing his seniority by service time.

Class is also applied to ships themselves, each new breed or type of ship is classified, e.g. Flower class, Tribal class, County class etc. and within these strictures, first of class, second of class and so on until last of class. Each subsequent vessel after first of class usually contained technical refinements that had been discovered by technological progress or in response to what had been found wanting in the earlier vessels. Vessels themselves thus confer more or less class upon those who serve in them, to be chosen to serve upon the first of a new class is 'a feather in the cap'[5] perceived as putting a crew member himself into 'first class' no matter how lowly a rank he may be.

Such a posting would invariably involve what is known as 'working by'. Working by is time spent by Royal Navy personnel who are not at sea working within the yard which is building the vessel and working with the shipbuilders themselves. This would be considered a first class or 'plum' posting offering all the delights of working 'normal' working hours in the days and taking advantage of the pleasures that any shipbuilding town has to offer a man in uniform with money in his pocket outside of working hours. In addition the Navy itself as a branch of the armed forces is classified and has always been so since the middle ages; it was then and is now always referred to as 'the senior service', more important to our island nation and older than the other branches of the military, the Army and the Royal Air Force.

Finally class means social class and is as rife in the British Royal Navy, possibly more so, than any other walk of life. David Mathew's *British Seamen* [6], published in the middle of the Second World War, is an obvious propagandist tract designed to whip up morale for and within the Royal Navy, but despite this it perhaps inadvertently illustrates the social make up of the Royal Navy: -

> There is no calling so rooted in the English mind and
> character as the Royal Navy, which now includes a vast
> mass and cross-section of the manhood of the United
> Kingdom. [7]

The reference to 'Englishness' and manhood are a clear pointer to an attempt to endow 'British Seamen' with the macho and patriotic image required in time of war who are 'called' to the Royal Navy. Almost as an afterthought those Scots, Irish and Welshmen who served in the Royal Navy are almost 'awarded' 'Englishness' by the all encompassing use of 'United Kingdom' at the end of the passage. Above all the social 'cross- section' is confirmed.

This melange of ranking class, class of vessel and social class is evident from many of the testimonies of those who served between the wars and after. One man, Gilbert Adshead on moving from one ship to another highlights the 'Navy way' and the discipline involved...

> The rules and regulations are so very strict, everybody
> knows them, and it's just like moving from one house to
> another... one ship is known as a happy ship; other ships
> are not so very happy depending upon the officers in
> charge.[8]

The Navy has rules for everything and it is clearly the officers who interpret and enforce the rules. Everyone knows the rules and no one shall break them. If the rules are broken then the Navy has a system for this too. The Navy has a curious habit of making the unpalatable palatable by using a similar system to Mathew of *'bestowing an award'* for minor and arguably major misdemeanours.

In my own father's experience, John Ifor Roberts' World War Two Royal Navy records or 'linens' as they are known (they are actually woven from linen) show this remarkable system at work. All the vessels he served upon with dates and rank are shown (he went from stoker 2nd class to stoker 1st class in about one year). After each posting he is signed off with a VG / Very Good. This is in fact a very standard navy signing off comment. However after one posting in December 1944 he received only a 'Good'. In Naval terms a 'Good' is the navy equivalent of 'The Black Spot' in Stevenson's *Treasure Island* which Blind Pew handed over to Billy Bones and is a sign that something has gone very wrong. Thus even problems with personnel are glossed over in Navy parlance with a 'good' comment that is the converse, that is, bad. In another section of the linens and within weeks of this date, John Ifor Roberts is shown as forfeiting seven days time, probably in the cells. The column headings for this time are headed Number of days Awarded and Number of days Served.[9] Old salts tell me that this probably means that he either returned to his ship drunk or has 'smacked' an officer/petty officer, or both. Once again the unpalatable is made palatable by *'awarding'* what is effectively a short prison sentence. It is the Navy way.

In an effort to understand life below decks during this period (although a submarine of this era only had one deck the divisions still apply), the work of Alan Ereira, Anthony Carew, Barry Duncan and the American maritime historian Leonard Gutteridge prove invaluable.

Ereira has produced a narrative history of the last major mutiny in the British Navy, Invergordon [10] in 1931 and it contains a wealth of testimony from those who were there including several junior officers. Carew's *Lower Deck of the Royal Navy 1900-1939 - Invergordon in Perspective* [11] specifically targets members of the lower deck. Both of these historians used their work as a contribution to the oral history archive recordings kept at the Imperial War Museum, London.

Barry Duncan is a Shetlander with a clear political agenda. Only in the Navy long enough to get his discharge papers Duncan was a full-time worker with the International Labour Defence, an ultra left-wing association for workers rights and the defence of 'the politically accused', when the alleged 'ringleaders' of the mutiny at Invergordon, Len Wincott and Fred Copeman, were recruited to that organisation. Barry Duncan's *Invergordon 31 - How the men of the RN struck and won* [12] was perhaps not surprisingly self-published; Duncan is a self-confessed communist and moreover was not even at Invergordon, nonetheless his 55 page booklet is valuable for its clarity about what he calls 'a victorious incident in the class war'.[13]

Finally the historian Leonard Guttridge, Cardiff born but long resident in the United States, provides a casebook of mutinies from the *Bounty* to the USS *Constellation* in 1972.[14] This naturally includes Invergordon. Whilst telling a riveting tale of mutinous deeds Guttridge also provides the researcher with an intriguing insight into the legal minefield that accords the term Mutiny to any naval 'unrest'. He further analyses the Royal Navy's reluctance to apply such a label as mutiny to 'unrest', The Navy's preferred terms are, 'unrest', 'disturbance' or 'incident', anything but mutiny, as the term mutiny infers a loss of control and a failure on the part of those who should be in control i.e. officers. Thus Guttridge highlights and underlines the Navy's inherent desire once again to make the unpalatable palatable, to do things 'the Navy way', a way that makes things look considerably less eventful than they really are and a way which will protect the 'face' and 'standing' of the status quo.

Whilst *Thetis* was not by any stretch of the imagination a mutiny there were elements of 'unrest' and 'dissatisfaction' with the conduct of the Navy and the Admiralty before, during and after the disaster; and in this attempt to look at the *Thetis* disaster and its aftermath from a new perspective contemporary research is at a premium. What the above books do provide for the modern day historian are glimpses of naval society and naval philosophy during the inter war period.

Similarly the transcripts of interviews with lower deck personnel of the time are few and far between. My own previous oral history books about working people, and this particular work in recording the testimonies about and around the *Thetis* disaster, has taught me that there is nothing quite like what Paul Thompson calls 'the voice of the past'. [15] Those who were there and were a part of events, a part of the whole that is being researched, carry a more authoritative weight than any others do.

The Department of Sound Recordings at the Imperial War Museum in Lambeth, London, holds more than any other sound archive for this subject area. In total sixty-five interviews are held here. Carew's work was recorded between 1974-1976 and Ereira's in 1980. Each archive has one catalogue[16]. These list the names of the men interviewed, their rank, dates of service, dates of birth, duration of tape and number of reels as well as a one or two line snippet of areas discussed, e.g. Family background, enlistment, training, actions, being torpedoed etc. The 'snippets' are no more than that, but they will provide a general target area to start at, as listening and rewinding are a lengthy process. Even so I spent many days doing just that.

The details of which tapes were chosen are appended in the bibliography but my main criteria for selection were:

1)If at all possible submariners. This proved a negligible number in that no submarines were involved at Invergordon.

2)Men who had served during the inter-war years who could perhaps provide an insight into a peacetime Royal Navy and a wartime Royal Navy.

The recordings paint a picture of terrible conditions and very definite divisions between officers, petty officers and men. Michael George Clarkson, Joiner 1st class is not untypical: -

> ...the term for officers was a pig. The Dartmouth boys, even though they tolerated the Warrant Officers, they more or less looked down on them. It seemed they despised them. They were officers and they (W.O.s) were not. They were in a funny position you see the Warrant Officer was. He couldn't be too friendly with the lower deck. But they were in a position to make life very uncomfortable for a lower deck man... when one officer left the ship it was the usual thing...Commander so and so is leaving the ship... and if he was popular of course the ship's company got up and cheered him as he got away... if not there would be plenty there that just spit over the side as he went away.[17]

Allan Arthur Clarke, a signalman, graphically describes the conditions aboard ship for the lower decks: -

> ... It (the heating and ventilation) was pretty terrible on the whole ship, especially at sea when we were battened down... after you'd been at sea for 24 hours you could cut it with a knife... and the toilets were just a great big tank and the seats were on top of the tank, you just sat there, next to each other in a long line...every so often

they would pull a plug, turn a handle or something and it just went into the sea.[18]

Clearly the conditions on the Lower deck would not be endured by Officers, who had their own separate toilet arrangements totally segregated from the men. What is of interest is the **'they'** who 'pull a plug, turn a handle or something'. Who are **'they'**? If an assumption is made that 'they' are either Petty/Warrant Officers, a reasonable assumption in that all lower deck personnel refer to Officers as 'they', then it appears that the lower deck man even had the responsibility for the disposal of his own waste taken from him!

The first speaker mentions 'the Dartmouth Boys'. Dartmouth is the site of the Royal Naval College, the Royal Navy's Eton, where only career Officers are accepted and, with ominous echoes of Orwell's *Animal Farm,* as Clarkson's evidence confirms, is a breeder of 'pigs', who despised anyone who was not of their class. This man's testimony is of particular relevance to *Thetis* as his service ended just two years before the events in Liverpool Bay in 1939. I have found no evidence to support the view that anything had changed by 1939.

War at Sea - 1939 - 1945 by Edward Smithies and Colin John Bruce[19] is a work of oral history that both enlightens and disappoints. However it does provide a very slight glimpse into the perceptions of the Navy, its men and its officers in the last years of the inter war peace. A contributor identified simply as Mr. Roberts recalls:

> It (the Navy) was a national institution. It was the Senior Service - legendary, beloved of everyone. Jolly Jack was tremendously popular ashore, and there were sailors to be seen everywhere. There were superstitions like touching a sailor's collar for luck. Abroad, honorary membership of clubs to officers of visiting ships was automatic. 'Gangway for a Naval Officer' was very much the order of the day.'[20]

Roberts' testimony reveals the vein of subservience, of knowing ones place, which runs through the Navy of 1939 as well as society in general. 'Gangway for a Naval Officer' bestows a kind of authority upon these men; almost a 'make way for the king' or 'all rise for Judge Bloggs'. The only parallel

- Aftermath of a disaster

I can think of in my own time would be one of giving up a seat on a bus/train for a female. It was expected and the norm for a young man in the 1960's. However, there is a very real sense of 'positioning' taking place here; a time when Naval officers knew best, when those who had reached positions of authority within the 'Senior Service' were believed to be invulnerable both in terms of intelligence and leadership.

However, George Clarkson says otherwise, having no truck with the 'born to lead' attitudes toward officers of any kind:

'The Master at Arms is known as 'the Jaunty' and the regulating Master at Arms were known as the 'crushers' or 'the body snatchers'.... They were the police [in the Navy]... they were recruited from people who were no good at any other job'.[21]

Or, after Invergordon was all over:

'After it was over we had a Captain of Marines, Captain Sparrow, he was a great fellow for running revues and all that sort of thing, a very clever man. But that was his only qualifications. Otherwise he was a bit dim'.[22]

Len Wincott, not surprisingly, goes even further and in the style of a 'people's champion' equates the 'ability to talk' as a weapon in the class war:

'The Admiralty had people who could hypnotise sailors when they speak...being articulate is the principle attribute of a confidence trickster'.[23]

Invergordon and the events of 1931 happened less than eight years before the tragedy in Liverpool Bay, but I believe it is reasonable to suppose that the Royal Navy had not changed overmuch in the interim. Invergordon was 'a dispute' over proposed pay cuts in the navy, cuts that were disproportionately large between the Officers and those from the lower decks. As stated earlier there is significant research on the incidents in Cromarty Firth and this can throw some light upon the months just before world war two in two ways:

1) The attitudes of those involved
2) The nature of the Navy's handling of the events

Those involved at Invergordon tell a story of unity, a fight against unfairness and class distinction, yet even members of the lower deck, like this particular participant, baulked against using the M word, Mutiny.

Charles Edward Wild was a 2nd class stoker:-

Interviewer: Was it a strike or a mutiny?

Wild: No it was a strike, we downed tools, we wouldn't do anything.[24]

Others, like Bill Woods a Boy Seaman, speaking of the events themselves and of Wincott himself, offer two perspectives upon Invergordon:

> There is always a character like that [Wincott] on any ship...but they did a lot of spouting but that was it... but he stirred it up and got it going and stayed with it... and he knew what would happen to him when it was all over.'[25] THEN: Interviewer: How did it end?
> Woods: They promised they would go back to their home depots...[26]

Wincott is thus seen in the same image as he sees the Admiralty Svengalis, a sea-lawyer and a fast talker, one who could and did incite others by his oratory; but most fascinating of all is the continued refusal to say the M-word. The 'incident', its inception, life and aftermath, is constantly referred to by both the interviewer and Wood as 'it'. Equally the previous speaker, Wild, insists that 'it' was 'a strike'.

Invergordon was serious enough for Britain to abandon the gold standard. The directors of the Bank of England wrote to the Chancellor and the Prime Minister with a formal request to cease exchanging sterling for gold:

> If the gold standard goes, the trade of the world would be plunged into a welter of depreciating currencies... revolution would follow in Central Europe, leading possibly to the triumph of international communism.[27]

Yet even here the M-word was avoided. Guttridge, perhaps the leading historian on Mutiny, chronicles the Invergordon events as described by the government, the Admiralty and the press; the word Mutiny appears but once in the conservative *Morning Post*.[28] 'Internal crisis', 'disturbance', 'unrest', a 'temporary suspension of exercises', were all thrown into the reporting of the situation by all concerned; apart from the *Morning Post* the most serious description given by officials was 'a refusal to obey orders'.[29] This was the Navy way of handling matters that appeared to 'threaten officership' [30] or threaten the iron grip of the class system on both the Admiralty and its agents aboard naval vessels. Guttridge perhaps encapsulates the whole ethos of both society and the Royal Navy in those inter war years in its [the Navy's] reluctance to use the M-word:

> Few reasons have arisen to explain this odd verbal abhorrence, the closest to the truth probably that which suggests a fundamental and primarily political fear of eroding popular faith in the state's control over its fighting forces. Another reason could be the conviction, perhaps justified, among those in ultimate command that their lofty vantage point better equips them for balanced assessment. Whatever the explanation, the fact is that while mutiny has its place in formal service rules and regulations, the lexicon of top naval bureaucracy appears at times to have omitted it altogether.[31]

Clearly those in authority in the Navy and the Admiralty in 1939 maintained their lofty vantage point by doing things their way, the Navy way.

In the summer of 1939 HMS *Thetis* was in trouble, as were the 103 men aboard her; but all offers of help were declined with disdain whilst the navy insisted on their own retrieval methods, their own retrieval personnel and even their own agenda when all aboard *Thetis* were lost. The Navy response system that did **not** move swiftly into action like a well oiled machine was known as 'Operation Subsmash'. Thus was the way in 1939; a time of 'Gangway for a Naval Officer'.

A final comment upon the year of 1939 might I feel be useful here. 1939 is a very strange year for historians / researchers. It is ironic that an almost 'lost' incident like *Thetis* should take place in an almost 'lost' year. Most textbooks either start at 1939 as the beginning of World War Two or end in 1939 as the end of the peaceful inter-war years. 1939 seems to fall into a 'gap' in history where everyone was simply waiting for the impending war to happen and thus the year was a time of anticipation rather than participation, a time of looking ahead instead of looking around. 1939 was also an unusual year and a year of huge changes for the armed forces in general. In May, the British Parliament adopted a Conscription Act, which maintained a system of military training in peacetime, but on September 3rd after the 'official' outbreak of war the new law conscripted all males between the ages of 18 and 41. Thus every naval man jack aboard *Thetis* in the summer of 1939 was a volunteer into the Royal Navy.

This was not the case for the others lost on *Thetis*. Some were civil servants including a Mersey Pilot, and some were employed by an outside contractor to provide a catering service; but the vast majority of non-naval personnel aboard that day were employees of Cammell Laird and Co. Ltd. - Shipbuilders and Engineers of Birkenhead : civilians. The Warren & Benson book, exhaustive in its time, was written by two former RN personnel and concentrates on the intricacies of the tragedy itself and the naval involvement. The role of the civilian shipyard workers and their ultimate fate is almost an aside.

Work was hard to come by in most parts of Britain in 1939 but those with the required shipbuilding skills in shipbuilding areas could participate in the rapid expansion of the Royal Navy in the last years of peace and at the same time feed their families. Archive material from the now defunct Cammell Laird shipyard is almost non-existent but I can draw upon my own experience of the yard and the arrangements for sea trials.

Sea trials were a bonus. To be chosen to go on trials was an accolade. You were, for a few days, a 'real' mariner, who knew something about and could contribute to the operation of a new vessel. Trials were also lucrative; payment was made for 24 hours out of 24 and trial crews would be fed and watered. It was also an opportunity to escape the confines of the yard for something a little different.

The sea trials of His Majesty's submarine *Thetis* were to be as different as it was possible to be.

In the summer of 1939 the month of June brought hot weather…. Marjorie Beattie (nee Watterson) was a little girl of eleven years old. Her home in Wallasey was 'almost on top of the prom'.[32]

She was an only child and was skipping with her friends in the road on that hot morning as she and her mother, as arranged beforehand with her father, waved goodbye to her father, Cammell Laird ships fitter Bill Watterson[33] who could not possibly see them from inside the steel tube of *Thetis* as she passed their family home on her port side while leaving the River Mersey, though maybe he gave his little wave as arranged. They would never see him alive again.

Sixty years later Majorie tells her own story.

- Aftermath of a disaster

Bill Watterson with his daughter.   Marjorie Beattie (nee Watterson) as a young girl

Marjorie Watterson DOB 17.9.1927.Daughter of Ship's Fitter Bill Watterson

I lost my dad on the *Thetis* in 1939, and he was one of them who probably went quite willingly, I think. But it was a terribly sad incident… I did go down to the prom where we lived, and waved him off that morning and I of course I was only 11 years old, and I waved him off as a little girl waving a skipping rope, hoping to see the submarine come back in the evening. I did go down with my mother and my auntie, about 7 o'clock in the evening, thinking it would come back, and those days there were loads of people on the prom. It was so busy and there were seats all along the prom, it was a beautiful evening. We waited and waited and of course it didn't come back.

Eventually I got sent back home to bed, and mother and auntie stayed till it was absolutely pitch black. And of course, they came home, and went to bed, like everyone does and it wasn't until the morning that she heard this dreadful news. Of course, she more or less collapsed in a heap. But fortunately my auntie and her husband were staying with us at the time and were a great comfort to her. She had two very good sisters. But it was a dreadful thing wasn't it, really.

I really should have been at school that week, but I was getting over scarlet fever. So I was going to school the following Monday, but I was off during that Thursday or Friday morning. That is why I was on the prom with my skipping rope. I did go on Monday, and mother didn't say anything to me at all but I could see that she was terribly upset. But when I saw the teachers at school, of course, they knew all about it and they were surprised that I didn't know. But they sent me home again, and said you take another week off, you've been poorly...and they sent this beautiful bouquet of flowers for my mother.

Of course, when I did go home, mother had to explain exactly that my dad wasn't coming back and there had been this terrible disaster. Fortunately my aunt and uncle were there with her. She wasn't entirely alone...but it was a terrible time for her...and within two or three days part of her hair turned absolutely white with shock. That did happen within the first week. Of course, things have go on, and I did go to school and everyone was very kind. But it was a dreadful time for my mother.

The War came in September, and I was evacuated first to Neston, I was there for about a year. Anyway there were no blitzes or anything in Wallasey at that time so like a lot of the kids, I came home. And I was home when we had the awful May blitz, in Wallasey. Anyway it was very very bad and people thought mum and I should be away and we did go to stay with some friends in Wales, just outside Holywell...of course I went to school there, and was very happy. It was a good thing for my mum to get right out of Wallasey. So we were there for over a year, but I do remember mum had to come home when they did get the *Thetis* up, about November, and she did have to go to Wales to identify my dad's body. My uncle went with her, and of course there was a man found with a couple of scars where my dad had his, appendix and something else.

Being so long in the water, it must have been a dreadful experience, but she just looked at his face, and said yes that is my husband... of course it was dreadful for her. But within two or three days they found another man with more or less the same scars. And they did write and say would she come and identify this second man... my uncle said there was no way could she go through that again, no woman should be put through that dreadful experience, so she didn't go. However, this second man, did turn out to be my father. And they only knew by things in his pockets, and his own cigarette lighter

- Aftermath of a disaster

with his initials on…also his boiler suit had the laundry mark, and it is a thing that sticks in my mind very much the mark was Z38. In a way it was a great relief for mum to know that she had really found her husband and he was buried in the little cemetery in Wales with 39 or 40 others.

They had the funeral, the full naval funeral. I didn't go to that because by then I was only 11 or so still. They didn't want children there anyway. But I believe the coffins were all very high up by the photographs I've seen and lead lined, also the sections of the grave were brick lined to accommodate these heavy coffins. They were all covered with union jacks and it was done very nicely. But it was a terrible tragedy to happen in peacetime.

Mum's Workman's Compensation was about £300… something like that, at that time, and very little help, and a £1.0s.0d. for me until I was 16…from Laird's I think. And of course, those days, I don't know why, but money was never discussed, especially with kids…I never felt hard up in any way, I had a supportive family, I mean I personally didn't go short of clothes or toys or anything.   But I do remember, just before my dad did go, I was pestering him for a pair of ball-bearing roller skates. He said you'll get them for your birthday, if you are good. Well, of course, that was one present I didn't get. When I was 13 mum did buy me skates, but these little things stay in your mind. You know, as a child.

There was a lot of widows who were very short of money, including my own mother, but I was an only child and probably not too bad. It was a struggle for my mum.

Occasionally we were behind with money for the rates, as it was then, and it was always my uncle, or close family friends who would lend her £5 or whatever…which she managed to pay back.

The only holiday she had was by this titled Lady that rang Laird's in 1939 and she was a Mrs. Dorothy Mack and she had been a Lady in her own right previously, and her husband had been a commander of the Cutty Sark. She wrote to either Mr. Johnson or whoever was the head of Laird's at the time, offering the widows a holiday…that if anybody would like to come and stay with her, they would have a change of air, good food, and a really nice time, and she'd make them as welcome as she could. Of course, a lot of women didn't want to go, and mum thought about it, and I think the family persuaded her to go.

She went with two other ladies, widows of engineers or something from

Laird's... I think, I'm not terribly sure, but I think one was a Mrs. Scarth...whether Mrs. Craven went, I don't know but those names were mentioned to me at the time. I think they had a fortnight's holiday and they had a wonderful time, and this lady made them most welcome...it was in Norfolk, at her shooting lodge. This lady had homes in London as well. But she gave the three of them a really happy time and took them to meet her personal friends. They also went to the Sandringham Estate belonging to the Queen...they had a picnic on the Queen's private beach, and when they came away, each lady got a small present, from Mrs. Mack as a memento of the holiday. My mother chose a small oak tray and I still have it on my tea trolley. So that was 1939, she died in 1977.

By that time, Wallasey had been blitzed and they brought firemen in from Durham, they were Geordies. And with us having quite a big house, and my mum couldn't possibly pay the mortgage, it was quite an expensive house at the time, but she took these firemen in...well I think it was a case of having to at first... there were 4 of them...and she had meals to prepare and worked very hard. But looking back it was a good thing for her. Eventually they went back and we had Polish refugees. It was a Doctor, his wife and little boy, they stayed about 2½ years. They were very friendly, and we met their friends. In a way it was good therapy for my mum.

We stayed in the same house, and I of course, grew up and married the fella over the road, Ralph, my husband, and of course with having a big house, we were able to have upstairs, it was a 10-roomed house, we had 5 rooms as a flat. Mother lived downstairs, and it was a very good help Ralph being in the building trade. He maintained the house as much as he could, and we helped financially, of course, which was a big relief to my mum. I think she was very very happy till she died.

There must be many other children of the victims, even locally. Perhaps we could get together sometime and talk all about it.

Authors note: *Sadly Majorie's last words on the subject will never be fulfilled as she passed away just a few short weeks before the publication of this book.*

- Aftermath of a disaster

The *Thetis* Disaster

Bill Watterson was one of the 99 who perished that summer's day in 1939. *Thetis* was to be lost because of a half-inch plug of black bitumastic paint that blocked the tell-tale mechanism on the inner door of No 5 forward torpedo tube.

Torpedo tubes, by definition, would be regularly opened to the sea and thus needed some protection against corrosion. This was achieved by the application of bitumastic paint followed by an enamelling process. The tell-tale mechanism was a small-bore cock attached to the inner torpedo tube door which, when opened, would reveal the presence or otherwise of water within the torpedo tube. For reasons which will be considered in detail later in this book a decision was made to open the inner torpedo tube door itself whilst the vessel was in Liverpool Bay. What was not known to those on *Thetis* was that the outer torpedo tube door on No 5 tube was also open. The sea came into the submarine with terrible force and those aboard sought refuge behind a watertight bulkhead between the torpedo space and the next compartment of the submarine. The fastenings to secure this door became entangled with their own housings preventing it from shutting properly, so the sea came even further into the boat before the watertight door to the **next** compartment could be secured. *Thetis* was dragged down into a position from which she was unable to right herself.

Thetis had left the River Mersey on June 1st 1939 preceded by a tug of the Liverpool Screw Towing and Lighterage Company *Grebecock*. *Grebecock*'s function was as a standby and escort vessel. She had a crew of seven and also carried the official Royal Navy Liaison Officer, Lt. R.E Coltart and a Navy Telegraphist V.J.Crosby. *Grebecock* went ahead because of her inferior speed and *Thetis*' Captain Lt. Commander Guy Bolus agreed to accommodate the speed of the tug to arrive at the dive site in good time.

The Mersey Pilot, Norman Willcox, was a third generation Mersey Pilot and at just 25 years old was the first of his family to pilot a submarine, so at the end of his pilot's responsibilities, as *Thetis* passed the Mersey Bar lightship, he decided to stay aboard the submarine to 'enjoy' a new experience. He was to be the first but not the last to invite themselves to a disaster.

At the dive site, some 38 miles out of Liverpool and approximately 15 miles off the North Wales coast north of the Great Ormes Head at Llandudno, Captain Bolus was on the bridge and passed the word through the boat that those wanting to disembark should do so. This was quite usual and normally those with no involvement with the technical side of sea trials would leave. There were no takers for Bolus' offer and he duly informed *Grebecock* by megaphone that this was the case.

The conning tower was cleared and *Thetis* prepared to dive. Orders were given to flood the various tanks around the vessel to achieve negative buoyancy, in other words to make the submarine dive below the surface.

In a submarine the basic idea is that water is admitted in a controlled mechanical process to various compartments and tanks around the hull until such time as the submarine achieves the depth required; more water equals more weight equals more depth. The reverse of these actions, less water less weight, less depth, in other words to surface, is achieved by blowing the water out of the various tanks by means of compressed air carried in pressurised steel bottles within the submarine.

But *Thetis* refused to dive. She was clearly 'light' at the forward end. Light is a nautical expression that means just that; *Thetis* was not heavy enough at the forward end of the vessel to take her down.

Astonishingly this was not the first time that *Thetis* had seemed reluctant to get wet all over. Nor was it the first time that she would manifest technical and mechanical problems with her new equipment. One month earlier on April 30th 1939, *Thetis* had her first set of sea trials in the Clyde estuary but before she even got to the Clyde a steering fault had produced a state of 'reverse thinking' for those aboard the vessel. Somehow the mechanisms for turning the rudder Port and Starboard had been connected in reverse so that an action designed to turn the ship to Port resulted in her going to Starboard and vice versa! This foul-up was *'The cause of some merriment amongst the crew, however the incident did not pass unnoticed by the more sober thinking persons on board'* [1] ... how had such a thing been missed by the army of Naval overseers whose function it was to monitor and police both quality of workmanship and the reliability of machinery systems?

To add to the problems with the steering gear, when *Thetis* was to undergo her first dive on this her initial sea trials, the forward hydroplanes jammed in the diving position. (Hydroplanes are a sort of short wing fitted either side of the vessel's forward hull at the forward end. They would act in

- Aftermath of a disaster

conjunction with the movement and speed of the submarine to force the nose of the vessel up or down; in much the same way as a human swimmer uses their hands to propel themselves up or down in the water). This was all very well for diving but *Thetis* would need the hydroplanes in the opposite position to get back to the surface once more. The upshot was that the diving trials for *Thetis* were cancelled for the moment. Subsequently the Admiralty approved a new diving trial at a later date: in Liverpool Bay.

Some explanation should perhaps be given of exactly what Naval overseers do. From my own time in shipbuilding and in particular on submarines (I spent two years working on nuclear-armed Polaris and nuclear-powered non-Polaris submarines in the late 1960's) I feel fairly qualified to provide some perspective upon these gentlemen. They were not liked.

The overseer was the one who was going to come and check your work and possibly find something wrong with it. That was his job, and shipbuilders are no different from any other workers and usually resent anyone checking their work for reasons of pride as well as for reasons of variety. Nobody likes being told that their work is not up to scratch and nobody likes having to repeat work until it **is** up to scratch; shipbuilders are no different and so the overseer would not be a popular man. Vital too is the fact that, unlike my time in the shipyard of the 1960's, shipbuilders in 1939 would be paid on piecework, that is, the more you did the more you got paid for. Nonetheless such was the job of the overseer, they were not there to win popularity contests but ensure that the job was acceptable.

Often during the Polaris building programme tolerances would be given for acceptable pressures/dimensions/degrees of noise/degrees of straightness etc. and equally often the results of an inspection of same might be around or upon the borderline of such tolerances. It would then be a case of whether the overseer would 'let it go'. Some did, some did not. I have no reason to believe that the role of and attitude of naval overseers and their systems of acceptance or otherwise had changed much in the 30 years between *Thetis* and Polaris. If anything, an argument could be made that the overseers would be run off their feet during the accelerated warship building programme of 1939 and thus potentially more prone to either missing checks and tests or 'letting go' other instances of 'borderline' test results. Certainly from the evidence so far of reversed steering gear and jammed hydroplanes things had been missed by somebody somewhere along the line. Before the defensive howls of protest about 'no shoddy workmanship' from shipbuilders nationwide hits this writer's ears remember that I was there. I know what went on.

However to balance the argument, it should also be pointed out the Admiralty/Naval specifications and tolerances are sometimes considerably in excess of what qualified shipbuilders, through many years of experience, believe are both safe and adequate. The naval 'belt, braces and if required the kitchen sink' approach to testing and acceptance procedures would often be at variance with the experienced shipbuilder and so a case could often be made to either 'let it go' or to dilute the naval specification through a so called 'change order', an official procedure whereby overseers, Admiralty representatives and shipyard personnel would agree to modify the specifications / requirements. It was not a new philosophy toward the building of ships...they had to learn to build as well as build to learn. Such a system of 'learning as things progressed' was definitely at work in the nuclear submarine programme of the 1960's and it was also recorded of the 1960's Birkenhead shipbuilder that there was a need to *indoctrinate the workforce'* amongst whom *'quality control was not an inherent feeling'.*[2]

If this was the case in the 1960's is it then a reasonable assumption to conclude that this same lack of inherent feeling for quality control was any better in the late 1930's? Unemployment was still high after the depression and there would certainly have been no love lost between management and workforce in any shipyard of the period. This did not just apply to the workforce directly controlled by the shipbuilding yard itself. Overseers too could be considered as a part of the workforce.

In the rush to war and the accelerated shipbuilding programme of the late 1930's Cammell Laird were, in some respects, building the 1939 equivalent of Polaris. The 'T' class vessels were the latest submarines the Royal Navy had; they were at the cutting edge of submarine technology and for Cammell Laird, *Thetis* was the first of her class. Therefore the overseers involved would be dealing with new innovations, equipment and procedures that they may or may not have encountered previously and so perhaps a case could be made that they should have been extra vigilant.

One of the overseers engaged by the Admiralty on the *Thetis* project was a Mr. Edward Grundy, and in the months after the disaster, during the official Tribunal Enquiry into the loss of *Thetis*, a sharp dispute arose between Mr. Grundy and the Cammell Laird chargehand painter Mr. W.G. Taylor.[3] The

- Aftermath of a disaster

actual date and time that Mr. Grundy had inspected the final enamelling of No 5 tube were disputed between these two men. The latest possible date was May 17th 1939. Nonetheless, whoever was correct, the damage had been done in time for the overseer to see it. He hadn't, and thus the inspection of the enamelling process of No 5 torpedo tube *'never took place in any effective form'*.[4]

One man who had the role of overseeing the overseers on *Thetis* was RN Commissioned Engineer R.D. (Roy) Glenn. Glenn had a reputation on *Thetis* of being a pushy character; he 'had a way of putting an inflection in his voice that could quickly get a man's back up'.[5] He was constantly 'driving' the shipyard foremen and the Admiralty overseers as though *Thetis* was 'his' boat.[6]

One thing that has happened time and again during this research has been coincidence and arguably fortuitous events, in fact quite the opposite of the lack of providential intervention that attended the events of June 1939. As a result of the republished version of *'The Admiralty Regrets'*, contacts were made, stories were told and retold and quite amazing things happened.

One such was a telephone call from Keith Roy Glenn, the grandson of Roy Glenn, who was lost on *Thetis* but was to play his part in the whole sorry episode that unfolded in Liverpool Bay. Keith Glenn enquired about obtaining a copy of the book and casually mentioned that his father John, (Roy Glenn's son), was alive, living in the United States and would be visiting the UK in March 1998. A short time later Keith called and asked if his father could meet me in Liverpool. The meeting was duly arranged and also present was Derek Arnold, the son of the survivor Walter Arnold.

The meeting and subsequent interview was recorded. This was a unique event in my view and I believe the first time that relatives of a survivor and victim have been recorded together.

The fathers of these two men knew each other and had worked in close proximity to each other during the building of *Thetis*. They were both aboard that day in 1939. Destiny however was to have a path for each of them that could not be more devastatingly different.

Derek Arnold meets John Glenn

- Aftermath of a disaster

Walter Arnold.   Derek Arnold

Derek Arnold, DOB 22.6.1938.

Son of Ldg. Stoker Walter Arnold, survived *Thetis*.

I was only one year old when it happened. He was very lucky to get out. Because the whole thing happened up here a lot of people think he was a Scouser but he was actually from the South, he came from Hampshire with a Hampshire accent. Later on, when I was a teenager, sometimes it would upset me when I would bring girls home to the house, and they used to fall in love with his accent, because he was a really nice guy and he had a lovely silky accent, but he was not exactly introverted, he was like an engine with a big fly wheel that took a while to get him going, but once you got him going he could open up. But he didn't often do so.

He wasn't a quiet guy, but if you knew him you'd think that he was... he wasn't ambitious at all which was a shame really, because when he came out of the Royal Navy he just took a fairly menial job as a rigger at Levers. And he had the potential really to advance himself. He had 22 years in an engine room so there was very little you could teach my father about engineering. If he'd have been of the ilk he could have gone to University as a late starter and taken a degree, but he was of the generation that thought University is not for the likes of us it is for the gentry, the upper crust, which I suppose in those days it was, but the barriers were starting to be broken down. On reflection it was a source of great disappointment to me that he never actually made more of himself than he did. But he was quite happy and contented in the sort of life that he led. He wasn't exactly introvert but he was not extrovert. He was not very demonstrative. And I suppose he was a product of the times...a sailor man, jolly jack tar and all that.

He married a local girl from Tranmere. He met my mother two years previously when he was working by Cammell Lairds on a submarine called the *Sealion* an 'S' class submarine. He met my mother at a dance that had been arranged for the matelots. They started going out and he asked my mother to marry him after a short period of time... and she agreed.

That must have been 1936, because the Spanish Civil War broke out and Britain sent a major naval force to the Mediterranean to protect their interests. So the *Sealion* did hurried sea trials and sailed straight out to the Med. He was gone for 2 years. But in those days when people promised to marry they stood by it. And she waited for him for two years and of course when he came back from that jaunt, they got married, and eventually I came along.

There are 7 years between my sister and I, and the war put paid to anything in between. When he returned from Spain he was lucky in a sense I suppose to be asked or ordered to stand by the *Thetis* which when you consider he was still a newlywed although he'd been married for a couple of years, standing by the *Thetis* in Cammell Lairds, it was a plum job for him. So of course he was made up with that. He worked by for the best part of a year. Then he went out on trials, and you know the rest.

After the event, he was treated quite badly...if I can give you a comparison between him and Frank Shaw the Cammell Lairds man, he escaped with Frank Shaw and the circumstances of that were by the time they had made their escape, Oram and Woods had already gone up... you've to imagine that they had been down there for about 24 hours, all afternoon and all night, and this was the next morning. So the air in there was getting a little bit hard to breathe, because there were twice as many people on there as would normally be aboard. Also it was an effort to move because they were at an angle of 45 degrees...just walking from A to B was something of an effort. Going for'ard again was an effort to stop yourself from plummeting. So whatever happened it was hard going and the breathing got heavy so therefore conditions were pretty bad.

After Oram and Woods had escaped, the rest realised that they weren't going to make it if they went out at this rate, because they had to get people ready, put them in the chamber, fill the chamber up with water, escape, close the hatch from inside, drain down, open up and two more had to go in. A lengthy process at the best of times but when you are intoxicated with CO_2 poisoning - very very lengthy. So they decided to try getting four men out...that failed and the men drowned.

Now there was never really any good explanation as to why these people drowned, but according to my father what happened was this - it is a frightening thing when you are in water, you are in a chamber, you are very very closed in especially with four crammed into a space meant for one. The water is creeping up, oxygen is not good to breathe, it is very sickly... you feel uncomfortable in every sense of the word. Father thought that what had happened is they tried to open the hatch before the chamber was filled. The weight of the sea-water on top would keep it down, it was necessary to wait for the water to equalise before you could open it...there was no way it could be opened against several tons of water.

It was believed that they had panicked at that point...there is a little sort of port hole in the side of the escape chamber, and when the hatch opens you would normally see a shaft of light, if you are escaping in daylight which they were... no shaft of light was seen, so they figured that something was wrong here...they drained down, dragged them out, and three were dead and one guy was close to death and before he expired he said the hatch had indeed jammed.

Well that posed a dilemma...what to do? The Captain of the ship, Bolus, said to my father, who was actually working the escape chamber, 'Would you like to have a try, Arnold?' So my dad figured, well, I'm going to die, possibly, down here, I'd sooner die trying to escape than just waiting for it to come. By this time some of the older shipyard men were starting to look a little bit the worse for wear, so he figured the end can't be far away...so I'm going to have a go, and if I'm killed getting out, then so be it...it will be quick and over. Bolus said, 'Take somebody with you.'

He looked around the space that they were in and about the fittest guy there, was Frank Shaw...if you see photographs of Frank at the time, he was rather portly, really... and he said to Frank Shaw 'do you fancy having a go'? Shaw agreed, but was not familiar with the equipment...Father said 'I'll do everything, you do nothing, just do exactly as I say'. They kitted up, went in the chamber and started flooding up. Frank Shaw asked 'shall we put the mask on now'? Father said 'no', knowing that they had to fill right up...at the very last minute father said 'OK put your mask on now'. I don't know how the Davis Apparatus worked in detail...but I think you had to whistle when going up, so that the pressure in your lungs was decreasing. Something to do with equalising of pressure inside and outside of your body. It was also necessary to undo a little valve strapped to your side on the way up... Frank Shaw was instructed to undo this little valve... as the chamber filled right up father operated the mechanism to successfully open the hatch.

The breathing oxygen was so sweet it made dad actually vomit into the mask...he was actually breathing vomit...he was semi-drowning if you like... he pushed Shaw out first but noticed that the all important valve was still closed, so as Shaw went up my dad just held his foot, opened the valve for him, and let him go... he shot up like a cork. Then he had to get out himself.

A submarine has a jumping wire that runs from the conning tower down to the bow and stern (they don't have them now). It has several different uses... to carry the radio aerial and also if the submarine went under a net, it would easily lift the net away from the sub...on the way up he snagged his foot on the wire for a second and it held him, but he kicked free and he went to the top.

Several small boats were waiting to rescue them... I don't know where Frank Shaw went but my dad was taken aboard HMS *Brazen* which was a destroyer. He stayed on deck for a short period of time, and the Brazen shoved off for Portsmouth. At Portsmouth, he was hospitalised, examined, and finally ordered by the Admiralty not to say anything as he was under the Official Secrets Act, and couldn't disclose anything without permission. The Press couldn't interview him, and even if they had, he was duty bound not to say anything.

Frank Shaw, on the other hand, did quite well out of the *Thetis* disaster. He received £2000 from the Daily Express for telling his story... in 1939, £2000 was a lot of money when you consider that the average weekly wage for a tradesman was about £5.00...well 2000 quid was a tidy sum. He was also promoted to foreman, which was a prestigious position in those days...he was also provided with a house by Cammell Lairds as a form of compensation for his trauma... in a time when not many people owned their houses... Frank didn't do too badly out of it.

On the other hand, my father, when he eventually got down to Fort Blockhouse, the submarine base, at Gosport, Portsmouth, he went to the

- Aftermath of a disaster

Paymaster for his wages...then he was asked for his pay book?'
My father replied 'Well, it's at the bottom of Liverpool Bay.' The Paymaster said 'Well I'm sorry, but I can't pay you unless you produce your pay book.'

Father said 'I can't, I'm a survivor from a sunken ship.' So the Paymaster said 'We'll have to apply for a new one for you.'

It took six months before it came through...for six months, my father received not a penny piece from the State, or the Navy or anybody else. Now can you imagine that, even in this day and age, and with a one year old baby, he confided to me much later, 'That's when you know who your friends are...we relied on relatives to keep the family fed and watered.'

The shipyards were booming because it was clear that there was a War coming and shipyard production was quite high especially in Naval ships. The shipbuilding fraternity in those days had been used to moving around following the work round, and when things picked up they just stopped where they were. My father was friendly with a boiler maker, at Cammell Lairds...Fred Verdis, and he was a real Geordie lad. I couldn't understand half of what he said as his accent was that thick...but he was a good friend to dad who made it his business to keep my father in his ale. He'd call round to the house and say 'Come on for a pint Mac'.

Father was always called 'Mac' because on one of his first submarines on exercises in Tobermory Bay...they'd go out in the submarine where a destroyer would chase round trying to find them and they'd do exercises trying to shoot the torpedo at the destroyer and between them they got the experience. He was up in Tobermory Bay for quite a long time, during which he had many runs ashore...which prompted his being deemed an honorary Scotsman by his shipmates.

After *Thetis* he went in the submarine *Spearfish*... but he found he was getting claustrophobia. It was too tense for him...In todays parlance it would be trauma. He was suffering from trauma...remember too that he had to identify the bodies when they were removed from *Thetis* in the September...that had a profound effect on him, which would have driven him round the bend, had not the Second World War broken out, and the sight of people who had been shot up, killed or maimed, became commonplace.

He served in every theatre of war so when the War broke out I didn't really see him all that much. He was with the Pacific Fleet toward the end of the War on the King George V which was the flagship of the British Pacific

Fleet, and did not return home until 1947...he was out of my life for a long long time, so I really didn't get to know him until I was somewhere in the region of around 11 years old. I took an interest in his wartime exploits and used to ask him things but he was very reluctant to talk about it, but once I got him going he used to talk about how he felt, and how the Navy treated him...never paid him, and things like that.

One of his main criticisms of the *Thetis* disaster was that there had been nobody who could actually say... look, sink or swim, I'll take charge of this, and this is what we are going to do. And that was the top and bottom of it all. Unfortunately, there was nobody there to say, let's bite the bullet, and we'll do this and I'll stand by the decision. Oram had been in submarines, but he wasn't a submariner at the time. He had been in submarines in his early Naval career and now found himself thrust in charge of the submarine flotilla that was being formed by this new T class of submarine. He was in charge of the building programme and was more sailing a desk...when he escaped from the *Thetis*, he wasn't even in uniform he was in civvies.

Father was given an injection aboard *Brazen*...and he was out for the count...actually, there was no need for him to go to hospital, he wasn't injured, he'd gone through a fairly traumatic experience, but by today's standards people do far worse things in the name of leisure and sport, he was just salted away so he couldn't open his mouth to anyone...he was actually told don't say anything, don't meet the Press. The Press were not allowed to interview him. And of course they got all the stories from Frank Shaw who was the only available person who had a first hand knowledge...Oram and Woods would be bound by the same code of secrecy as dad.

Of course with both Woods and Oram being officers, they stood by the code of conduct that the Navy officer class was a closed shop anyway, and my father being a mere stoker, was not bound by that, and would probably have been pumped full of rum by some reporter, would probably have spilt the beans, that is why they had to salt him away...afterwards he told me about when it took several days to get those bodies out and as they brought them out they had to be identified, that is what he was doing back there. And before they went on board, they took the people who had the job of getting the bodies out to the local boozer and got them absolutely pie-eyed so that it wouldn't be too horrendous to them. ...If you sit in the bath a bit too long, the ends of your fingers go wrinkly, just imagine if you were immersed from

1st June 'til sometime in September, what you'd be like? My father said the bodies were that bloated because the inside decomposes and forms gas which builds up and eventually they burst or decompose but when he got them out these bodies were not like human forms at all they were just things.

My father had a folder with all the identifying marks of all the people as far as he knew...relatives volunteeered information such as... he's got a ring with a snakes head on it...a tattoo of a skull on his forearm...they were laid out somewhere in Holyhead where he had to peruse the remains for these items and marks.

He finished his working life out at Levers...he never received any kind of compensation...nothing. ...that's a sore point actually... he was never recognised.

Some years after the war there was a submarine named *Artemis* ...she was tied up at *HMS Dolphin* with most of the crew ashore, they normally do that when they tie up and there was a skeleton crew left on board. Because they were taking on fuel and water, it was sinking lower and lower in the water until the water lapped over the hatches. Still tied to the side,down she went, sinking at her moorings. The crew that were left on board acted quite courageously, I suppose, in that they shut all the hatches, and they affected an escape...divers went down, pumped air in, blew all the water out, brought her up, no big deal. But the man who was in charge of that ship, received some sort of quite high gallantry medal...some may take the view that a court-martial would have been more appropriate.

My father escaped from a submarine in quite trying circumstances and indeed brought somebody else out, who had no idea how to operate the equipment, and didn't get any compensation, medals, or certificates for gallantry. Nothing at all.... that to me seems quite unfair.

He was more or less due to finish his span of service coinciding with the beginning of the Second World War, so he had to stay on to see the War out. They just extended his service, so it wasn't hostilities only it was an extension of his service. At the end of the War, they said you are due for discharge now but if you stay on another couple of years it will bring you up to 22 years which will give you a higher rate of Naval pension and that is what he chose to do.

There was another occasion actually which really highlighted not so much the bureaucracy of the Navy but the subtle class system if you like.

Shortly afterwards there was a memorial service and Captain Oram was there. I think it was in London, not Holyhead, somewhere or other, but it was on shore. There was a meal and some form of ceremony and all the participants were invited up to the top table. So there was Captain Oram and his wife, and there were several high ranking Naval Officers, and their wives. My mother and father had been invited but because he was only a rating mother would not be afforded a place at the top table with Admirals' wives...father declined.

That continued for some time after really because he told me about an event on a ship long long afterwards when there was a notice put up on the ship to say that there is a certain function at which would be Officers and their Ladies, Petty Officers and their wives, and sailors and their women! The sailors went absolutely mad...as you can imagine.

But they did recognise not so much my father but the Arnold family name. In 1990 before the end of the Cold War when there was still a face to face with the Warsaw Pact Countries, when the submarines tied up at Fort Blockhouse the sailors didn't live on board, they lived in accommodation ashore, and what they decided to do, they built a number of accommodation blocks and in Naval tradition need to give them names. What are we going to name them after. So they said let's name them after submariners of note. Gus Britton, was the curator of the Submarine Museum at Gosport at the time... I don't know how he got involved, however he suggested to the great and the good that they call it Arnold block...the family gave up three sons and I think it was three sons-in-law to the submarine service...what greater service can any family do than give up its sons like that? So they were persuaded and the last accommodation block became the Arnold block.

I think if father had had more acumen he could have made more of himself than he did, but he was of that persona that when he came out of the Navy, he got himself a job which paid him a certain amount of money on a Friday night and he was content with that.

He got what he was due from the Navy, nothing more nothing less.

- Aftermath of a disaster

Stoker Walter Arnold and the man he saved from *Thetis*, Cammell Laird's
Frank Shaw, on their way to the Tribunal hearings in London.

Comm Engr. Roy Glenn   John Glenn.

John Glenn DOB 21.09.1927. Son of Commissioned Engineer
Roy Demetrius Glenn

I became aware on 1st June 1939. Mother came in and looked at the newspaper and there were drawings that Captain Oram had brought up. That's your father's writing. He's your father. That's before we actually had the telegram. The telegram came through – Mrs. Glenn the Admiralty regrets that your husband ....aboard HMS *Thetis*, and has failed to return to port or something like that. Then she of course got on to her brother, my uncle. He drove up to Birkenhead over night. She was outside Cammell Laird's yard waiting for news like everybody else. We were left with my grandmother...Yes we were in Leamington Spa at the time... me, my brother and my sister. And of course when we went to school, we were pointed out. It was throughout the country. The whole country was aware of what was going on up here. So at the school we were, how should I say, looked after, and people would say Oh dear, dear and all that sort of thing.

  We weren't allowed to go to father's funeral...children were not allowed to go there. I would have loved to have gone but we weren't allowed to. I don't know how mother managed....We did a lot of midnight flits, out of furnished houses...without paying the rent...she had to survive...but the

Admiralty did pay for the education. We had pretty good schools. We went to good schools. The Admiralty I understand did pay for the fee paying schools. Public Schools. We were looked after on that aspect of it.

Mother never married, because she would have lost the Navy pension. Which I think was probably enough. But of course the War came along and everything went haywire then. Had it been during the War I think things would have been different. I'm not sure but probably would have been different...I can't remember how much it was... Brenda, my sister may have the details. She'll probably have some bank drafts or something like that.

In the old days if you were on leave you couldn't wear your uniform, you had to wear civvies. And if you were a matelot you really wouldn't walk on the pavement, you had to get off the pavement to let an Officer through. 'I suppose you could say we were middle class... those were the days when rank and class strata was very very...

I remember father on one occasion he was away in the China Station and another when he was up here in Birkenhead. I can only really remember one occasion that we had any diligent contact really. He was always away doing something or other. But when he died, we had a sheaf of letters from throughout the world where he had been...people who were engineers of the fleet and stuff like that. But he did cause quite a bit of...and I think it shows itself at the beginning of the book...that he was not a man to, how can I say...wouldn't suffer fools. He had the same thing as I have...unfortunately, I've inherited...I can upset some people very easily without meaning to...I think that is in the book...but he had a standard...that wouldn't necessarily make him a very popular man ...he wasn't.... He was a stickler for things to be right. He was an engineer, a very good one too. But he had this about him that he made enemies very easily without really wanting to...he would put people's backs up.

The Fund I think was very small. They were always trying to get more out of it but couldn't, it seemed to be blocked half way down the line somewhere. The money was there but you couldn't get it out. They were giving excuses like the money has been transferred to another fund, King George Fund for Sailors. But you never heard any more about it. It just died....she got very little... I think she had a monthly cheque but it wasn't very much... she tried to get details from Winston Churchill, from the King, she wrote to all sorts of people trying to get information.

But nobody would do anything about it.

She never got involved with any court cases because she was a Navy wife. It was hushed up so badly…The Admiralty really didn't want to know it happened.

You had to be careful not to upset the Navy in those days. You start doing things like that and they'll say your pension is going to stop if you carry on. Things like that could happen in those days.

This thing was always there as we got older…we were never satisfied and we wanted to meet Stoker Arnold more than anything else… but I think I did meet his father once. I can't really remember, but I think I met him at the memorial service. He was there at Holyhead. I think mother introduced us… My brother and my sister were there, I was a teenager then. In 1947. My brother put the flowers on the memorial. Dad is there in Anglesey. When my mother died my sister in Australia said well the Admiralty is going to pay for her funeral. They didn't though. They should have done.

I'm disgusted at the treatment they received. I really am. The more I look into it, the more I've heard, even today I'm disgusted they could have been subjected to this sort of thing. I am disgusted really. And if you bring it to light, it will make a wonderful revelation of what can happen. And how many times has this happened since then on like the Aberfan Disaster. The *Herald of Free Enterprise*, things like that, have been covered up.

I suppose I could point the finger at Lieutenant Woods. But I point the finger more to the Admiralty Salvage Team and all the red tape they went through before they brought any help and the Salvage Team. They could have saved it had they injected air, oxygen in there and weren't so concerned about saving the boat, and more concerned about saving the men inside that is my contention.

I've no bitterness now…Proud… very proud of my father….but no bitterness now.

I'd like to see what you are doing made public… I'd like to see all these things coming out into print and I think the papers will do it. They are talking now about having a pardon for all the soldiers in the First World War that were fined for cowardice, giving them a pardon. Well let's expose a little bit of this going on now, and let us see what they say about this. We aren't asking for pardons or anything like that, but we are asking for a little respect for all those widows who didn't get anything after it happened. I think the world

- Aftermath of a disaster

should be told what really happened to the people who were left behind...because the world doesn't know...they don't know these things. There was a lot of hurt after that, not only for those who died, that was bad, very bad, but it was those who were left behind, they went through hell. They must have done.

Derek Arnold: I've worked under Admiralty Overseers and they are very demanding people. Because they are spending the taxpayers money basically and it has to be spent correctly. Your father was the engineer on the ship for the navy, effectively overseeing the overseers. He was the man who would ensure everything worked correctly and as you are aware and have said, he was a very demanding guy. That goes with the job. But being like that you don't make very many friends. Now one of the things that interested me re-reading the book, was that he was a pain in the neck.

John: I can believe that.

Derek: People got to the point where they wouldn't tell him what was ready for inspection because they didn't want arguments with him. Their bonus depended on this and if he said he wasn't happy with it they'd have to rework it. So they didn't tell them things. Having told him what was finished, what hadn't been checked and things like that, I feel your father might possibly have been in a position where he could have said I'm not happy with the indicator system on these torpedo tubes. Let's run through it again.

John: I think he did do that. Actually, what happened, he wrote reports. These reports actually showed up on that, and that is why the Admiralty sealed his digs off when things went wrong...they took everything...these reports where going through to the Admiralty.

He was in digs in Birkenhead and as soon as it happened, or the disaster went on, the Navy took their Navy Police in there and sealed his digs. Took everything out. Took all his paperwork and everything. Everything was ripped out of drawers... my mother told me that...she was up here in Birkenhead. She wasn't allowed in to his digs. Because he'd written down all his reports of what was going on. He said to his father, this submarine is sabotaged. On many occasions there were instances where work was shoddy or was wrong or something was definitely done to avoid the submarine being launched. He reckoned that it was sabotage.

I guess in retrospect we shouldn't blame Woods...he shouldn't have been allowed to do that job, really...but he did do something he shouldn't have done.

He was exonerated by the official public enquiry into the loss of the *Thetis* for the same reason Oswald was accused of shooting President Kennedy… It just didn't happen like that I'm sure it didn't happen… He was exonerated because he was Navy. That was it.

Derek: And an Officer.

John: And an Officer…They wanted to put it under the mat and get on with the War. That was it. They wanted to get the submarine up, refurbished, and sent out to War. It was an embarrassment to the Admiralty.

*   *   *   *   *

John Glenn, now in his early seventies, was very much aware that his father was a 'difficult' man; however more thought provoking still was Glenn's own opinion of his father and even himself:

> He did cause quite a bit of… and I think that comes
> through strongly in the book…how can I say…he
> didn't suffer fools…he had the same thing as I
> have…I can upset people very easily without meaning
> to…he was a stickler…he would put people's back
> up.[7]

John Glenn was certainly a 'chip off the old block' and as the interview progressed it began to become clear to me why his father might have attracted such dislike. On the other hand Derek Arnold is a quieter man, much as he describes his father, who sadly I never met. Derek is also a very big and well-built man like his father, a build which served Walter Arnold well in his escape from *Thetis*. Derek has a significant collection of ephemera on *Thetis*, (cuttings, photographs etc.), and is in possession of perhaps the most ironic and unique 'souvenir' in the world. When Walter Arnold was involved in the identification of the bodies of his shipmates he 'liberated' the brass numberplate with the number '5' on it from the fateful torpedo tube. This is mounted on a polished piece of wood and is now in the possession of Derek Arnold.

Roy Glenn knew stoker Walter Arnold. They had after all been working together for the whole 'T' Class building programme. According to Walter Arnold's son, his father had told him that 'although he and Glenn worked together, the 'master and servant' attitude prevailed… it was Glenn's job to find fault... so he wasn't the popular man on the boat'.[8] In fact Glenn and his function was so disliked by both Admiralty representatives and Cammell Laird men that they even resorted to waiting for him to go home before conducting some of the requisite tests.

Incredibly Glenn too had been the victim of the Navy's obsession with class and rank. He was a commissioned Warrant officer, a senior rating from the lower deck. He had one stripe on his arm and immediately beneath this a coloured band to denote his trade. As a 'tradesman' he was in a halfway house or no mans land between Officers and men. Although accorded Officer status he was never invited to the daily luncheon given by Cammell Laird management for his 'brother' officers and this 'rankled very sorely with him'.[9] Once again we have a prime example of the divisive nature of the 'Navy way', excluding a man purely because of his background in the 'trade' of engineer. Glenn's son tried to put this in perspective in his own father's case;

> I suppose you could say we were middle class… but those
> were the days when class structure and rank were very
> very... (unfinished sentence)[10]

In what proved to be a vein running through the whole aftermath of the *Thetis* affair, the subject of what happened afterwards, when Glenn's mother had to get along on her own with three children is worthy of note here, in Glenn's response to the question 'How did your mother manage'? ;
After a very long pause...

> 'I don't know…but we did a lot of moonlight flits…without paying
> the rent… she had to survive.'[11]

So it was against this whole backdrop of division, the 'Navy way', and the pressures of war that *Thetis* found herself flooded in two of her forward compartments and without the ability to resurface. Like *Titanic* a quarter of a century earlier, she could survive with some of her hull flooded but should that be exceeded she was powerless. *Thetis* could survive with one compartment flooded but not two. The only help she could expect would have to come from the surface and the only people who were up there were on the tug *Grebecock*, Navy men and tug personnel. None of the observers had liked the look of the dive yet nobody did anything about their doubts until 16.45pm, almost three hours after *Thetis* had made her 'unnatural' dive, Coltart on board the tug sent a simple message to Gosport, which he described as 'not wanting to cause alarm'; it read: 'what was the duration of *Thetis'* dive?' The message was not marked urgent.

For a multiplicity of technical reasons and atmospheric conditions the radio telephone equipment of the day failed to get even this bland message to Gosport Post Office, until 17.38pm. *Thetis* had been down for almost 4 hours.

*   *   *   *   *

HMS Dolphin at Gosport, Hampshire, on the south coast of Britain, was then and was still in 1998, the home of Fort Blockhouse, the submarine Headquarters for the British Navy. Incredible as it may seem the duty telegraph boy at the Gosport Post Office was busy when the telegram arrived. He was fixing a puncture on his bicycle! The telegram was not marked urgent and so nobody rushed him! Puncture repaired he cycled down the long road to the Navy's HQ on that lovely summer day and delivered his small orange envelope with its devastatingly simple contents. The telegram eventually arrived at its destination at 18.15pm. *Thetis* had been down for more than four and a half hours.[12]

Those in Fort Blockhouse were already aware that *Thetis* had not maintained the regular contact that she had said she would before diving; but a 'wait and see' policy, if such a stance could be described as 'policy', was adopted. Upon receipt of the apparently innocuous telegram a navy response was eventually initiated; 'Operation Subsmash'.

The sobriquet of 'Operation Subsmash' is of course manna from heaven for the writer of a thriller or an author of tales of military heroism and daring. It conjures up images of rapidity, slick action and perhaps most of all **a plan**, a system of men, equipment and experience that is triggered into activity like a well-oiled machine... everyone knowing exactly what to do and how to get it done quickly. Perhaps those self-same writers would use expressions like 'swung into action' or 'the full might of Operation Subsmash and all its expertise was now primed and ready to sprint to the aid of the stricken submarine'.

In reality what actually happened is that Operation Subsmash lumbered into action in the same way as a drunken man strikes out at an adversary: directionless and ill-judged. The lack of urgency that started with a humble telegraph boy and his punctured bicycle pervaded the whole of the following 48 hours. Operation Subsmash was a total failure. Operation Subsmash was a Navy operation conducted 'the Navy way'.

Warren and Benson detail the litany of 'mishaps' that contributed to the failure of Operation Subsmash and the ultimate loss of *Thetis* in their work. In brief, surface vessels, aircraft, submarines and some specialist vessels were all alerted to the distress of *Thetis*. The destroyer Brazen, steaming south through the Irish Sea received a signal to 'proceed to position ... establish contact with *Thetis*'... Brazen's skipper had never heard of *Thetis* so checked his Navy Lists.... She wasn't listed... *Thetis* had not officially been commissioned into the Navy... So a junior rating signalman and former submariner piped up with 'I think *Thetis* is a new submarine Sir'... The Navy and the Admiralty had not told an ignorant skipper what *Thetis* was, but a young rating with his ear to the ground knew her! [13]

Captain I.A.P. MacIntyre, Chief of Staff to Flag Officer Submarines, was second in command at Blockhouse; the Rear Admiral was ill. MacIntyre eventually left Blockhouse to take command of Operation Subsmash in Liverpool Bay itself. He left the south coast of Britain aboard the duty destroyer *Winchelsea* a veteran vessel with no turn of speed at her disposal. McIntyre left at 22.00 and arrived in Liverpool Bay the following afternoon. Why not use the train or even a plane to get to the scene? This was though the 'Navy way' of using the 'duty' destroyer, the one that is on hand for just such a purpose, according to the regulations; this is how to do it by the book. *Winchelsea* is the duty or nominated vessel, it would be a brave stand-in for the Rear Admiral who would choose not to play it 'the Navy way'.[14]

The specialist diving vessel HMS *Tedworth* was based on the Clyde. Her crew were ashore playing football. On receipt of the 'Subsmash' signal they returned to their vessel which then proceeded **NORTH** up the Clyde some 70 miles to fill her almost empty coal holds for the voyage south to Liverpool Bay; there she had to wait for almost four hours for civilian staff to undertake the bunkering operation. *Tedworth* was perhaps the most crucial of any of the vessels that would be required that day and she too was delayed to such an extent as to make her role in Liverpool Bay when she eventually did arrive one concerned more with salvage than with life-saving. Why was such a speciality vessel allowed to sit at her berth not ready for a seagoing voyage? Probably because a ship full of coal has to be paid for and a stationary ship full of coal would be expensive in the Navy's eyes.[15]

These were the systems and these were the methods of Operation Subsmash, the Navy was in charge and the Navy would do things ' the Navy way'. Regardless of whatever or whoever offered assistance or ideas of any kind it was a Navy operation. Responsibility would later be apportioned in a way that seemed to look around for any excuse or combination of circumstances that appeared to take the spotlight away from those who had been coordinating 'Operation Subsmash', the Admiralty, the Navy, and officers of the Navy.

The whole tragic situation was made doubly frustrating by the common knowledge throughout the country of the successful American submarine rescue just one week before *Thetis*.

The USS *Squalus* had sunk in 240 feet of water and the 33 officers and men left alive after the initial incident were rescued by a new American emergency rescue system. A rescue pod with its own pressure hull was lowered from the surface to mate with an escape hatch on the submarine, thus providing those aboard the sunken vessel with a safe haven for their ascent to safety.

In the *Daily Express* of June 6th 1939, just three days after all hope for those on *Thetis* had been abandoned, the Prime Minister, Neville Chamberlain, was reported as saying to the House of Commons apropos *Thetis*: 'it is evident that the accident occurred while the vessel was submerged…while adjusting the trim AFTER diving, the rear door of [one of] these tubes had been opened for reasons that cannot be fully explained'.

Even taking into account the comparative sketchy knowledge of the situation on *Thetis* during the diving trial, three days later Chamberlain was clearly very wrong considering that the vessel had flooded AFTER diving, compounding this error by going on to publicly announce that the open torpedo tube could not be explained.

In other words 99 men had been lost and nobody knew why. Not only did this fail to deliver any confidence in 'the establishment' and in particular the Royal Navy, but on the very same page of the same newspaper adjacent to this report stands a report headlined:

'Squalus will be raised in a month'.

Experts from the U.S Navy said today that the submarine Squalus, which sank on May 23rd, and from which 33 men were saved, will probably be raised to the surface
within a month. The progress made is regarded as highly …satisfactory. The submarine lies in 240 feet of water.[16]

Within ten days of the *Squalus* rescue *Thetis* was in trouble in Liverpool Bay. She was in water shallower than her own length and was actually sticking out of the water by some twenty feet yet 99 men were lost.

Could more have been done? The list of 'if onlys' is constantly being added to as time goes on. There were many offers of help in the investigation that followed the loss, none of them acted upon and as far as is known, these documents have never seen the light of day since 1939.

Patrick Strevens contacted the BBC after hearing the radio play about the disaster, and I made contact with him. His father William was the Captain of the THV (Trinity House Vessel) *Beacon* based at Holyhead, Anglesey, in 1939.

Patrick states:-

> If only the Royal Navy had called in the services of Trinity House right at the outset. Just a few miles away at Holyhead was the nearest Trinity House depot and the THV Beacon equipped with heavy lifting gear required daily to lift heavy buoys, towing capacity - the tenders had to tow light ships to their stations - and Oxy-acetylene cutting gear to cut through metal. In addition Trinity House had links with diving companies and a knowledge of servicing divers while they carried explosives down to wrecks that were a danger to shipping. All of these abilities would have combined to give assistance at very short notice...I was a week short of my eleventh birthday and I remember my father regretting that nothing was done to request his assistance. He felt quite helpless as the tragedy unfolded....remember that in 1939 there was no instant exposure to television and it was probably only in the newspaper **the day after the Navy released the news** that my father knew of it. Although the Beacon would have been unable to haul the *Thetis* to the surface my father's contention was that at the very least he could have kept the stern as high as possible while the tide rose over it and cut a hole at the next low tide... A year later my father resigned his post. He was a conscientious objector and when a cannon

was to be installed on the Beacon, for which he would have to give the order to fire, he left the service he had been a member of since 1920.

The possible involvement of Trinity House was never even mentioned during the Tribunal of Enquiry, despite the fact that one of those sitting on the tribunal bench to assist and act as Assessors was Captain Archibald Hamilton Ryley, a so called Elder Brother of Trinity House, that is a member of the governing body of that organisation !

Trinity House Vessel *Beacon* 1925-1960

- Aftermath of a disaster

The managing director of a major Salvage company, Cox and Danks of Fulham, London S.W.6 wrote to the Chairman of the Tribunal of Enquiry, The High Court Judge Mr. Alfred Townsend Bucknill, the day after the Tribunal first opened on July 3rd 1939.[17]

Scapa House,
Park Royal Road,
London, W.10.
4th July, 1939.

Mr. Justice Bucknill,
Royal Court of Justice, W.C.1.

Sir,

My name is Earnest Frank Cox. I am Managing Director of Messrs. Cox and Danks Limited, Salvage Contractors of Fulham, SW6.

I am justified in writing to you giving my views of the disaster when I advise you that I undertook the salvage of the German Fleet at Scapa Flow and lifted 32 ships, spending over £500,000 on the salvage work. I also lifted for the British Admiralty the Battleship *'Emperor of India'* which sank off Bognor in 1931, after the Admiralty had tried to salve her for seven or eight weeks. Therefore, I claim to know what I am talking about.

I only gave up the salvage work at Scapa Flow in 1933 because I was, at that time, only getting £30,000 for a battleship delivered into Rosyth Dockyard when the cost of lifting the ship was at least £45,000. Therefore, you will see this was not a paying proposition for me.

To summarise the whole position these disasters could be avoided by having a salvage man on the Admiralty Staff, and I have no hesitation in saying that this would have meant the lives of all those men being saved had the salvage men been present. My view of the 'Thetis' is as follows:-
When the 'Thetis' was found with her stern up out of water the ship, as we would say in salvage language, was a gift. All that was required was someone with salvage experience, to take charge and direct operations.

The first thing was to get out on the spot with compressors and tools, and drill a hole in the stern of the Submarine. This would be child's play as we have done similar jobs hundreds of times in worse conditions and my divers have done the job under water. The time at the very outside should be 15/30 minutes.

The hole would then be tapped and a ¾ bend or straight piece of pipe screwed in same, and a check valve, if one had been thought of but it is not very essential. I am positive compressed air could have been put into the ship within one hour after the arrival of the tug or ship with compressing plant. If this had been done, there is no question that everyone in the Submarine would have been saved, also the Submarine itself.

I am aware at the stern of the Submarine there is a bulkhead, but, in all my experience of hundreds of bulkheads, I have never found one airtight, and I am confident this one was no different to the others I have dealt with.

As further proof of what I wish to stress the men in the Submarine were still alive and it would be a simple matter to signal by tapping that you were putting in compressed air, and it would be a very easy matter for the men in the submarine to take off the manhole on this bulkhead and so let in all the fresh air you were passing into the ship.

The compressed air would serve two very vital **purposes.** Firstly, all men would be revived very quickly, as fresh air will disperse any gas. I have had ample proof of this at Scapa Flow. The next very important point would be as follows:-Assuming only one compressor was available, say, 100 cubic foot capacity, this would build up a pressure in the Submarine and, in 5/6 hours, there would be enough pressure in the Submarine to force the water out of the Submarine to enable the men to go through the first door they had closed, and eventually the second door, and go right to the torpedo tube door and close it again.

This is not a theory as we have done similar work hundreds of times.

The maximum pressure that would have been in the Submarine would not exceed 50-lbs pressure. This would probably be rather unpleasant to the few elderly people inside, but as the pressure will be built up slowly the effects might not be very serious.

Had this single operation been carried out it would have been a very simple matter to place one or two wires round the bow of the ship, without divers, and as the bow would have been only 20/30-tons of dead weight on the bottom, this could easily have been lifted off the bottom and the Submarine carried ashore.

Instead of doing this simple job, the men in charge actually sank the Submarine, not deliberately, but owing to lack of experience.

When the stern had been lifted to the surface by the splendid action of the men inside, the serious error of the people in charge in trying to hold up the

- Aftermath of a disaster

stern by means of wires, resulted in actually causing the Submarine to sink. The explanation is as follows:-

When the stern was on the surface any movement of the tide simply lifts the stern with it, therefore, the stern of the ship would have arisen and fallen with the tide. If the compressed air had been put in the ship, the stern of the Submarine would actually have come further out of the water.

The simple explanation of why the submarine was sent to the bottom is as follows:-

The stern of the Submarine on the surface was only buoyant to the extent of say, 20/50 tons margin. This surplus was in the side tanks. When the two tugs were trying to hold up the stern, one of the wires on one tug broke, this threw the strain on to one side of the Submarine which, naturally, twisted her and the air in the tanks on the highest side of the submarine partly escaped. This caused the Submarine to lose the small margin of buoyancy, and, at the same time, moved over the loose water in the Submarine to one side of her, and these two items caused the Submarine to slip sideways to the bottom, but on the way down she naturally righted herself.

This was a tragedy caused solely through lack of experience and could easily have been avoided had experienced people been present. The ship even then, at the bottom of the sea, could have been easily lifted had the proper apparatus been available or if the first air pipe had been fixed to the stern as I have mentioned before.

The tragedy was caused, in my opinion, because the whole thing was badly handled and a lot of things want altering on Submarines from a salvage point of view. I think I have sufficient knowledge to suggest such a change. The suggestions are briefly as follows:-

No Submarine to go into commission without a connection to the oil tanks so that oil can be released when required to show the Submarine's position. This is so apparent I am amazed it has not been carried out after the Admiralty's experience on M. 2 in Portland Bay in 1932 when they hunted for several days to find her.

The same with the THETIS. If this oil connection had been in use, the tug would have kept in touch with the Submarine at the time she was under test, and would have been on the spot when the accident inside the Submarine happened. This was about 5 p.m., - therefore salvage men and plant could have been on the spot that same evening and the lives and Submarine would have been saved.

The next very important point is that the Air Connection on all submarines should be altered and made so that the standard connection of all air compressors all over the Country would fit any Submarine instead of the special connection as at present (if any). Also, at the same time every compartment of a Submarine should have two inlet connections for air and two outlets for letting the water out.

Also most important is that the upper deck of a submarine should have a Bulb angle welded all along the top as that a diver can hold on to this when he gets down on the submarine so that he can pull himself along quite easily to get to the connections or to any other work. This bulb angle to have holes in same so that a diver can lash himself to when he is at work so that he can have both hands free. Had this been on the THETIS a diver could have walked down the deck of the Submarine to get to the Air Connection even if the tide was 2/3 knots per hour, because he could have held on as he was walking or sliding down.

Also the entrance door on all submarines should be altered so that a diver can fasten them easily with bolts from the outside, because when you put Compressed Air inside the submarine the air lifts the door off the sea(l) and a lot of air escapes. If this is done there is no question that it would be very easy to lift the ship by Compressed Air without any lifting pontoons.

It should also be compulsory for a small 200 **cubic** feet Rotary Compressor working up to 150-lb. to be in every Navy vessel for use with Pneumatic Tools and ready for emergency use anywhere.

If you wish, I shall be pleased to go further into any of these points, as something should be done to stop further mishaps. I can assure you that I am not out for Publicity but consider the valuable knowledge which I have, and had to pay dearly for, can be used to avoid further disasters. I would like to make the suggestion that seeing you have been inside a Submarine with Admiralty Officials, you could spare the time to go inside one with myself and I could then give you the salvage view of the matter. Please do not think this impertinence as I am sure I could stagger you with known facts if we could meet actually on a submarine.

Yours faithfully,
E.F. Cox

Mr. Cox's expertise is probably beyond challenge. It came obviously too late for *Thetis* but apart from demonstrating with pinpoint clarity what should have been done that was not done, he also indicates areas where simple protective procedures like the release of oil to show a submarine's position could have helped the situation.

As far as I am aware Mr. Cox never had any meeting with any Admiralty Officials on a submarine to illustrate his ideas, and his letter was summarily dismissed.

Offers of assistance to the Tribunal from other sources were also declined and dismissed. An example, offering eye witness accounts and aerial photographs of the scene from Utility Airways, a company based at what was an aerodrome at Hooton, Wirral in 1939, is shown here. Today the giant Ellesmere Port Vauxhall Motor Company factory sits on most of the site of what was Hooton aerodrome.

UTILITY AIRWAYS LTD.
AIRLINE · CHARTER & TAXI AIRCRAFT OPERATORS.
MERSEYSIDE AIR PARK
HOOTON
CHESHIRE

DIRECTORS:
W.F. ORMSON
E.J. DAWSON, F.R.S.

TELEGRAMS: Utility Airways-Little Sutton
TELEPHONE: HOOTON 2264

YOUR REF:
OUR REF: UA/WFD/RJ

1st July 1939.

The Secretary,
The Admiralty,
Whitehall,
LONDON, S.W. 1.

N.L. 2304
1939

CENTRAL
3 JUL 1939
REGISTRY

ack.
CW/P3/7

For the attention of the Chief Press Officer.

Dear Sir,

We understand from the News Editor of the "Daily Express" Manchester, that you are anxious to obtain first hand evidence regarding the sinking, and subsequent attempts to salvage, the Submarine "THETIS".

Our Aircraft were engaged during the night of the 1st June, and all the following day, June 2nd., in searching for the missing Submarine, and after it had been located, in flying various Press Representatives to the spot, for the purpose of obtaining photographs and eye-witnesses' accounts. As a result of this, we have on our Staff four Pilots who had frequent opportunities of observing the operations through-out the day of June 2nd., and we hope that if we can be of any assistance to you, you will advise us accordingly.

Yours faithfully,
For UTILITY AIRWAYS LIMITED,

(signature)

Letter offering assistance from Utility Airways of Hooton and (overleaf) the 'thanks but no thanks' reply from the Lords Commissioners of the Admiralty.[18]

N.L.2304/39   10th July   9

Gentlemen,

In reply to your letter of the 1st July, 1939, UA/WFD/RJ, I am commanded by My Lords Commissioners of the Admiralty to inform you that they appreciate your offer of providing evidence obtained by representatives of your Company during the salvage operations on H...Submarine, THETIS.

In reply I am to state that it is not at present considered necessary to call upon the evidence of your pilots, but, in case it is considered desirable to obtain their evidence at a later stage, My Lords would be grateful if they could be held available for this purpose. Not less than 24 hours notice will be given should their evidence be called for.

I am, Gentlemen,

Your obedient Servant,

Utility Airways Ltd.,
   Hooton,
      Cheshire.

The older brother of the Mersey Pilot lost on *Thetis* also believes that more could have been done and his evidence is given added strength from the fact that he too was a Mersey Pilot and knew Liverpool Bay 'like the back of his hand' and he also had first hand knowledge of the submarine having been pilot aboard her when she was moved between the wet basin and the dry dock at Cammell Laird's yard during her fitting out period.

'I had two brothers and three sisters. There was myself, Norman Douglas, who was lost in the Sub, and John Holland Willcox, or Jack, who lives in Florida now but John wasn't a mariner like Norman and I. Norman was my immediately younger brother. He would have been around 83 years old today.

Norman was a Pilot the same as myself. A pilot on the River Mersey. He was lost on the Submarine *Thetis*…I was around 28 years old then, was married at the time, but my brother Norman still lived at home with my father and mother.

I remember the day it happened …just before the outbreak of war, I had bought my wife a radio set which was capable of receiving all bands from 0 - 2000 metres you see... she used to listen in during the afternoons the Pilot boats would report the number of Pilots on board and she could always tell whether I had a chance of getting home you see... I came home that day...when I got home she said 'Is there a Submarine in trouble in Liverpool Bay.' So I said 'Not that I know of.' So she said 'Well there have been messages going on between the Dock Board tender, I think it was the Vigilant, and the Dock Board all afternoon'…I smelt a rat.

So I rang Seaforth Radio and there was a very peppery Welshman at Seaforth Radio and he upbraided me for listening in to commercial wave bands. He didn't like it, although the set I had was perfectly legal because it was produced mainly for trawler men to ring their wives at home.

With that I went home to my father, …the family home was in Prenton, 22 Carlaw Road, Prenton, off Swan Hill. Roads were named after the sons of the Brewers, Osmaston Walker, Carlaw Walker... and I said 'I'm sorry to tell you dad, but Norman is in trouble…there's a Submarine gone down in Liverpool Bay and he is on it.'

My father said 'Oh my God!' So we rang Cammell Lairds and we knew Mr. Woodward, who was the Secretary of Lairds and we spoke to him on the telephone and he said 'Yes the Submarine has gone down but we are hopeful of getting them all out.' So with that my father and I we went down to Cammell

Lairds. We waited with all the wives, and sisters, and brothers, and relatives.

Eventually word came through, a false word, that they were all out of the Submarine, that they were all rescued...which was poppycock.

It was still daytime, the afternoon of the second of June. So anyhow, with that I went home with my father and a message came through that the sixth destroyer flotilla were leaving Portsmouth on their way round and his remark to me was 'What the bloody hell can they do?' So I said 'Father, I know what I would do if I was there in charge of that operation.' I said 'There's a ....tug there, a salvage boat, I would place one on each side of the stern when it is out of the water get chains round it, tow it into shallow water and they'd all walk out.' 'That's precisely what I'd do son,' he said. He was pilot for the City Line at the time. So I said 'Yes...but whether these humbug Navy people will do that I don't know.'

You see the Dock Board had a lien (no outside operator was allowed to touch a wreck without their permission) on every wreck which foundered in their waters. Whether that was overcome by the Navy I don't know, but that was the law at the time. Anyhow, from there, we waited and waited and waited and of course the news came through eventually, probably two days later I would think… that all hope had been abandoned.

The weather was perfect, it couldn't have been better. It was as flat as a carpet, and so anyhow, shortly after that, I went round to the pilotage office on Canning Wall and abutting our pilotage office was the headquarters of the Liverpool and Glasgow Salvage Association. Now these people had salvaged the submarine on the Clyde previously… K 33 I think it was, K something, it was a K class submarine…and had in effect fed hot chocolate down tubes into the submarine to keep the men fortified inside.

I met Mr. Batten who was the manager and he pointed to the Dock Building and said 'That man over there ought to be flayed (meaning the Marine Surveyor of the Mersey Docks and Harbour Board). Do you know, Mr. Willcox, we have this vessel Ranger (a wooden salvage vessel which belonged to the Liverpool Salvage Company… The Ranger was the Liverpool and Glasgow Salvage Company's own vessel. The Vigilant was the MDHB vessel as was the Salvor.) and it was such an efficient vessel it could pump coal. He said he'd called the Ranger back to Canning Wall and said you better take another set of burning gear in case you've got to do any fast burning to get them out. Which they did.

Anyhow, he said do you know what happened eventually, he said, we sent the Ranger outside to standby in case they were needed for any burning. So in the end the Captain of Ranger got so exasperated that nothing was being done, that he walked on board the Vigilant or the Salvor, I'm not too sure which of the two salvage vessels it was, and he said Hart was sitting there, Commander Hart RNVR with these naval officers who had now arrived with the sixth destroyer flotilla, and he said 'Gentlemen, when is something going to be done?' Captain Hart looked at him and he said 'Who invited you here? Get out!' Those were his exact words.

Mind you, the pilots as a body had no very cordial feelings towards Commander Hart because of a certain incident which had happened sometime before, subsequently their mistrust was quite well founded. But by the time I found this out I knew Norman was gone.

Norman was a single man. So, mother and father took it very very badly. They never got over it. Father was retired by then. My mother was invited to participate in the *Thetis* fund which she drew almost until she died. She didn't apply but she was invited to.

My mother and father got his body eventually from Holyhead, and he is buried at Woodchurch, the graveyard just by the Arrowe Park estate...Woodchurch Parish Church. They used to go to his grave and talk to him, which used to upset me very much... because my brother and I were very close, very close together.

I know that at the time we were amazed that the funeral people were bringing him home, and I have an idea that my father got in touch with Charles Stephens (funeral directors) who finished the job off, with their usual panache...I wouldn't be surprised if we didn't get the right bodies. Because they were so badly decomposed by that time especially with the acid and the fumes in the submarine, you know.

I expect my father paid for the funeral. I wasn't party to that. I suppose he would pay for it cheerfully. Knowing him. As far as I'm aware he didn't get any help with this.

There was a man, a local man, who came from the Disaster Fund...I would have known at the time because his name would crop up quite often, you see. But I can't recall the gentleman's name who was in charge of it. But he did say once that it was worked out to such an extent that ultimately the last dependant would see the fund out to its limit. In other words there would

- Aftermath of a disaster

be no surplus. I think he was a Bank Manager, who was appointed from Barclays Bank, I think so, I'm not sure about that though.

Father was still a working pilot…in his 50's…Maybe 5 or 10 years away from retirement. He was bringing a wage in, supporting his wife and family… There were 2 sisters, and Norman.

I've no idea how much they got. It wasn't very much. If I say it was £5.00 a week I might be exaggerating. I really couldn't put a figure on it. But it wasn't very much. She appreciated it, because naturally when the old man retired, inflation was rife and that little bit of money came in handy for them…I never enquired about the total, but I know she said it wasn't very much, just a small appreciation by the public of what had happened. She got that until the day she died…around 1967 or 1968…I think it was paid into a Bank account.

We had a service at the Town Hall, and also I've been to several services in Liverpool Cathedral for instance…I didn't go out on the *Hebe*…The loss of my brother upset me so much that I wouldn't even read the book… I wouldn't… no… It would bring it all back and it is very painful still…you can understand.

There were a lot of newspaper headlines, a lot of interest in what had happened. There was a little article by a gentleman in the Daily Mail, to criticise the inefficiency of the operation. But apart from that there was very little criticism at the time. Although my father and I as practical men we knew that something could have been done…we felt that something could have been done. I'd served nine years as an apprentice of the Liverpool Cutters and I recognised the seaman to my fingertips… my dad certainly was…because he'd been a sailing ship man… I know Liverpool Bay like the back of my hand…we felt, if she'd been towed into shallow water, with the rise and fall of the tide, at that spot being 18 feet, it would have possibly exposed the conning tower.

Blame from certain sources from time to time has been levelled at the Admiralty. The Admiralty have never confessed that they forbade any other outside influence to attempt salvage. Otherwise I would say the MDHB having charge of the wreck should have done something more about it…they had a lien on any wrecks in their waters…it has been suggested that the Admiralty had forbidden any other outside bodies to interfere with the submarine, when it was out of the water…whether that is true or not, I'm not in a position to say.

You see, that far out in Liverpool Bay the bottom of the sea is not mud. It is sand and gravel. So they can't say the bow of the submarine was in mud...which has been voiced in the past...but looking in the bay chart you notice that it is sand and gravel there. So that towed inshore, at 3 to 4 knots there was no reason why they couldn't have walked out.

There was also carelessness obviously in the shipyard, at not making sure that those test holes were clear. The naval overseers too were careless...I know they have to pass a vessel that has been constructed for the Royal Navy...and they are supposed to be very, very particular.

They seem to think that the ship had a jinx on it in any case, but whether that will hold water, I don't know. I actually took the ship from the wet basin into the dry dock. If I'd have known what I know now I'd have wrecked the bloody thing.

It was always in doubt whether my brother was opting to leave the vessel at the Bar...you see compulsory pilotage finishes at the Bar lightship. There was a Pilot named Tregenza, and he told me that the Commander who went out on the original trials with her (up to the Clyde) was very unwilling to let the small boat come alongside it in case he damaged the plating...but even so that wouldn't hold water because the classical method of disembarking or going aboard a submarine is over the bow where if you notice there are little holes at the bow of a submarine and you could climb of and on ...and this is the way we always used to do them. We made the submarine go astern while we drove the boat into it and then the Pilot would climb up and pull himself on board. On trials it was normal for the Pilot to accompany most ships on trials and come back with the ship to save picking up another Pilot.

I could never read the book about it *(Thetis - The Admiralty Regrets)*. ..because of the bad memories it brings back'.

- Aftermath of a disaster

The world learned of the *Thetis* disaster in Liverpool Bay from their radios but not everyone got the news from the BBC. Jean Beattie was the nine year old daughter of Bill Beattie, a Cammell Laird Boilermaker Caulker, and Jean was with her mother at the fish and chip shop in Old Chester Road at the top of Union Street in Tranmere, Birkenhead.

Bill Beattie

Jean Newton (nee Beattie)

Jean Newton.(nee Beattie). DOB 23.10.1930.
Daughter of Caulker Bill Beattie

We lived in Clare Street, near Union Street Birkenhead and when I finished school at 12 o'clock and he finished work and he always used to hide in the same place to try and scare me. He was a workman in Cammell Laird's when he went on one of the *Thetis* dives and just never came back. He was a caulker, a boilermaker. He'd only been back in the yard 5 or 6 years, with the depression and that, and he'd just been made up to chargehand about 8 months before he went. Very traumatic. I was nearly nine years old.

I remember my dad. He was fair. I never, never remember him smacking me. He'd tell me off ...but from what memory I've got there used to be a picture house just off the New Chester Road and on a Saturday night, every Saturday night, he'd walk me and my mother up and pay for us to go in the Palace, and he'd come back down and have a few pints, then he'd come back up and meet us and I'd sit on his shoulders and call in the chippy on the way home. He always used to say he wanted a son, as he was surrounded by women. There was the three of us girls, my mother and my gran. We lived with my granny, it wasn't his own house. His sister lived over the road, and he'd come in at night and think there are all these women, why can't I have a man here!

At the time when he went out that day... two or three weeks before or a month, a big submarine had gone down in America, and there had been talk for weeks. My sister Nancy worked in Littlewoods in Liverpool and she used to finish at 9.00 pm and my mother said to me come on we'll go up to the chippy and get some fish. That was in Union Street. My mother was in the chip shop and I was outside waiting for her, and another women came in and said 'Oh have you heard about the submarine that hasn't surfaced?' And my mother took no notice at first. She thought about the American one. The man behind the counter said 'The American One?' She said 'No. The one that went out of Laird's this morning.'

Well I can see my mother and all these people around her and somebody got hold of me and took my mother home. It wasn't 5 minutes walk. But all I can remember that night was, sitting on the step, it was June, it was very warm, and these people coming in and out, my mother saw the doctor who called, the Vicar called, and then somebody got hold of me and took me down and I got as far as the Tannery on New Chester Road, I never got to Laird's. I never seen what was going on at Laird's so whoever it was must have changed their mind... when you are a kid, I didn't fully understand really what was going on.

Then an uncle got hold of me, and then a lady who lived opposite a Mrs. Derman, she got hold of me, and I can't remember this, but her daughter told me a couple of years later, she got hold of me and took me into their house. Then of course, I can remember them all, around the wireless, people coming in and out, in and out. That went on for a few days.

The worst thing I can remember, my eldest sister Peggy, she got hold of me, and I don't know if it was the next day or the day after, and said to me 'You won't see your dad any more.' That is all I can remember, you won't see your dad any more.

But the thing that sticks out, most vividly in my mind, is when we got the bodies, I think it was, August or September, but the coffins were awfully big. Awfully deep. When they brought the coffin to the door, and I came out,

- Aftermath of a disaster

that mesmerised me because a few weeks before I had seen a funeral of a neighbour, and I couldn't take my eyes off this coffin that was so big, so deep, and we went up to Bebington and go up Town Lane, and turn left into the cemetery and as a kid, it looked a very very long road. There were all these men, and some had bowler hats, some had caps, and as the coffin and the cars passed, the hats came off in unison as it was going passed. That stayed with me. But coming home used to be the worst, from school. My mother never got over it.

I have a vague recollection and I'm not sure, but my mother said it had to be a special coffin. I don't know whether it was Laird's or the Government, my mother had to pay for the funeral, I know she got his wages, I don't know if it was a month or six weeks, she got his wages.

The workmen's compensation … Oh yes. That was hilarious...they went to Court and one Court blamed Cammell Laird's and the Navy and Cammell Laird's again. It must have been about 2 or 3 years later she got £300 for herself and £100 for me. But you had to go to Court over that…, you had to go to Chambers in Hamilton Square in the Birkenhead Town Hall. The Court was in there, the Judge's Chambers. You had to go, put it in writing, how much you wanted. Then you had to go before this Judge, I can't remember his name…I never ever went, my sister went...my mother only went once, and it made her ill...she never got over it my mother...she always said it was as though it wasn't their money. I think it depended how he felt at the time. Sometimes you'd get it, other times you wouldn't.

My sister used to go [to the court]…they would ask all sorts of questions… I remember one time she wanted a bike for me… it was Christmas time, I'd be about 12 or 13, my sister went down and the Judge said 'God gave you two legs. Your sister is only 13, she should be able to walk' and she didn't get the money.

That lasted about 6 or 7 years. They gave her stuff like bedding, and she became a diabetic, and I can remember, my sister went, as my mother wouldn't go as he used to frighten her to death, this judge. I used to be a bit like that before I got older, my older sister was very strong and used to say it's my mother's money...The judge told her not to be cheeky more than once.

But the laughable part of all this, is people thought that my mother got a lot of money. And she didn't. I mean, when I was 21 years old, somebody stopped me at the bus stop and said to me 'Are you giving your job up now,

Jean?' I looked at her and said 'I'm not getting married.' She said 'No, but you'll come into your money now, from the *Thetis*, won't you?... it was hysterical... because I got nothing.

She got money from the fund and the widow's pension and I think at the time, I think it was 10/- from the widow's pension, and I think it was 12/6 from the Fund and she got 2/6 for me. That was per week. That came by money order. It had the *Thetis* Memorial Fund, and the Lord Mayor of London on it, and it came every Friday which you could cash at the Post Office. Through the War that then went up. To about £3.00 and then up again. I mean, my mother was of the 'old school'. All the men would say, my uncles, a lot of whom worked down at Lairds, The boilermakers down there are on £25.00 - £30.00 a week... but my mum used to say 'Aren't they good to me'.... but she wasn't like that. She wasn't money grabbing, my mother. She got the money until the day she died. She got the money for me until I was 14...my sisters were 19 and 21....I started work when I was 14 ...then it stopped.

In the 1960's...I can't remember, I'd say 1964 at a guess, it was changed over, it wasn't the *Thetis* Memorial Fund anymore. She got a letter to go down to Laird's, my sister and I went with her. They explained to her that they were turning this money over to an Insurance Company. She had to sign this letter, because they said they had to get everybody to sign accepting it.

I went up to my dad's grave once at Christmas time with my mother, and we were talking to this man, and his son was a young apprentice. He was one of the youngest ones there. I can't remember his name. We got talking to him. My sister happened to say she wanted to go and identify my dad, at Holyhead. He said to her you want to pray and thank God you never went. He said he'll never ever forget the sight of my young son. He said that with the shock he now had this big white piece of hair. That happened within two days of identifying him. It was a terrible sight. He'd said he didn't know whether it was lack of oxygen or what, but he said they were all like a brown vase sort of thing. The colour of them was shiny brown and bulbous.

My mother was so upset. He said it was terrible. He shouldn't have said that really to my mother...twelve months later she had another set back. She met a woman out shopping who said to her, 'How do you know you've got your husband in that grave? You could have somebody else's husband in that grave.' I'd be about 11 then and my mother had to have the doctor again.

- Aftermath of a disaster

She never got over it…. I hope you are successful trying to find out what happened to the fund money…there are a lot of people my age now… why should an Insurance Company reap the benefit of it… I just wish you luck.

I never thought my dad was dead. I was 14, I'd started work, and I always used to say to myself that dad had got off that sub, and he'd been picked up and he was either in America or another country and lost his memory. You know, you think childlike things. I mean, it has a lot to do with how dreadfully my mother took it. I just say that he was such a good man, that I missed out such a lot. Nobody knows unless it is you inside, especially a child.

The *Thetis* Disaster Narrated

Jean Newton (nee Beattie) will always remember the conversation in the chip shop, when she learned she had lost her father,[1] and then like everyone else, people tuned into their radios for the latest updates on the situation in Liverpool Bay. Then as now, the media is highly influential and media responses can often colour public perceptions and vice versa. How did the media report the *Thetis* disaster, what were the implications of the language used at the time and how did the media treat the so called 'human angle' of the tragedy; the mourning and the funerals? How did the media report the beginnings of the call for a public enquiry following the disaster? Were perhaps, the signs already there that *Thetis* was to be 'submerged' from the public gaze?

Looking at the newspapers of the time is the only way of obtaining verbatim reports of the official tribunal of enquiry. Although the 60 page report itself was published in April 1940 I have not been able to find, in either the Public Record Office or the Royal Navy Submarine museum at Gosport / Fort Blockhouse any transcripts of the proceedings. However the newspapers were full of the enquiry at the time and I have used their reporting of questions and answers at the enquiry as being as close to verbatim as I can get. The sources of these quotations are noted later.

Radio was the main source of information for most people in 1939 and a close look at the language of the BBC radio bulletins is extraordinarily revealing.

The BBC News bulletins mixed dour reports about the disaster with coverage of the Royal Visit to Canada by the King and Queen. It must be mentioned at this point that fortune once again played a part. The BBC archives for such material can be difficult and / or expensive to access. However through my work for BBC Radio Merseyside, and meeting and talking with Fred Lawless [who had been commissioned by the BBC to write the radio play about *Thetis*], he was able to supply me with the photocopies of the 1939 broadcasts which he had requested from the BBC to provide background material for his dramatisation. In Fred's own words he had asked his producers at the BBC 'I don't suppose that you can get your hands on the actual broadcast scripts of the news for me?' and they had replied 'this is the BBC, we can get anything'. And they did.

- Aftermath of a disaster

From the 10.45pm Bulletin 2.6.39

The submarine *Thetis* is now lying in Liverpool Bay with her nose on the bottom of the sea and her stern projecting several feet above the water... The Admiralty issued a statement this morning which said 'HM Submarine *Thetis* has been located in position 328 degrees 14 miles from Great Ormes head. Her bow is in 130 feet of water and her stern is on the surface. Captain Oram, Lt. Woods, Leading Stoker Arnold and Mr. F. Shaw of Cammell Lairds have escaped by Davis escape apparatus. Captain Oram escaped to direct salvage operations and to make a full report on the state of the submarine. The commanding officer and the remainder of the crew were alive at 10 o'clock and salvage equipment is being rushed to the spot'.[2]

(This bulletin was at least 12 hours old.)

The next morning's bulletin at 10.30am on 3.6.39:

Before I read the weather forecast here is a short news bulletin: -

'The Admiralty issued a statement early this morning saying that divers had reported at 2.00am that they had heard faint tappings in the submarine *Thetis*, the statement added 'salvage operations are proceeding and a further attempt will be made to raise the stern when slack water provides the next opportunity'. The latest news from the Admiralty half an hour ago [thus at 10.00am real time] said there was still hope that some of the submarine's crew might be rescued alive. More news is not expected for some time.[3]

At 9.00pm on 3.6.39 the bulletin reads:

The Admiralty announced at 4.30 this afternoon that there was no longer any justification for hope that any further lives could be saved from the submarine *Thetis*...the latest information is that salvage work is proceeding and that the submarine will be either towed to the nearest shore and beached, or brought back to Birkenhead.[4]

The motivation for the Admiralty manoeuvres on and around *Thetis* seem to be more concerned with 'salvage' rather than 'rescue'. Each of the bulletins refer to 'salvage work' whilst only one refers to 'rescue'. Dictionaries define salvage as: -

a) 'The rescue of a ship and cargo at sea from fire, shipwreck etc.'.
b) 'Compensation paid for such rescue'.
c) 'The ship or cargo so rescued'.

It is generally regarded to be a fine line between the saving of life and salvage. When does one end and the other begin? Certainly the presence of the *Vigilant* and the *Salvor,* the salvage vessels of the Liverpool and Glasgow Salvage Co. that were used on the scene, meant that company would incur costs, and indeed the invoices from that company to Cammell Laird and Co. after the event follow considerable correspondence between the two companies upon the exact point in time that invoicing for costs incurred should commence.[5] Furthermore it is a more than reasonable assumption that human life would **not** be regarded as 'cargo'. Could the BBC of 1939 be so slipshod in their use of language? This seems unlikely. Working for the BBC myself in my own small capacity I am aware that the BBC and most of its broadcasters, producers and directors are very vigilant in the use of their language, especially in the wake of human catastrophe. I cite the reporting in the aftermath of the Hillsborough football stadium disaster in 1989 in support of this assertion.

All of the reports in the bulletins of 1939 are taken directly from Admiralty statements. Surely then the Admiralty would be aware of the distinctions and nuances of the use of the word salvage as opposed to rescue? Or did the Admiralty unconsciously betray the real driving force behind the operations in Liverpool Bay. What the (late) flotilla of vessels were really briefed for, sooner rather than later than the actual announcement that all hope was lost (4.30pm on the 3rd June). Salvage! The rescue of the ship, the vessel, the boat. Brand spanking new, worth £350,000 and with a war around the corner.

Perhaps conclusive evidence of the primary intentions of the Admiralty can be heard from a television interview given to Granada Television upon the occasion to mark the 50th anniversary commemorative service for *Thetis* at Holyhead, Anglesey, in 1989. Mr. Sam Gawthope was a switchboard operator at Liverpool Police Telephone Exchange in 1939. He recalls a Naval Officer standing next to him at his console as he relayed calls between all the concerned parties during those fateful hours while those aboard *Thetis* were dead or dying.

> I remember them saying that on no account is the
> submarine to be damaged and I said to the officer
> 'surely you are going to ignore that. I mean you have
> to ignore that.'
> The officer replied 'I have to obey orders...[6]

Thetis was indeed worth a great deal of money and the press coverage did not ignore the financial implications of the disaster. The newspaper coverage of the disaster and its immediate aftermath in the following days and weeks, chose, not unlike today, different 'angles'.

From the Daily Express of June 6th:-

'Such was the confidence of the marine underwriting markets that *Thetis* would be salved, that on 6th June 1939, just three days after the 'all hope is lost' statement, they refused to pay out the forty guineas percent, approx. 40% of the costs of *Thetis* on the claim, agreeing to pay only 20% or 20 guineas percent'.[7]

Similarly other contemporary reports seemed to endow more importance to the price tag of *Thetis* before reporting upon the tragedy itself. On the 2nd of June the following article appeared in the *Sporting Mail and Morning News*. The banner headline is in capitals :

'HOPE FOR ALL ON BOARD'

followed by the statement in a lower point size but still in capitals,

'IT IS OFFICIALLY STATED THAT THE CREW IS SAFE'. [8]

Apart from being wildly incorrect these two statements are diametrically opposed to each other. If all are safe then why is hope necessary? Hope is only required when something that is desired is possibly still attainable. Assuming that the desire was to see those aboard *Thetis* safe then according to this report they already were!

At this time only Oram and Woods had escaped from the submarine and the rest of those aboard were in a terrible condition. The Admiralty never issued any statement to the effect that all were safe. *Thetis* had been *found* at last but that was all.

After printing a list of those aboard, which was also incomplete, a sub-headline was '*THETIS* COST £350,000'. Under this sub-headline was a brief report about the emergency telephone system that *Thetis* carried to communicate with the surface in such circumstances; there is no reference at all to financial matters which begs the question why is the sub-headline even included?

Another newspaper cutting from Derek Arnold's collection must be included here even though sadly it is not known which newspaper it came from. Derek was not to know that a researcher would come along in 1997 and comb his material with a detailed eye. It is stapled to the *Sporting Mail and Morning News* article so a connection can be made to the date only, 2nd June 1939.

The headline once again in capitals is

'DRAMA IN RACE TO SAVE 79 MEN'.

There are a minimum of 20 men missing from this figure but on 2nd June information was hard to come by, yet nonetheless the piece begins:-

> Anxious search began today over the area where at the bottom of Liverpool Bay lies Britain's £350,000 new submarine *Thetis*, with 79 men entombed in her steel hull.[9]

Clearly the only hard fact available and certainly one to lead an article with was the building cost of *Thetis*. Money, as stated earlier, was hard to come by in 1939 and such figures could probably be equated with National Lottery winnings in 1999. They would literally be a King's ransom to the general public and thus would grab the attention by their headlines and arguably attract customers to purchase the newspaper in question.

Yet despite this apparent fixation with the building costs of *Thetis* it is the unspoken and unwritten costs that perhaps focused the attention of the British Admiralty. Indeed *Thetis* **had** cost in the region £350,000 and this money would all have been paid to the builders, Cammell Laird of Birkenhead. They in turn would buy the steel, the machinery, the fabrication apparatus that would be required, pay any subcontractors and of course pay their own employees for their time and effort expended upon the building of the submarine. The British Admiralty had used the expression 'salvage' instead of 'rescue' time and time again. The evidence of Sam Gawthope is irrefutable and irresistible, and the newspaper reports, however inaccurate on some counts, place a significant amount of emphasis of the building costs of *Thetis*. Why?

I believe I can use the above analysis to conclude that apart from human life the only commodity that could not be salved from *Thetis* was time. Ships are not built in a week or two and arguably moreso submarines because of the additional work demands of fabricating the pressure hull and the resultant extra thickness of materials and specialised welding procedures required. *Thetis* had taken some 20 months to build as part of the general expansion of the British Navy, as a response to a similar German expansion of her own navy. This time was now lost, dead time. Dead time ran parallel with dead men. But men could be replaced, machinery could be replaced, faults could be rectified and paint can be retouched, but the time it takes to build a submarine from scratch cannot be replaced, it is gone, it has passed and become dead just as those aboard *Thetis* had become.

Whilst it would be fair to argue that experienced submariners could not be replaced straight away by raw recruits, other 'T' class boats were under construction at the same time as *Thetis,* both at Cammell Laird and at the Vickers yard in Barrow. Indeed some of those lost on *Thetis* were 'drafted' from those boats to 'get the feel' of the latest 'T' class boats. The crews of these vessels would be 'standing by' their own boats and would be available to the navy; submariners were simply 'moved up the line' to serve on what *Thetis* was to become; *Thunderbolt.* It should also be remembered that almost all sailors in the submarine service were volunteers; for one simple reason; the submarine service paid more than surface vessels.

However as Sam Gawthope recalled from his switchboard days '*On no account is the submarine to be damaged in any way*'. The only conclusion that can be drawn from this evidence is that **'they'** wanted the submarine more than **'they'** wanted the men! *Thetis* was an expensive weapon of war, in just the same way as a rifle is a weapon of war. To ministers, strategists and those in command of the British armed forces it is of little consequence who is holding and controlling the rifle. The rifle has first and foremost to be in a working condition.

In the comparative absence of any real hard news in the early hours and first days contemporary news reports also looked at the disaster in human terms and in disclosing brief details about the homes, families and backgrounds of those who were known to be aboard the submarine *Thetis* . A close look at the reporting of the 'human angle' is also quite revealing in that different notices reflect social class. Printed 'word- sketches' of victims included :-

Leading Wireless Telegraphist Allen aged 24, married. His home is in Cardiff. 'I did not believe that anything could happen to my husband', his wife said yesterday 'He is a fatalist, I hate submarines but he loves them'. She added that he nearly failed to join the crew owing to a skating accident on Wednesday.[10]

Mr. George Scarth. Ship's Fitter. Son of Mr. G. Scarth, a prominent member of Birkenhead St.John's Ambulance Brigade. Home is in Randel Street Tranmere.[11]

Mr. William Bath of Meade Road, West Derby, Liverpool. A member of the City Caterers staff. Married with children.[12]

Mr. E.Lewis. Aged 24. An Electrician of Raffles Road Birkenhead. Married with one child.[13]

However most telling of all are those entries at the top of the listings, the officers.

Lieut.- Commander T.C.C. Lloyd. Eldest son of Colonel and Mrs. John Lloyd of Dinas House Brecon, South Wales. Was married to Miss Marie Smith, daughter of the late Major W.A. Smith and of Mrs. Richmond Temple of Park Street W1, in 1937.[14]

Lieut. P.E.J. Ryan. Only son of the late Lieut. E.W. Blackwood Ryan R.N. and Mrs. Ryan of Ivybridge Devon. His wife is the daughter of Mr. and Mrs. Cecil Cookson of The Grange, North Curry, Taunton. They had a son in April 1937.[15]

Clearly the entries for the officers read like an announcement in *The Times* for a society wedding and are a far cry from the one line entry for Mr. E. Lewis, Electrician. The newspaper report was from the *Daily Herald* and not *The Times*, but what is glaringly obvious is the respect given to the social standing of the Officers to include even a potted genealogy.

Contemporary media comment also addressed the vexed question of the opening of the fateful No. 5 torpedo tube. This was a literally crucial issue so a very close look at the press reports following the disaster which covered the official response, that is the Enquiry held by a tribunal in London, brings out many of the 'omissions and anomalies' that seemed to surround this disaster.

This form of tribunal for the official enquiry had only been used on two previous occasions; when the R101 airship exploded in flames on its maiden flight with the loss of 48 lives in 1930, and the second time to investigate a leak of budget information involving the then Chancellor of the Exchequer, J.H.Thomas.[16]

A scapegoat was required and the commentators of the day tried hard to pin one down but there was the whiff of cover up as early as a week after the event. During the first days of the proceedings the Attorney General of the time, Sir Donald Somerville, is reported in The London Evening Standard of July 5th 1939, under a headline of 'Documents may have to be kept secret'

> There are details in connection with the design of the submarine which it is undesirable should be made public. They would have to be dealt with in camera'.[17]

Perhaps this was an attempt to use the cloak of impending war to protect military matters and prevent possibly sensitive details of the submarine design and building programme from becoming public. Perhaps it was thought that the whole affair would be morale sapping within the services and for the public in general. Or perhaps this was the first attempt at cover-up. One can only guess that there was a public outcry against hearings in camera as eventually the proceedings were public, however the hint is clearly there that secrecy, for whatever reason, was considered very early on.

It is now known that the disaster happened because of a blockage in the test cock of No. 5 torpedo tube and a failure to use the rimer (pin) provided to prevent such a blockage, so in 1939 the test cock itself was the place to start looking.

The Official Tribunal of Enquiry into the loss of HMS *Thetis* opened its proceedings on Monday 3rd July 1939 and lasted for almost the whole of that month. It was then adjourned awaiting the salvage of the boat; it was reconvened in December 1939 and concluded in the same month.

During the *Thetis* Enquiry that followed the sinking, Mr. A.M Lyons KC., MP, acting for the relatives of a 16 year old apprentice, questioned the man who had actually given the order to open the door and survived the disaster. Lieut. Frederick Woods was asked about the test cock and the riming apparatus to ensure that the test cock had not been blocked: -

> **Lyons:** You said you tried No. 5 test cock on three occasions?
> **Woods:** Yes
> **Lyons:** There is no doubt that on the third occasion the cock was blocked?
> **Woods:** I think that must have been the case.
> He agreed that the test cock might have become blocked with dirt.
> Lieut. Woods said it did not occur to him that the hole was choked because he considered that the employees of Cammell Laird would have seen that the holes were clear.
> Mr. A.T. Miller KC. (for Messrs. Cammell Laird) suggested that in using the test cock in the way in which Lieut. Woods demonstrated yesterday he was neglecting the proper use of it as a test.
> Lieut. Woods replied that he considered that the way in which he used it would indicate if the test cock was clear and water was in the tube. He had previously found

this to be sufficient.

Lt. Woods agreed that if he had used any of the apparatus in addition to the test cock he would have found that the torpedo tube was not empty. He said he had not noticed that a rimer (pin) was fitted to the test cock.[18]

It seems from the above that there is a clear scapegoat available and that Lieut. Woods failed to use the apparatus correctly. If he had used the rimer it is very likely that the whole *Thetis* tragedy may never have happened. What is puzzling is the apparent contradiction in the report. Initially it appears that Woods actually says the words 'I think that must have been the case' in reply to a question claiming that the hole was definitely blocked. The report then goes on to state that 'he agreed that the test cock might have become blocked with dirt'. Did Woods say these words? Is the reporter paraphrasing Woods' earlier reply that 'He thought that must have been the case', or is this sentence a paraphrase of another reply from Woods that is not reported as direct speech? Later in the cross-examination Woods appears to distance himself from not using the rimer by saying that 'he had previously found this to be sufficient'. Yet one sentence later he agrees that if the rimer had been used he would have found the tube to be full of water! He even admits that he did not notice that a rimer was fitted to the test cock!

The other Naval Officer who escaped from *Thetis* was Captain H.P.K. (Joe) Oram. His autobiography was published posthumously in 1993, he having died in 1986[19]. The dust jacket to the book reveals - 'During his lifetime Joe Oram steadfastly steered clear of all attempts to extract the '*Thetis* story' from him....in old age however he felt the need to set the record straight within the context of his long and remarkable naval career.'

Almost sixty years after the events Oram confirmed that it was clear in the immediate moments following the inrush of the sea into *Thetis* what had happened and why,

It quickly became evident that a very serious mistake had been made. However it was vital to get accurate information about the condition of the two flooded compartments and to maintain positive morale among all members of the crew. Blaming people was not going to get us any further on.[20]

- Aftermath of a disaster

He goes further and attempts to explain why Woods, after the flooding, had volunteered to try and shut the rear torpedo tube door of No.5 tube on two occasions at great personal distress and pain. (The plan to try and do this was by using the Davis Submarine Escape Apparatus [DSEA] to breathe and first entering the rear door of the for'd escape chamber, closing the door behind them and then trying to re-enter the submarine's flooded compartments via the forward door of the chamber. Both attempts failed but Oram recalls that when Woods responded to a request from *Thetis'* captain, Captain Bolus, for volunteers to accompany Oram in his escape attempt, two seamen also volunteered. Oram selected Woods because of Woods' greater knowledge of the submarine.

Oram recalled:-

> I still didn't realise at that time that Woods
> knew he'd been responsible for opening the rear
> door of the tube that resulted in *Thetis* going to
> the bottom. This would not be revealed until some
> weeks later. In a way he was ready to volunteer
> for anything to redeem this error.[21]

Clearly both the press at the time and Oram toward the end of his life saw Lieut. Woods as culpable; yet at no time did the enquiry apportion responsibility to any individual, preferring instead to list a series of highly unfortunate events which standing alone would not have resulted in the loss of *Thetis* and the 99 men aboard her, but which collectively, conspired toward the tragedy. If any individual (or several) **had** been found responsible then the way would have been open for dependants to sue.

This particular area of the 'investigation' into the tragedy will be closely considered towards the end of this story as will the subject of accountability and claims for compensation. However as far as 1939 officialdom went all that was on offer for public consumption was, among the six reasons given as the official causes of the disaster, unbelievably, **'The failure of those on board the *Thetis* to escape'**. [22] It wasn't enough to die on *Thetis*, you had to take the blame as well!

Meanwhile those lost on *Thetis* were to be mourned. For obvious reasons the mourning was undertaken in the main by women. The loss of their men was marked in the time-honoured way and in this section a close look at the treatment the press gave to those lost and their relatives at this distressing time is valuable too.

Preparations for the funerals were covered in a sensationalist manner. Under the headline in capitals the *London Evening News* stated:

'THETIS WIDOWS GIVE UP THEIR DANCE FROCKS'

and a sub-heading also in capitals

'BUYING BLACK ON DAY FIXED FOR FAREWELL PARTY'

filed from our special correspondent. Birkenhead, Tuesday, (June 6th 1939)

> As no attempt can be made to lift *Thetis* from the bottom of Liverpool Bay before Thursday - perhaps it will be Friday - the arrangements for the funeral stand. About 200 relatives and friends of the 99 victims will leave Liverpool at 10.00am tomorrow in HMS *Hebe* and the service will begin over the *Thetis* at 2.00pm.
>
> From an early hour today drapers and milliners shops in Liverpool and Birkenhead were filled with women buying mourning.
>
> They were ordering black in exchange for the pretty dance frocks that had already been delivered and were waiting for the great farewell dance that given by all those who worked on the *Thetis*. It was fixed for tonight in the Kingsland Hall and 700 people were expected. From the drapers the women hurried to the flower market or to the florists where extra staffs are engaged making hundreds of wreaths.[23]

A ticket for the 6th June 1939 farewell dance for *Thetis*, that was never held.

- Aftermath of a disaster

Exactly how many milliners and drapers were in Birkenhead and Liverpool in 1939 is not known to me, but I would venture to say that there would certainly be sufficient to provide relatives with the required 'mourning' without filling or overunning the relevant trader's premises. Furthermore the memorial service aboard HMS *Hebe* was for relatives only and not friends, so further reducing the numbers of articles required and the number of people wanting them.

What is fact is that the Kingsland dancehall is still a dancehall in the centre of the town and that the farewell dance was obviously missed. Walter Arnold himself referred to the dance in a television interview shown in 1989 but filmed at an unknown earlier date as Walter Arnold died in 1974.[24]

This mixture of over exaggeration, celebration and frivolity in the same report as bereavement and memorial services is the press' idea of 'the human angle' or 'the human touch' and is further echoed in another 'human interest' story that concerned Roy Glenn's daughter, Brenda. Headlined :-

'Girl Dances Unaware Father is Trapped – Her Mother did not Tell her'.

A 12-year-old girl is dancing in a children's concert at Coventry Hippodrome this afternoon, unaware that her father is trapped in the submarine *Thetis*. She is the daughter of Mrs. Glenn and Commissioned Engineer R.D. Glenn whose home is in Coventry.

Mrs. Glenn who travelled by car during the night to Birkenhead to wait at Messers. Cammell Laird's yard for news said today 'We have three children, the eldest a boy of sixteen. I did not tell any of the children anything about their father being in the submarine before I left Coventry, and I think it is best to let my daughter dance just the same. I want her to enjoy herself while she can.[25]

Perhaps the most interesting aspect of these highly emotionally charged articles is the reference to 'extra staffs [at florists] engaged making hundreds of wreaths'. There are very direct comparisons here with the events following the death of Princess Diana in 1997. I know from a reliable press source that at this time there were calls from many members of the public asking newspapers to provide free space on their pages for public condolences for the Princess by telephone. Newspapers both in 1939 and 1999 are not in the business of giving away free space. Advertising pays for a considerable slice of the costs of production, distribution etc. This commercial dilemma following the events in Paris was circumvented by printing a coupon in many newspapers which could be filled out and posted into the papers concerned; the effect of which was to drastically reduce the numbers of readers who 'could be bothered' to fill in and post the coupons. Internally, and privately, advertising executives posed the question 'Are all those florists giving away their flowers?' [26]

It is equally unlikely that the florists of 1939 would be similarly disposed.

The similarity with the events following the death of the Princess of Wales does not end here. Following her death a publicly subscribed fund was established to provide for the charities that the Princess was known to be involved with or sympathetic to. The administration of this fund is now the subject of intense media interest, being criticised for parsimony as well as 'cheapening' the memory of the Princess by allowing, among other things, a margarine company to print a facsimile 'Diana' signature upon the packing of their product. Whilst this book is not the place for any judgements upon these matters, there are still parallels with *Thetis*, as *Thetis* too had a publicly subscribed disaster / memorial fund that was set up immediately following the disaster. This fund too has been heavily criticised for parsimony and poor management.

The *Daily Herald* within days of the loss of *Thetis* reported the early birth of the fund. Headlined- **'Aid For The Victims'**

> Wires from all parts of the country reached Sir Frank Bowater, Lord Mayor of London yesterday promising support for the *Thetis* Fund that is being opened at the Mansion House today… Sir Frank sent a letter to the editor of the Daily Herald last night ** in which he says…. we can…join together in a practical course of action and raise a fund from which special provision will be made for their [the bereaved] future – provision of a sort which, had they but known of it, would have comforted the men themselves in their last hours.[27]

**As I am sure he sent to each and every other newspaper, but why not claim an element of exclusivity here!

- Aftermath of a disaster

The administrators of this fund operated in a world that did not have television, computers or a Freedom of Information Act. They had nobody looking over their shoulders and were accountable to nobody. The *Thetis* Fund was never a registered Charity.[28] These administrators could do as they thought fit and they did just that. I have spent many hours and days trying to trace the whereabouts and distribution of these monies, which within days of the disaster amounted to over £115,000, an absolute fortune in 1939.[29] I have encountered numerous brick walls and more than my share of 'buck passing'; whilst support has come from some surprising sources, other avenues have been equally surprisingly less than helpful.

Having found what I believe to be the truth about the distribution and management of the Fund, the only thing can be said with any degree of certainty is that the one thing that those men who died aboard *Thetis* would definitely **not** have had in their last hours, had they but known of the administration of this fund, would be any comfort.

To conclude this look at how things were reported and narrated at the time it would of course be ideal to consider the views of eye witness reports but after 60 years these are naturally almost non existent. There are very few voices around today that can remember the disaster and the immediate events afterwards that were actually 'on the spot'.

Most relatives found out about their loss after the events and were spread around the country. The only people who were actually there or thereabouts would be living witnesses of the beaching of *Thetis* and the burials of her dead.

Both of these events took place on the island of Anglesey. Some might say that the island is an isolated place even today, though I would disagree with that view as I have been fortunate enough to visit the island many times and continue to do so. However, what is true is that Anglesey certainly was a fairly remote region in 1939 with a population of approximately 49,000 people. (The estimated population for 1995 is only 67,212.*) Talking to local people I interviewed some living witnesses of the events on Anglesey immediately after the loss of the *Thetis*. Mrs. Eluned French, of Holyhead, was a 14 year old schoolgirl in 1939. Mr. Owen Aled Owen, of Pentraeth, now a farmer, was a 24 year old insurance salesman in 1939.

* Anglesey in figures, Anglesey County Council.1997

Mrs. Eluned French. DOB 3.11.1924 Holyhead, Anglesey.

We were strolling down to town as usual on a Saturday morning, a glorious day. We got to town and everyone seemed to be so hushed and still. We realised straight away that something was amiss. Of course, we eventually got to hear what had happened...that the *Thetis* had sunk, and people were in tears and were already grieving for them, although there was then, still hope that they might be brought out alive. But unfortunately they didn't.

One of my uncles used to work in the marine yard... he was devastated by the whole affair and he wondered why the Admiralty wouldn't send some welders, actually he said the ship hadn't been taken over then by the Navy and why didn't Cammell Lairds take action themselves and cut a hole in it and get the people out, because at that time I don't think the ship had been taken over by the Navy. My Uncle was very angry. He was very angry, yes that no action was being taken to save the men.

After we found out the men had been lost, the submarine was pulled onto the beach at Traeth Bychan...and eventually they brought it to Holyhead.

I didn't go and look at it........ at the time and you know.. there was an awful lot of military people around, I don't think I would have been able to get there to see what was going on, really...there were sentries everywhere, you know...to stop people from going, from approaching the dock...of course by then it was also a naval base HMS *Bee* was established there on shore. That was at 'Turkey Shore' what we called 'Turkey Shore'. It was a shore base for the Navy, they had motor launches and Beta boats based here during the war, just at the beginning of the war. Everything happened so quickly...within what seemed a few days a whole little sleepy port was transferred to a very very busy naval port.

I remember the cortege as well... I think it was either the end of September or the beginning of October, in 1939...I'm not too certain of the date...but I remember it was another glorious autumn day. Lorries had been commandeered

- Aftermath of a disaster

from all the tradesmen around about the villages and Holyhead, and of course they were cleaned up and polished and the drivers or owners drove them. There were two massive coffins placed on each lorry draped with flags and it was very gruesome really the sight of the coffins...they were very high about three feet, at least 30 inches, or more near enough...and quite long of course.

We had some evacuees staying with us at the time and the wife whose husband was in the Merchant Navy ...and he happened to be here on leave with her at the time and of course he met some of the people involved in the beaching and bringing the bodies ashore...they said that the bodies were in a bad state ...they were hands clasped and embracing each other ...they had to cut them apart. I heard that from the people who were involved in it, you know...that some of them were old acquaintances, embracing each other. So they died like that, it was awful wasn't it. Very sad.

I stood by the road, with my parents and watched the cortege.. All the brass hats were there, they led the procession... but we weren't allowed to go to the cemetery then. It was opened later on. We were allowed in then... but we weren't allowed to go to the service itself...that was just a navy affair...there were too many people in the funeral, families and navy personnel.

When it happened at the time, everybody was stunned by what had happened and there were some talk of sabotage as we were so near a war, and lots of people thought, you know...the sinking of *Thetis* was the first declaration of war, more or less, lots of people thought of it that way...it's going back a long time now. I think the whole nation grieved you know and everybody seemed to think the Admiralty were at fault and that they could have been saved... I should imagine the Admiralty wouldn't given them permission to cut it open, would they. They wanted to save the submarine. With the war imminent, I suppose.

We used to attend the anniversary parades every year. Up until the 50th Anniversary. The naval authorities organised it. And after the 50th most of the families had gone, so they stopped it then, but Holyhead still carries on, the Royal Naval Association always have a service led by the Sea Cadets band who sound the Last Post. They go to the cemetery and one or two of the old submariners who are still alive come up from Birkenhead...It's still a very very sad thing to remember.

Mr. Owen Aled Owen. DOB
30.9.1915. Pentraeth, Anglesey.

In 1939 I was 23 or 24.. I was called up
to the RAF in 1940. I was in the insurance
business with the Pearl Insurance...I 'd
go a round the island collecting most days
and nights...I was single then. I remember
in the summer of 1939, hearing the news
about the submarine that was lost off
Anglesey...I think it was on the radio, it said that it had gone down, with all
hands...so many years ago isn't it?
You could see the boats, coming to where it had gone down. They were there
for weeks and weeks...I don't know what kind of boats they were, but I could
see that they were quite decent sized boats. You could see from the land.

There were all sorts of stories about it... that they were celebrating so
there were a lot of extra people on board, that shouldn't have been on it at the
time. That's what they said at the time. Celebrating because it was a new boat
just launched from Cammell Laird's. But they'd forgotten to close the torpedo
tube... That is what they were saying then... I don't know if there was any
truth in it. That was the story that was about.

There were some cars going about, but you don't know if they were
Navy or Merchant Navy. I don't know what they were...but there were more
cars than usual on the island... they were going backwards and forward, like,
you know.

After a few weeks They brought the submarine *Thetis* into Traeth
Bychan, that was only a few miles from my home at Pentraeth...so I went
to see it...I was surprised how small it was. I thought it would be bigger.
With all those people on board. First time I'd seen a submarine, anyway...
There were quite a few local people going down to see it ...but after that

- Aftermath of a disaster

they stopped people going to see it.

They kept it quite quiet, didn't make a splash about it, as War was on by then, wasn't it.

They said there were miners from South Wales coming to get them out.. there was a lot in the news about the War... but the submarine business was quite quiet...kept it quiet. I was going out with my job and I could see those two boats out there for a couple of weeks. I used to watch them. I didn't see the submarine arriving at all, only heard that she had been beached...at Traeth Bychan.

There were these two boats out there all the time in the same position. I suppose that was quite near the point were the submarine went down. There might have been more boats but these two were there all the time. There might have been more boats coming and going. These two were there every day. It was something new to get ships up then, they couldn't do much about it could they. I don't know how deep was it down there...If it happened today I suppose they'd be more clever.

I know the bodies were taken to Holyhead... people talk don't they...they used lorries to take them at night...these miners had come from South Wales to do the job...The people around Traeth Bychan ...on my rounds... They tell me there were lots of smells.

Then I was called up... you had to go. I wasn't farming. If I was farming I wouldn't have had to go. I preferred the RAF, well, I'm not very fond of the water.

I remember small things like seeing the submarine. It was exciting to see a submarine for the first time... seen plenty of cruisers and all that you know when I was sailing in Malaya from India to Malaya...we had big escorts taking us...but it was upsetting at the time, of course, with all these people down there, couldn't get at them, very very upsetting at the time...Well I suppose there were a lot of mistakes made then, in a panic...and this was before the War started, really. After that it all went quiet. Other tragedies happened very quickly after that.

In 2000 Dave Walker and his wife Val ran the cafe and shop at the busy beach of Traeth Bychan, Moelfre, and are naturally interested in the events that happened on their doorstep in 1939...the shop sells copies of *Thetis - The Admiralty Regrets'* and this book. One of their long standing customers has been a regular visitor to the island for more than 60 years, Shirley Grimsdale (nee Roberts), who today lives in Brighton, Sussex.

Shirley wrote to me and told that she was an eight year old on holiday on the island of Anglesey in 1939. She remembers how 'quiet and sad all the adults became'. She was also kind enough to allow the use of her father, Marshall Roberts' photographs of the wrecked *Thetis* at Traeth Bychan. She tells in her letter that 'dad took the photos from a little rowing boat owned by a man named David Thomas who actually took the people around the bay for a shilling. David Thomas eventually bought the Penrhyn Point Headland, at the other end of Traeth Bychan from Dave and Val's place, and was the first owner of Penrhyn Point Caravan site, where we have had a caravan since 1964'.

Unfortunately David Thomas died some time ago, but he would certainly have been able to tell us a great deal about those lingering summer months of 1939.

above and overleaf:
Various views of the wreck of *Thetis* at Traeth Bychan, Moelfre, Anglesey.
Courtesy of Marshall Roberts / Shirley Grimsdale.

- Aftermath of a disaster

Aftermath and Today

Sixty years on what happened to the Thetis Fund? Who got the money and why? Who was in charge of the distribution of the Fund and how did they make their decisions? What was the treatment meted out to those left behind?

For clarity, it must be emphasised that although some institutions did make donations to the Thetis Fund the vast majority of the sums collected came from Joe Public...ordinary men, women and children who gave what they could in the hard times of 1939.

Those left behind from this tragedy are, for obvious reasons, a rapidly diminishing and a very disparate group of people who in the main have rarely or never met each other. They are dotted around the UK and the world, from Birkenhead to Portsmouth, Australia to North America. Finding them and finding the Fund were to prove a lengthy, complex and very time consuming business. In many ways this may read somewhat like a detective novel and at times it must be said that I felt like it was. There were so many red herrings and dead ends in an effort to trace the administration, use and even the whereabouts of the publicly subscribed Thetis Disaster / Memorial Fund.

The only starting point I had was the republication of the Warren and Benson book and my telling of the story over a period of some six weeks in September / October 1997 on BBC Radio Merseyside. This was the spark that ignited and inflamed interest and opinion in this disaster from sixty years ago. The telephone lines to the station were jammed and many people wanted their say and an opportunity to respond to the story. Some were relatives of those lost and naturally these contacts were maintained by me to contribute to this book. Some were from a generation who, like me, knew only the bare bones of the story and were shocked to be made aware of the startling details of the disaster. Yet others heard the story for the first time and comments like 'I just don't believe that these things happened this way' or 'Why didn't they do x, y or z?' were commonplace.

Many letters were received in a similar vein, some offering information whilst others simply expressed their sympathies to those left behind or offered congratulations for bringing the story back to public attention. Most striking of all was the deep resentment about the whole affair still felt on Merseyside and, after the national broadcasting of the radio drama *'Close Enough to Touch'*

- Aftermath of a disaster

in September 1997, both nationally and internationally.

As the publisher of the book I became the inadvertent focal point for those with an interest in *Thetis*, relatives, retired submariners and sailors, museums and historians. Engaging with these parties it became clear that there were still many unanswered questions about the *Thetis* disaster. Relatives felt that apart from the annual remembrance service in Holyhead that ceased on the 50th anniversary in 1989, they had been forgotten, that they had been let down and that there had been a cover-up, but most of all that they had been shabbily treated by either the Royal Navy, the 'establishment', Cammell Laird or the Thetis Disaster Fund.

The first shocks came when relatives of civilians talked about the immediate aftermath of the disaster and the interment of their loved ones. Families were given a choice for the remains of their relatives to be either interred in the mass grave at Holyhead or privately at their home town or other place of their own choosing. If the latter were chosen the Navy would arrange to transport the remains to the nearest mainline railway station where a local undertaker would then take over the arrangements for transport, burial, cremation etc. From the moment that the remains were handed over to local people all costs incurred were borne by the families. This almost incredible state of affairs was never questioned by anyone at the time. So it was that Victoria 'May' Summers a young woman of 27 years old with three young children under the age of seven was made a widow, with no income, and had to pay to bury her lost husband George, a Cammell Laird electrician.[1]

This applied to other civilians too, like Norman Willcox, the Mersey Pilot who voluntarily stayed aboard *Thetis*. His older brother recalled:

'Mother and Father never really got over it…they got his body from Holyhead… he is buried at Woodchurch Parish Church, …I wouldn't be surprised if we didn't get the right bodies back…they'd be in such a state…but my father paid for the funeral himself.[2]

The Thetis dead, if not interred at Holyhead, were buried at home with the costs borne by their loved ones and it was the treatment of those loved ones left behind which would both shame and shock any sensible human being.

During the course of my interviews with relatives I asked if they had received any help from anywhere else such as the Thetis Fund. Asked if she received any help from the fund, Victoria 'May' Levelle (formerly Summers) replied that she had received £1.00 a week for herself and 7s 6d (36p) each for the children. These payments took the form of a redeemable money order so the recipients kept no records. She also received, in common with other dependent relatives of Cammell Laird employees, £300 Workman's Compensation from Cammell Laird. However this money was never actually put into the hands of the relatives of lost shipyard workers but paid into the County Court at Birkenhead. Recipients or claimants were obliged to make a written application for funds, be this for clothing or furniture or whatever.[3]

The cold reality of what happened when the bereaved made their applications for help to the court in Birkenhead is remembered by the widow and daughter of George Summers, a Cammell Laird electrician.

Victoria 'May' Levelle (formerly Summers) DOB 19.2.1909 Widow of George Summers, Electrician, and Agnes Gaul (nee Summers) DOB 1.3.1932. Daughter of George Summers.

May: We lived in a flat in Gilbert Square in Birkenhead. That day George went to work at about 6.45am on the morning of the 1st June. It was a marvellous morning, a beautiful morning. He'd been away a week up in Scotland, when it went on trials, he'd come home rather depressed because it hadn't took the trial and they brought her back to Cammell Laird's to fix her up again.

I didn't hear the news until teatime. My mother heard it. I went down to George's dad, took the children with me about 7 o'clock at night. I said George hadn't come home...Mr Summers said go home...they must have missed the tide. Whether he'd heard anything, I don't know...he had his own wireless. He said you take those children home. We didn't hear anything for three days then heard everything was abandoned.

When my mother came the next morning, I knew then...she said they'd heard (my dad and mum) what had happened.

I went on a minesweeper, the *Hebe*, to the Liverpool Bay where she'd gone down... there was a service...we got a meal and everything.

When they did get George after 6 months, I got a letter to say that the remains had been passed on to Woodside... Alec Smith was the Undertaker, who told us the coffin was a terribly big, zinc lined coffin... The letter said Woodside...he probably came home on the train and then Mr. Smith had to pick him up at Woodside to bring him home. Then I paid for George's funeral so he was buried nice...he's in Flaybrick Cemetery.

They gave me £1.00 a week and 7/6d each for the children. I went three years and got married again…but when I wrote and told them that I'd got married again, they took the £1.00. off me… It carried on for a few years the 7/6d. for the children… until they were 16…nothing else…then it stopped.

My second husband…he went down to Lairds to ask about the lad, my son Bill, getting a job, he wanted to be a joiner. They did give him a job. He had to do his National Service, Bill, he still came back to do his apprenticeship. We did ask for help with the tools, which he had to have. His dad took those down with him on the *Thetis*. He had a big box as he was an electrician…they went down with him…so we wrote to the fund to ask for help with the tools for Bill to start his time, we sent a stamped envelope end everything… but we got no reply.

Agnes: I was 7 when it happened. Of course, I think I realised when all the commotion was going on. My mother had to go down and wait for news at Cammell Laird's gates, I used to go with her. I was missing my dad and I wouldn't let my mother out of my sight, and I wanted to be with her, and I remember going down to the big gates at Cammell Laird's…waiting for news.

Mum got £300 for compensation from Lairds, £100.00 for me, £100.00. for Betty and £100.00 for Bill. I was the one who had to go down…I was working then and we used to have to put an application form in, to the County Court in Birkenhead, and then the Judge would decide whether we could have anything out of the fund or not. One time I went down there, asked for a dress I think it was about £10, and put an application form in, his secretary who was a nice lady…she sometimes shake her head as though to say 'be careful, he's in a bad mood today'…the Judges' name was Burgess, I can still remember him… depending upon what mood he was in would affect if you got the money. I remember going one day to ask for some money for a new dress; I was about 16 at the time. He said to me 'Do you really need a new dress?' …and I got a bit 'fed-up' you know, and so I said to him something like … 'but this is my money not yours, it's for me because my dad died' or something like that… anyway he just got hold of the paper that you had to fill in and ripped it up in front of me saying, 'You're a very cheeky young lady, you'd better come back when you have calmed down'. So I didn't get the money.' [4]

We'd get little bits. My mother used to go down for £4.00 a month. Couldn't have it all in one go, the £300.00…she got George's Pension too - 5s.0d. for me 3s.0d. for my sister Betty and 3s.0d. for Bill…that was the Widow's

- Aftermath of a disaster

Pension paid by the Government.

After we lost my dad, mum's sister, Evelyn, her husband was going in the Army, and she decided to come and live with my mum. We lived in Townsend Street then. The other sister, Nance, wasn't married, she was younger. So she came to stay with my mum to help out...buy shoes or help the family out...they were very good. It always made me think twice about when I saw people collecting for funds, I'm not giving to funds... it made me that way. We got nothing out of the fund... I don't believe the people who need the money, get the money from the funds, but where does it go? Maybe backhanders or something like that. The people who should get it don't get it...it made me think that way...so as I say I would never give to funds after that.

May: There was a cough mixture company...I can't think of the name of the company ...who sent me a cheque directly rather than through the Fund.. it was for £20.00...they wrote a letter saying they would sooner send it directly to the widow, rather than through the Fund.

Mrs. Craven, she appealed, she fought. When it first happened, it was brought in as damages...and we were supposed to get a lot more money from Cammell Laird's. Cammell Laird fought the case because they didn't know whose fault it was on that ship... ill fated I think... too many on it I think.

Agnes: The Craven's had just one boy... I don't know where he is...He was older than me... I think his name was John.

George Summers, Cammell Laird Electrician.

- Aftermath of a disaster

Archie and Mabel Craven with John (8)   John Craven

John Craven. DOB 5.6.1929. Son of Ships' Fitter Archie Craven

I was just coming up to 10 on the 5 June. We lived in Landsdown Road, off Tollemache Road… Near St. James' Church, Birkenhead. I was the only child. My father had two brothers and his birthday was on 2nd June. He was the younger of the brothers.

Well my father never came home that day, and my mother thought he must be working late to get something finished, and they'd stopped to work. But nobody from Cammell Laird's got in touch to say that the submarine had gone down. She knew he was going on trials, but she thought he might have come back, and doing some work. Now and again I think he did stop and do some work. But it was the next day, she picked a newspaper up and it was the Headline, right across the paper and that was the first she knew about it. Nobody came and told her.

She just said the first thing she knew was when she picked the paper up and saw the Headlines across the newspaper. She said I'll never forgive them for that as no one had come to tell her.

I think I first realised that something wasn't right here was the next day after, my mother said to me, 'you'll have to go to school.' Of course I went to school and my mother stayed at home. I realised something, but it didn't sink in when you are young. It gradually comes to you that he's not going to come back again. She never said the words to me, not really, I think being only a young lad, my grandmother lived 4 doors away so she was seeing her all the time. It must have been a great shock for her…I remember her saying I'll never forgive them for that. She said to me you are never going to Cammell Laird's.

They got me out of bed one day and that was to meet Sir Robert Johnson. But it was night time and they came late…just after it happened this was…there was him and a few directors with him, he said 'There will always be a job in Cammell Laird's for you, son. Soon as you are old enough.' Years later, and I just walked in there (Lairds) and asked for a job and I was there for about 3 years. They were short of men.

Four months after it happened the bodies were recovered, and you don't realise until you see that coffin, and then you realise, that is it… I remember going to the funeral, opening the door, and the road was full of people. You look at all these people, looking at you. It does come home to you then.

Over the years I met different people that my mother knew and they were in the same position as my mother. She did go to Cammell Laird's one time, I think it was one of the visits by the Duchess of Kent, the mothers went before them. They were invited to go and meet her. She went in and out of court a few times, and I remember she went to court and she told them that my son wants to be a joiner. Is there any chance of any extra money to buy tools or anything? That time I think my mother got £1.10s.0d. They said that isn't a problem, we will take 10s.0d. off her and give it to your son... she said that's no good… I'll have no money then. They could only sue Lieutenant Woods couldn't they, because you couldn't sue the Crown. I've only realised after why they didn't sue the Admiralty, which is because you weren't in a position to do so... You couldn't... It seems ridiculous. If you sued Lieutenant Woods he'd probably declare himself bankrupt. So you wouldn't get any money off him anyway… they used my mother's name... and there was another lady probably if I looked in the book…I think mother went to London, but they weren't called to do anything.

When it first happened, they got in touch with my father's eldest brother. Years ago it was always the eldest son. Charlie Craven. They asked him to go to Anglesey to identify the bodies. It was years later, before he died, he said to me, I thought I better tell you, I never ever seen your father. He said I went to Anglesey to identify the bodies and there was a Policeman there, and I told

- Aftermath of a disaster

him who I was, and the Policeman said well if I were you I wouldn't go in there. You won't identify him anyway, because they've all grown beards. It was four months before it was recovered. He said I'll bring some things out and show them to you. He said you can just say yes or no. If anybody asks if you've seen the body just say yes. This is what we did. My father broke his leg one time, playing football, and he always had a pad on his leg, well he still had this pad on his leg. He showed him his watch and a few things, and said that was it. The Policeman said just tell them you've seen the body. But he said, they've all got beards, you'd never recognise anyone. It was four months before they recovered the bodies from there.

Dad's in Flaybrick Cemetery... I think my mother, Mabel, wanted him to come back. But what they did do, they would send the body back to the nearest Railway Station, at that time was Woodside. From then on you paid the rest. You had to pay for the funeral as well. They never said they would pay for the funeral or anything like that.

I think mother got 7s 6d a week for me...She did take a cleaning job because there was no money and it is only when the money came up from the Fund. They collected money didn't they? I remember I had a relation in the Army, and all the soldiers gave about 6d. each towards it, at that time. He said there must have been an awful lot of money.

She got a widow's pension. And from the Fund about £1.0s.0d. a month and the Compensation because they'd lost the case I think she got £300.0s.0d. Workmen's Compensation from insurance. That was from Cammell Laird's but she never got that money. My mother said when she was in the court in Birkenhead the Judge said if I give you this £300.0s.0d you'll spend it and you'll come back on the town to keep you and your son. So they decided to give £1.10s.0d. every month.

At the time they asked my mother do you owe any money to anybody? And she said no I don't. People didn't have a lot of money to spend, and they said it's a pity because if you'd had any furniture or anything on Hire Purchase they would have paid that off. But of course she didn't owe money. Never got anything. She went a few times, I think...They wanted to see what your position was as time went on. She used to have to go to court down in Birkenhead ..she used to go and I always remember she had to take this oath on the Bible they put in front of you, she said you had to pay a shilling (1/-) to take the oath. They used to give her the 1/- and she paid it in and took the oath on the Bible, then he'd ask you questions about your means, I suppose.

That £300.0s.0d. was doled out to you and once it had gone, that was it, finished. It was a damn cheek saying you'd spend the money if we give it you in a lump sum.

I remember one time I got a new bike. Thinking back now, probably perhaps her father's brothers had paid something towards it. When you are young you say you'd like a bike, but you don't realise people haven't got money, do you to buy you these things. Anyhow I did get this new bike, and I realised after, when I was older, that somebody else must have helped pay for it. Because my father's eldest brother, Charlie, he came with me down to the shop, and we got this new bike.

My mother used to talk about it. She'd talk about the money, but when you are young you think money is endless you don't think about where it comes from. There were a few firms that sent money. I remember there was a fruit firm, I remember her saying about this fruit firm. They sent her some money and said that we are giving you this money because if we pay it into the Fund, you may never ever see it. I don't know if a Newspaper, the *Daily Herald,* my mother used to buy, ...not sure if they gave her some money.

I was only a lad, but there was someone sitting on our garden wall, waiting for us to show our face out of the door. We had a back entry to where we lived, and she used to sneak out through there up to her mother-in-law's. They don't give up, they just hound you. I often thought about other people, and to me sometimes they aren't very bothered about upsetting people, they want a story as it is their living. They'll just hound you till they get a story. My mother's sister lived in Wrexham, and they must have found out where she lived, as they went to the house...there was an article in the paper... There was a write up about my father, mother and me. My mother came from Overton, outside Wrexham. My grandfather had a small holding.

I went to Lairds when I was about 27,... I never told mum till I went home. She said to me, 'They've offered you a job there, but I don't want you to go.' That day I had run round quite a few places, trying to find a job, and in the end I went into Cammell Laird's, in fact it was on the Friday. And they said I could start on the Monday. I never told anybody who I was and it was only this chargehand who knew my cousin, same name, and put two and two together. He came to me and said 'Was your father on the *Thetis?*' I said 'Yes.' I left it at that and then the next thing people were coming up to me saying 'I

- Aftermath of a disaster

knew your father.'

Somebody told me about this one fella, I think he was a fitter, and he had a bad heart. They gave him a job on the shore gang, or something. I went down to see him. Of course, he was made up to see me and said to me, 'I'm glad to see you. I was a great friend of your father's.' I think he told Frank Shaw that I was in the yard. Then I met him and he asked could he come and see my mother. I said yes and he came to see my mother.

I went to his house one day, to see him. I went round and there was only him and me. We went in his front room. He'd moved house by then, in Prenton. We just had a talk, but he never ever mentioned the *Thetis* once. And when he came to see my mother, he asked her would she go to the service. They started having a service every year. But my mother wouldn't go.. Then they gave him the British Empire medal. He said he was going to Australia to see his son. He said that he was taking the medal with him to give to his son, cause I'll probably never see him again. Then later on the first I knew was that it was in the Birkenhead News, he had died and there had been a funeral. I hadn't heard about it, otherwise I would have gone to it. I didn't know anything about it.

I never spoke to my mother much about it. I thought I didn't want to drag it up in front of her. In case it upset her. She was upset... She never said a great lot. She used to keep a lot to herself ...I don't think she ever got over it... She never ever got married again... Just never bothered.

She lived to a ripe old age of 97...she got a cheque for about £8.00 a month till the day she died...They used to send her the money every month through an Insurance Company. Actually it started off with the Lord Mayor of London's Appeal Fund. Because my mother said 'Why should they call it the Lord Mayor of London's Appeal Fund?' I said well someone will get paid for administering it. I said that is more money going out of the Fund. It came through Cammell Laird's...I remember one time, while I was working there, I went in one day and I said my mother has gone on her holidays. They were sending letters to say, she must have had to sign something and send it back to say that she had had the money... I went in the office. They said 'Come in,' and I went in and I saw the Head Cashier or someone like that in Laird's. I said to them my mother has gone away for a few weeks. I said this thing she filled in, if you are waiting for it to come back, she is away. They said it was OK. Then they asked if I was getting on alright.

I remember when she died I rang them up and told them my mother had died. They said to hang on a minute, and they checked and said she'd been paid up to date, so there would be no more money forthcoming. That was the end of it. They never even wrote a letter to acknowledge that I'd rung them up. They just said she'd been paid up to date. That is it.

When my mother died, I rang the *Birkenhead News,* and said a lot of people knew her. My father died on the *Thetis.* Some lad said 'well what's that, can you explain it to me?' I said it doesn't need explaining…I just said forget it… I just put the phone down, I won't bother.

I think she was badly done to. When I think of all that money that was collected, there was no such thing as we'll share it out. My mother used to say I bet them officers got a lot more money than your dad who was only a fitter. So they never knew what people got.

I always remember somebody from Laird's came to see my mother when it happened…They said we are very sorry but there are no tools, somebody had smashed his toolbox open, and pinched all his tools. When you think afterwards, they thought, well he's dead anyway he doesn't need them. And they just smashed the tool box open. They were very apologetic about it, but somebody there pinched all his tools.

I blame Cammell Laird's as they built that boat and all the other people were sub-contractors. They were the main contractors. To me what Lieutenant Woods did I thought it was crazy. I thought to myself, somebody who is a sailor, you'd go and open a torpedo tube knowing full well that if there is water there, you'll never shut it again! I mean you'd get a little bar or something and give it a poke to see if any water came through first when you open the drain hole. It would give you the indication that the torpedo tube is open or if it was closed there would be no water coming through. Once you've opened that door, and water comes through, there is no way of closing it. Which they couldn't, could they?

They did argue in court about that, and then they came to the conclusion they couldn't really blame anybody. The Admiralty should have been responsible for Lieutenant Woods' actions, what he did.

I wish I'd been older. I could have got up and done a bit more shouting about it. Or could have gone with my mother. They just seemed to tell you what you are going to do. I mean, that money, they said we are passing it to an Insurance Company, and they just said sign here. You are going to get this money monthly.

- Aftermath of a disaster

At one time I did think about going to see the local MP. Ask him what is happening to all this money and all these people.

I remember seeing in the paper at one time, '*Thetis* widow caught stealing'... They must have had her in court... and I thought, perhaps she was hard up, had no money. When you look back, I could have gone to see her or help her or do something... but you just let these things go, don't you... we are all full of good intentions... but we don't carry them out.

CAMMELL LAIRD & CO., LIMITED.

Shipbuilding & Engineering Works,
Birkenhead.

3, CENTRAL BUILDINGS, WESTMINSTER,
LONDON, S.W.1.
TELEPHONE WHITEHALL 3008.

IN YOUR REPLY PLEASE REFER TO

SEC/ARM.

2nd August 1939.

Mrs. Craven,
231, Lansdowne Road,
Birkenhead.

Dear Madam,

We are instructed by the Committee of The Lord
Mayor of London's "THETIS" Relief Fund to make provisional
payments to dependents of those who lost their lives in the
Disaster.

The weekly amount to be paid in respect of yourself
and child is £1. 7. 8. and this amount will be remitted to you
each week commencing Friday next, August 4th, 1939.

Yours faithfully,

FOR AND ON BEHALF OF
CAMMELL LAIRD & Co. LIMITED,

SECRETARY

Letter from Cammell Laird to Mabel Craven informing her of her payments
from the *Thetis* disaster fund.

THE LIVERPOOL & GLASGOW ASSOCIATION FOR THE PROTECTION OF
COMMERCIAL INTERESTS AS RESPECTS WRECKED AND DAMAGED PROPERTY.
(THE LIVERPOOL & GLASGOW SALVAGE ASSOCIATION.)

G.R.Critchley, *Joint Managers.*

Established 1857.
Incorporated 1881.

TELEPHONE NOS. {0143 & 2053 CENTRAL.
{2328 CENTRAL (CARGO SURVEYORS).
TELEGRAPHIC ADDRESS: SALVAGIUM LIVERPOOL.

A.19,20,21 & 22. Exchange Buildings,
Liverpool.

ALL COMMUNICATIONS TO BE ADDRESSED TO "THE MANAGERS."

12th Sept. 1939.

Dear Mrs. Craven,

H.M.S. "THETIS".

You will have received notice that we
are recovering the bodies of victims from this vessel, and
every effort is being made to identify them by representatives of Messrs. Cammell Laird & Co. Ltd. and the Admiralty
at Holyhead.

We have not yet received a list of the men
identified up to date, and you will be receiving direct
notice from the Admiralty Representative if your husband
has been identified.

The object of this present letter is an
earnest desire arising from our experience in these matters
to try to save you unnecessary distress, and with this
object we strongly advise you to try to overcome any desire
you may have to see the body. If you see the coffin you
will find that it is larger than you probably expected, and
we wish to avoid your feelings being hurt by this, and to
assure you that owing to the action of the sea water upon
the body this state of things is quite unavoidable, and
is in accordance with our experience. The coffin is zinc
lined and the zinc lining is hermetically sealed, and we
are sure you will accept our word based upon our experience
that the state of the body renders this sealing essential.

Yours sincerely,

George R. Critchley

Mrs. Craven,
231, Lansdown Road,
BIRKENHEAD.

Letter to the widowed Mabel Craven to 'save her any unnecessary distress'.
Sent by the Liverpool and Glasgow Salvage Association to dissuade her
from seeing her husbands body and describing in shocking detail the
condition of the body.

Mary Kipling and her husband Bob lived in Rodney Street Birkenhead. They had a seven year old son, also Bob, and three girls, Mary, nine, Jean eight and Evelyn aged just one. Bob Kipling was foreman at Cammell Laird who was lost on *Thetis*.

Robert 'Bob' Kipling Foreman Caulker at Cammell Laird. Lost on *Thetis*.

Robert 'Bob' Kipling DOB 26.10.1932. Son of Robert 'Bob' Kipling

Dad was a Foreman Caulker at Lairds' ...he was on the *Thetis* in 1939 during the trials for the submarine. I was just six when it happened... my other two sisters were Jean who was seven and Molly who was eight and the baby Evelyn was 9 months old.

I remember my grandmother she was more or less hysterical at the time when we eventually found that they weren't going to come back ...she lived just down the road from us, in Rodney Street in Birkenhead.

Mum was very level headed and she hid a lot rather than bring it out into the open with young children...she hid an awful lot of feelings...there was workmen's compensation set up and the relatives, particularly the wives, and mothers of those who were single, who went down on *Thetis*, they could go and withdraw money from the Fund but they had to have a good reason for drawing it. They had to go more or less cap in hand to request cash from the Fund and give reasons as to why they wanted it....I think is was the local county court.

She went down for books for me for school.... and clothes, and they were always given alternatives, couldn't you make do with this or buy second hand books rather than take money out of the Fund. But mother was quite strong actually, so she more or less got what she went in for...anybody with less will would have been fobbed off and chased away with less than what they wanted...but life wasn't easy, that's for sure.

My mother more or less put the children first and her second...she did go out to work during the War...we moved from Rodney Street up into Rock Ferry in Bedford Place, it runs parallel with Bedford Road. She took a job at a munitions factory Fawcett & Prestons...she used to work 12 hour days then 12 hour nights. There was a local woman who lived in Bedford Place who used to look after us...she made sure that we got home alright and had something to eat before mother got home.

Mother never really talked about it much...only if we asked...she'd answer whatever we used to ask. We asked once about my father what he did before he took his apprenticeship with Cammell Laird's or after his apprenticeship with Cammell Laird's and apparently, and I can't confirm this, but apparently he went to America during the depression and he worked as a rancher, mechanic, carpenter, anything he could get his hands on, until things started picking up in this country and then he came back.

I can only remember him vaguely... little things stay in the mind...I remember going down the bottom of Rodney Street where we lived when he went to Cammell Laird's and swinging on his fingers when I was only tiny. We used to swing on his fingers one on each side of him and we used to look forward to him coming home on a Friday night and Saturday night cause he used to call at the Market and buy chocolate which was, I don't know whether people remember it now but there was chocolate on sale in the Market called Snow White and the Seven Dwarfs...there was another chocolate called Double Six and he'd bring those home as well. On a Saturday he used to bring little toys, if you like, they were only a penny or tuppence... whatever.

My mother once had an interview with one of the national newspaper reporters, either the *Daily Mail* or *Express*, I can't think now...it was a long time after...it was about the life of a *Thetis* Widow... I'm almost sure the heading was 13 years on and wife of a *Thetis* Widow which tells an awful lot about how they coped for 13 years..so that has got to be somewhere in the region of 1952.

She never remarried and when she died we got in touch with the Boilermakers Union and Cammell Laird's and they said that they would inform all the relevant people who needed to know…I would say she didn't give the impression of being bitter but I would say she probably was…we were very young at the time and it doesn't affect children as it affects people who are a bit older.

What I feel about it now is I'm sorry I never asked my mother more questions when she was alive…but obviously you think they are never going to die. There is an awful lot I really need to know now which I didn't know at the time, and I should have asked but didn't…because it would have been probably traumatic for my mother to speak about it, even such a long time afterwards and I didn't want to put her through that.

There was an awful lot said about who was responsible for the disaster itself, I would say it was probably an accident waiting to happen with regards to what did happen. With regards to the tell-tales of the torpedo tubes…I think basically each one tried to blame the other. Cammell Laird's probably tried to blame the Admiralty, the Admiralty probably tried to blame Cammell Laird's as to who was actually in charge of the submarine who was responsible for it…but basically I would say the Admiralty should take full responsibility because until a submarine is handed over, Cammell Laird's are the owner of the submarine, but the Admiralty had control over what went on within the ship as they were actually going through the trials with it…a lot could be said the other way round if you like, as it hadn't been handed over it was Cammell Laird's responsibility.

I don' think I'm bitter about it really…bitter, no…curious, yes…curious with regard to why the relatives didn't get more help than what they actually did get.

- Aftermath of a disaster

Robert 'Bob' Kipling's children

Robert 'Bob' Kipling

Molly Kipling

Jean Kipling

Evelyn Kipling

Engine Fitter Richard Homer was on *Thetis*. He was the only man aboard who lived in the rapidly developing town of Ellesmere Port, about 10 miles south of Birkenhead. In 2000 his son John still lived in Ellesmere Port and still feels very aggrieved at how he lost his father Richard.

Richard Homer

John Hanley Homer

John Hanley Homer DOB 10.3.1930. Son of Engine Fitter Richard Homer

I'd be nine years old in the March as my dad was killed in June 1939, three months later. At Lairds he was down as a fitter, but he was actually an Electrical Engineer. When it happened I got no information off my mother whatsoever. A chap in the street told me as he was passing. He said, is it true that your dad is on that submarine that's gone down? Obviously I can not remember verbatim what was said then but my answer would have been 'I know nothing about it.' And I didn't know anything about it. And that was about the second day after it had gone down. As I say I was just playing in the street, in Cambridge Road, Ellesmere Port... just as a kiddy and that is how I found out. It didn't register with me obviously at that age that there was something wrong. That he was going to die, or something like that. That didn't occur to me at all. It is just something that was said in passing and just didn't realise what it actually meant.I can remember that when they brought the body home, in this darned

- Aftermath of a disaster

big coffin, because they were massive compared with a normal coffin... there is a little tale there, as I said my father was an Electrical Engineer, and built his own radios, so we had a type of cat's whisker (a bit better than that) he'd built himself. I can remember in 1938, he went up to one of the local shops, and he bought a radio...he brought it home, and my mother hit the roof because he put it on a table, a small table, underneath the window, and it was shaped like a coffin, standing on edge, and she went berserk. I'm not having that in our house she said, it's exactly like a coffin. Less than 12 months later that's where his coffin rested on two trestles when they brought him home.... in the family home in Cambridge Road, in exactly the same place underneath the window.It was just a story that always stuck in my mind. I was only eight at the time and memories of children of that age are not all that brilliant, normally. It was in the room they lived in not in the sitting room...

It was a wooden coffin, and we were told, rightly or wrongly, that it was lead lined...It would be about half as big again in all ways than a normal coffin. It was deeper, wider and longer. It was a massive thing. That was the first coffin that I'd ever seen in my life, so I wasn't comparing it with anything until later on in life, I think myself it would have been there for about, the best part of a week, before the funeral. I'm not sure of the exact date of funeral.

I had to go to the local undertaker's, it was Walkers in the Port to start making arrangements for him to come down to make the burial arrangements, at nine years old, I had to do that myself, because my mum was in, well, a hell of a state, obviously. I had to do that work myself... there were two younger brothers. I was the eldest. It landed on my shoulders to have to do the running around...I don't think it would be heard of nowadays, really. I think, people were hardier in those days. I don't think they showed their emotions as much as they do nowadays. It was life. They just had to get on with life and you just didn't get the sort of soft treatment. I don't mean that wrong, you just didn't get that sort of treatment in those days. You had to stand on your own two feet and this is how it went.

They were the only undertakers in the Port then. I can remember speaking to the chap, the exact words I just can't remember obviously. But I can remember speaking to the undertaker and then he came down later on in the day to see my mother and obviously then, make the proper arrangements...Dad is buried in the local cemetery at Overpool.

As I said my mother never divulged any information whatsoever. In fact I was coming up to 21 years of age before I even knew that I was entitled to some compensation out of the *Thetis* Fund. I never knew before that date. It was only a matter of weeks before I was 21 when I was entitled to a sum of money. It was only a matter of weeks before she said we've got to over to Liverpool to the court. That is what it was for. I didn't know before that.

I've always been given to understand that she got so much from Laird's and so much from the *Thetis* Fund. Now whether the *Thetis* Fund was paid out in a lump sum to her, I don't know. But I know that when she remarried and I think myself it was more a marriage of convenience, that she had three kids to bring up, and I think this was the reason, main reason, that she remarried and I understand that was when money from Laird's ceased. So after that date, there was no monies coming in from anywhere... but what she did say once, more or less in passing, the monies that I received and my two brothers were going to receive, which amounted to about £160.00 each, she was getting the interest that money was generating, those three sums of money... which would be very very little I should imagine. My brothers got something similar, within pounds, because they'd be an extra few years before the next brother was paid out, and then the youngest was paid out so there might have been just a little more interest on that money... I know that we had to go to court. Not into like going to court if you'd committed a crime, but we had to go to the court to see a Judge, or a Registrar or whatever he was…

I did get a new bike. The first year after dad died. He died in 1939, and mum took me and we went up to a cycle shop, and I had a smaller edition of a full-size bike, not a junior one...brand new. Now where the money came from, I know it cost nearly £5.00.

It was tough going. I can remember that. I could come home from school and all that would be for dinner in the evening would be a piece of bread and jam. That was about it. Just a bit of something at midday because there were no school meals until I went to the Grange school at the age of 11. There were no school meals till then. Then I started having a dinner at school. I think that was about 2s/6d a week. Even then, all that we got in the evening, coming home from school, at 4 or 5 o'clock, was a piece of bread and butter. That was about it. Nothing else.

We never went bare-footed or anything like that, we never went without. But by God if you tore clothes or got it dirty, there was trouble. Because we couldn't afford to replace things. I can see that interval up until she remarried, the lads that I played with, as a kid from nine years onwards, they were just that little bit better off than we were. Not a great deal because nobody was well off in those days, no working class family. But they had a few little extras that we didn't have. The parents were a little bit lenient, now my mother couldn't afford to be as she had three little reptiles to bring up, so life was really tough, there was no doubt about it.

They were sympathetic at school …they were at first but then the War started and there was a lot more people getting killed, there were children coming to school that their dad's had been shot or what have you, drowned at sea... so life became rather cheap I think, then, and you certainly didn't stand out in a crowd, like you would have done had the War not started.

Dad was a musician and a bloody good musician if I say so myself. That was him when he was in the Band. The band was called the Melody Makers. He was self taught, all the way along the line. He never had a music lesson in his life, he never had a lesson in writing or reading music. He could transpose any piece of music that came along for all the other instruments in a band. He could do all the arrangements.

He was a good bloke. No two ways about it. He was strict like they all were in those days, but my life and the life of my two brothers, would have been entirely different. Prior to getting killed, we had a junk shop in Ellesmere Port called Daddy Halves (sic) and he had put a deposit on a 3s/4d violin for me, to teach me to play violin. And of course it never materialised. Before he picked the violin up, he got killed. Mother had to go and cancel it.

He was completely self taught in all the musical world and the sax was his instrument... he only started to play the sax because work was a bit short, and him and a friend, a chap called Bob Corson from Ellesmere Port, his wife was the local midwife who always went about on a bike. She was a big, stout women, a marvellous person The family were a musical family in Ellesmere Port, they had music shops. They were planning to go busking to Blackpool until my mother found out. She put the blocks on it!

But this business of *Thetis*... I'm willing to gamble there's never a week goes past without it is in my mind...I'm talking about the whole of my life from nine onwards. I'll willing to bet there is never a week will go past without something comes up. Something comes into my mind over the *Thetis* and what went on. I still feel very bitter about it… I've always said they were murdered. My own feeling was that murder was committed there. I've looked at it in that vein for as long as I can remember. Especially after reading the transcript of the enquiry. I don't know whether you've read it or not, even up until then I always considered it murder, but when I read the transcript...and it should never have happened.

The accident was an accident, all life is full of accidents. The means of the submarine going down in my mind was a pure accident. Human error, which all accidents to me are committed by human error...but the actions from it being lost until all hope was abandoned, well that fell far short of what anybody could expect...that was dreadful to me.

In my mind, total responsibility is on the man who did the spraying inside of the bitumastic that clogged that bleed hole up. He knows who it is, and I feel sorry for him if he is still alive. Because he knows what he did, or he should do. I think that was the total responsibility of the submarine going down.

Reading the original book, and the transcript, right from leaving base, the whole lot just doesn't sound right. The way it wouldn't dive. It was built to dive! It was supposed to be ballasted out in the trim basin, to dive. I could understand if it had gone down and they couldn't get it up because it was too heavy, under a normal dive... I cannot understand the Captain, Bolus ...he should have finished the test, and said this is not right. He was an experienced man, he'd got an experienced crew, because it wasn't just Laird's men that were aboard, it was all submariners that were aboard, he'd got good brains in the crew that knew what they were doing and when they found out that it wouldn't dive, it was common sense. If you took a car out and found it wouldn't stop, because the brakes had gone, you don't continue driving. Or you shouldn't do! So as I say they were partly responsible, but I still think the poor bloke that did the spraying, he was the man responsible, cause if that water had come out of that bleed tube, then there is no way that the inner door would have been opened.

As far as the fund goes... from *Thetis* going down, until the Manchester United Munich air disaster there was never a fund collected. I can always remember reading when they decided to start the fund for Manchester United, the trustees of the fund said we are not having a *Thetis* here. When the fund is closed, the money will be shared out between all the dependants, pro rata, and the fund will be finalised. There will be no money left in the fund

- Aftermath of a disaster

whatsoever. Now I understand that is what happened, I don't know for 100%… it could have been on TV.

I think it was in the national papers. They said we are not having the same situation where people would only get minimal money and there was a big lump sum sitting there doing no good to anyone only the trustees that managed the fund. Then after that came the Penlee Lifeboat Disaster… That was done in exactly the same way as the Manchester United fund. It was handled in exactly the same way. It was opened, it was closed, it was shared out, it was finished.

I suppose, looking back, and being wise after the event, that was how the *Thetis* fund should have been used, but unfortunately nobody knew any differently then, as far as I know. I'm not a big financier, and don't know the workings of their minds, but it should have been done the same as the other funds, but unfortunately it wasn't. But it has always made me bitter that people, not for my own sake, because I read in the local Echo and over the years, especially when I was in the steel mills, of widows trying to get money, knowing there was £100,000 plus sitting there, and couldn't get a ha'penny. They were practically destitute. I'm talking about the widows now not the sons and daughters, like myself. They couldn't get a bean. It has always annoyed me, very much annoyed me.

Barbara Moore (nee Robinson) remembers that she was to have a music lesson at school that day. She knew something was wrong when her grandmother and her uncle arrived at the door to her home in Baytree Road, Tranmere and she was sent out of the room...but like any ten year old, she overheard...

Arthur 'Archie' Robinson

Barbara Moore (nee Robinson)

Barbara Moore (nee Robinson) DOB 15.6.1929.
Daughter of Cammell Laird Chief Engineer Arthur 'Archie' Robinson

I was almost 10 years old when it happened...my father was Arthur Bailey Robinson....Bailey was his mother's name before she was married...her maiden name. He went down on the submarine, *Thetis*, he was chief engineer at Cammell Laird's.

I was at school, it was a very warm summer that year...dad was never in of course, when I got in, because we used to get home from school about 4.00 pm and we'd just have a drink, and then wait for him to come in for our evening meal... He always walked across Mersey Park to Cammell Laird's and back, we lived in Baytree Road, off Downham Road, Tranmere.

My first memory of something being wrong was my grandmother and uncle arriving on the scene at about 8 o'clock in the morning...they came down from Prenton to our house, Uncle Alf had a car and they came down...because they'd heard it on the radio...at the time my mother didn't

- Aftermath of a disaster

know...the submarine was due home the same day, later on, so that evening mother didn't know, she just thought he's late, or delayed...we didn't know until the next morning.

I was getting music ready because I had a music lesson that day...my sister had already left for school she was at the senior school by then... they came in and asked me to leave the room, which I didn't like. But I listened, of course, outside, and I heard them say that the *Thetis* was down and wasn't coming up, they said. Then I went to school, and later that day, I don't know whether you know this, but they sent messages round all the schools, in Birkenhead, saying that *Thetis* had been lifted. I ran all the way home from school to mum, because I wasn't far away from Mersey Park School to Baytree Road, ran all the way, rushed in, and mum told me then that it wasn't, that four people had got off the *Thetis* and my father wasn't one of them...she knew that then.

She was quite calm, actually she was marvellous...she always was.. As far as we know she didn't know then what had happened. They still hoped then more would get off of course. She didn't know that my father was already dead, until we saw Frank Shaw... he was my father's best friend.. he came to our house and told us that my father was one of the 4 that died in the escape hatch... we never saw Frank Shaw again after that...I think he thought it might be not pleasant for my mother. They used to have a card school every Tuesday night the four of them, dad and Frank Shaw were two of them...he just came to tell us...that he hadn't suffered perhaps as long as some would have done. ...we were all in the room when he came...which wasn't very nice at all... I've had claustrophobia ever since. And that was it.

All I knew was a girl at school had lost her grandmother previously, and my mother said you know it is like Hilda's grandmother...that's how she explained it.

Dad is buried at Landican cemetery... my grandfather had died two years earlier and they bought two plots, so of course when my father died, he was buried next to my grandfather. My mother wouldn't let me go to the funeral. I was back in Birkenhead because I was evacuated and I hated it... I just wrote and said I couldn't stay there. Mother came and brought me back. So I was here when they raised the *Thetis* and when they brought them home for funerals... people come back to the house after dad's funeral... I was in the back garden, sunbathing, this is why I knew it was so hot. Mother just wanted me out of the way, because there were no other children there. My sister Eileen was evacuated and she didn't come back... She did eventually... She was away for four years.

The receipts and things I've got are all in my mother's name... she had to pay the funeral costs. She never really mentioned money much...all I knew was that she got a pension. She got a widow's pension from the state, and she got a pension through Laird's. ...that is all I knew... she wouldn't discuss it with a 10 year old. I mean she would discuss it with her family. My sister was away, evacuated, for the first 4 years. There was only mum and I at home. I was a lot younger if you see what I mean.

I knew later that she got something from the fund...I know it was very little... I think I remember her saying once it is funny you should say that, cause when my sister first started work, she got 28/- (£1.8s.0d.) and mother said and I only got thirty shillings (£1.10s.0d.) for a whole family...but I know she had to go out to work...she worked right through her life.

They offered me this place at Chatham Naval College, Laird's did...not the Navy. This was all done through work... Robert Johnson I think... we said no we didn't want to split the family... I was quite happy here. Then he said if ever we wanted any help to get in touch with Cammell Laird's. Well I left school at 16 with 'O' levels and I wanted to go full time for a year at Liverpool Tech... mother couldn't afford the money... So we applied to Laird's and they paid the fees...that's all I ever got. It was just a year's fees at Byrom Street Technical College, Liverpool. I was 16 then, and at 17 I started work.

She never remarried...maybe because she came from a big family who helped...I think probably because she was quite happy bringing us both up and with the family, we were always a very close family...so we always had company. Her younger sister's husband went to sea... so she was virtually a widow, he was away a lot. So they went about a lot together... so she did always   have   company.

Some times you think why did it happen to us, that sort of thing, but it is just one of those things isn't it? There is nothing you can do about it. But I often wondered what would of happened if he'd lived, what a different sort of life we might have had...but you can't change it.

Other kids lost their fathers because the War came...so I wasn't on my own in that position if you know what I mean...which probably helped. Now I've got two daughters, Kathryn 42 and Lindsey 40, they often say they wish

- Aftermath of a disaster

they'd known him. They have both read the book…it was one of my daughters that insisted I got in touch about it…

I would say really that the Navy were responsible…the Navy… that is the impression I got from my father…for a long time before *Thetis* he was dissatisfied. They'd taken him off the Mauritania and put him on the submarines which he said he hated… He said they were looking over his shoulder all the time.

I knew Stan Orton, he was in my class at school and his father was in charge of the cranes at Laird's at the time… He was absolutely furious that the Navy wouldn't let him go out…they insisted on sending boats round from Portsmouth, before they'd let Laird's people do anything. There was a lot of ill feeling about that…a lot…I'm sure they should and could have done more…

After listening to people who were the relatives of the working class folk who worked for Cammell Laird any scepticism I may have had completely evaporated. These people had been treated abominably. Women had lost husbands and breadwinners and children had lost fathers as well as childhoods together with mothers and fathers. All had suffered deprivation, both financial and emotional and all had been looked upon with disdain by anyone they ever turned to for help. Bill Watterson's widow accepted the offer of a 'change of air' in the country from a philanthropic 'titled' lady... Mrs. Dorothy Mack of 'The Shooting Box, North Creake, Fakenham, Norfolk. Mrs. Elizabeth Watterson kept a short diary of her stay and her daughter Marjorie has permitted these extracts to be printed:-

July 1939

Holiday in Norfolk. Staying with the Duke of Westminster's cousin. The now invalid Duke of Westminster is claiming none of the rights and privileges of a Duke - a title he inherited from his cousin last year, but it is a different matter with his sister, the four times married Mrs. Dorothy Mack.

She has applied for a warrant granting her the precedence she would have had if her father had succeeded to the title... this will give her back the right to call herself 'Lady'- a title she lost 34 years ago. In 1909 she married Lord Dalmeny- the present Earl of Rosebery... but then there was a divorce, she married a commoner, and them became plain 'Mrs.', and she has remarried that way to men without titles. Family motto is 'Virtue not Ancestry'.

Saturday July 14th 1939

Met Mrs. Mack at the station, it took me nine hours to arrive at Kings Lynn station at 8.30pm, from there Mrs. Mack took me by car to her home which was 30 miles from Kings Lynn...she stayed there during the shooting season. It was called the 'Shooting Box', North Creake. We arrived feeling very tired after such a long journey, but after having a wash, and a beautiful dinner waiting for us, we felt very much better. Went to bed about 11o'clock.

Sunday

Down for breakfast at 9.30, went to Church Service, back to lunch. As it was very cold we stayed in the rest of the day, reading, playing games and being entertained by Mrs. Mack herself, she was a perfect lady to us.'

Elizabeth Watterson refers to 'us' frequently and I have not been able to confirm or otherwise if any other widows accompanied her. Dorothy Mack certainly seemed to be the only aspect of 'the establishment' that ever did

- Aftermath of a disaster

anything to help the ordinary working class relatives of Birkenhead, and she did this voluntarily, out of 'the goodness of her heart'. From what I had found so far 'goodness of heart' was in short supply in 1939. I would have liked to try and contact her family and one day may well do so, to express my own thanks to them for the apparently lone gesture of Christian kindness shown to *Thetis* widows.

The Shooting Box, North Creake, Fakenham, Norfolk

Mrs. Dorothy Mack in the Norfolk Countryside

COPY.

5/6/39.   SOUTH WESTERN HOTEL,
                                      SOUTHAMPTON.

Messrs. Cammell Laird & Co.Ltd.

Dear Sirs,

            I know of no other way to get into touch with
the widows left from the dreadful disaster. I would be so pleased
if I could help them to get through these dreadful weeks and all
I can offer is to have two to stay with me for a week and keep
on having two for as long as I can. I can offer them comfort and
a change of air and good food all the time they would be with me.
My husband is Commander Mack and is going out on the "CUTTY SARK"
at once. I would like to hear if this would give any of them
pleasure or at least a change of air and scenery.
We live in Norfolk and my address after Wednesday will be:-

                    The Shooting Box,
                        North Creake,
                            Fakenham,
                                Norfolk.

I do not mind who comes, Officers wives or who ever you think
it would benefit. I cannot put up children as I have no convenience
for them, but if you care to send two at a time they come as my
personal guests.
Please reply to address in Norfolk, I return there on Saturday.

                    Yours very truly,

                        (SIGNED.) DOROTHY MACK.

Letter from Dorothy Mack to Cammell Laird offering 'comfort and a change
of air' to the *Thetis* widows.

The terrible and tragic stories of those left behind after *Thetis* seemed to be never ending...May Levelle (formerly Summers) herself recalls that as soon as she remarried her weekly allowance from the Disaster Fund stopped but she still got an allowance for the children. She wrote 'to London' once in about 1953/4 (May was 90 years old in 1999 and cannot remember where or to who) to ask for some help in providing her son Tom with the expensive tools he had to equip himself with to start his apprenticeship in the Cammell Laird yard as a Joiner. (Apprentice Joiners still had to do this even in my time at Lairds in the 1960's). May never received a reply.[5]

Other relatives told of similar instances... For example, Jean Newton (nee Beattie) in her interview:-

> ...she never got over it my mother. I remember one time
> she wanted a bike for me... it was Christmas time, I'd be
> about 12 or 13, my sister went down [to the court] and
> the Judge said 'God gave you two legs. Your sister is only
> 13, she should be able to walk' and she didn't get the
> money.' [6]

Such was the treatment meted out to relatives of working class people. They couldn't be trusted with such a large sum of money and might well squander it on alcohol or gambling or heaven forbid, a children's bicycle. In order to prevent such an occurrence the money was handled by a formal legal system that equally played god and made judgements upon who could have what, when and why. This was social engineering and control on a grand and scandalous scale.

Some of the Cammell Laird widows even tried to get some form of recompense for their loss and were the subject of test cases against Cammell Laird, Lieut.Woods, Wailes Dove Bitumastic (The contractors responsible for the enamelling of the insides of the torpedo tubes), Mrs. Bolus and the widowed mother of Seaman Hambrook. Action was also attempted by the family of David Norman Duncan, an employee of Brown Bros. Ltd, a sub contractor to Lairds. Initially these cases were deemed valid against Cammell Laird only. Cammell Laird appealed against this decision and this appeal was allowed. At the same time two widows cross appealed against Lieut. Woods and this too was allowed. Woods appealed to the House of Lords and this appeal was eventually allowed. Negligence had not been established.

What was not apparently recorded is the particulars of what the plaintiffs wanted to use to reinforce their claims. You have to look into the House of Lords records to find the case. Duncan and another Vs Cammell Laird 1942 (p624.) This case established the principle, in laymans terms, that if a member of the government wanted evidence for a civil trial to be withheld from the public domain as 'not in the public interest' the court had no right to question their reasons!

The families were stymied every direction they took as the establishment closed ranks. On January 29th 1941 Mr. Alexander, the First Lord of the Admiralty swore an affidavit concerning the disputed documentary evidence stating: 'All of the said documents were considered by me with the assistance of my technical advisors, and I formed the opinion that it would be injurious to the public interest that any of the said documents should be disclosed to any person.'(p626)

What were these documents that the families needed so much to press their claims for damages, but which the establishment thought so sensitive that they deemed them 'injurious to the public interest'? They are detailed in the same House of Lords records (1942 p627) as:-

1) The contract for the hull and machinery of the *Thetis*.

2) Letters written before the disaster relating to the vessels trim.

3) Reports as to the condition of the *Thetis* when raised.

4) A large number of plans and specifications relating to various parts of the vessel

5) **A notebook of a foreman painter employed by the respondents** *(Cammell Laird.)* [my italics]

War was around the corner and it may have been prudent to perhaps restrict access to plans and specifications on a 'need to know' basis...perhaps they could have been used in the court hearing only and under strict supervision. It is hard to know how the actual contract for the vessel build could be 'injurious to the public interest'.. this would be simply a commercial agreement. Letters relating to the vessels trim *before* the disaster may well have been injurious to the case for **the defence** if it could be shown that the vessel had a history of such problems!

Yet most damning of all was item 5, in another remarkable irony, the same number on the list as the fateful torpedo tube. Arguably the best legal minds in the country from the High Court to the House of Lords as well as the First Lord of the Admiralty expended huge amounts of time, effort and taxpayers money on keeping from the public gaze a notebook of a Cammell Laird foreman painter !

We can only speculate on what the effect upon the case may have been had the painters notebook been made public ... clearly there was something in there that could have implications against the defendants and just as surely they made sure that it would never get out !

More secrets and yet more scandal!

Letter to Mrs. Mabel Craven confirming that the claim against Cammell Laird had been successful and (overleaf) a newspaper report on the same subject.

Page 126

Y. OCTOBER 23, 19

THETIS WIDOWS WIN ACTIONS

BUILDERS LIABLE FOR SUBMARINE'S LOSS

Judgment for the plaintiffs, two widows, against Cammell Laird & Co. Ltd., for an amount to be ascertained, was given by Mr. Justice Wrottesley in the King's Bench Division yesterday in the consolidated test actions arising out of the Thetis submarine disaster in Liverpool Bay on June 1, 1939.

The hearing of the case lasted eight days and the costs amounted to between £15,000 and £20,000.

The plaintiffs, Mrs. Rose Duncan, of Edinburgh, and Mrs. Mabel Mary Jane Craven, of Birkenhead, claimed damages for the deaths of their husbands, due to negligence.

The proceedings were to determine liability for the loss of the submarine as between the builders and various other persons concerned.

In addition to Cammell Laird & Co., the defendants included Mrs. Matilda Ann Hambrook, widow of a leading seaman, Lt. Frederick Greville Woods, R.N., one of the survivors, Mrs. Sybil Bolus, widow of Lt.-Cmdr. G. H. Bolus, captain of the Thetis, and Walles Dove Bitumastic Ltd., of Hebburn, Durham.

99 LIVES LOST

The Thetis, which was undergoing submergence trials, had on board 103 persons, and all except four lost their lives. In the autumn of 1939 the Thetis was refloated, and, under the name of Thunderbolt, rendered valuable service in the war. She has since been lost.

Mr. Justice Wrottesley said that it was a matter of doubt whether the vessel, when she left Birkenhead for her trial, was in the condition stated in the "trim" sheet.

Lt. Woods, who was in charge forward of the control room, saw that something was wrong with the trim. It did not occur to him that the test-cock of No. 5 torpedo tube, which indicated the amount of water in the tube, was out of order. In fact, the hole in the test-cock had been filled with paint.

When, with the assistance of Leading Seaman Hambrook, the rear door of No. 5 torpedo tube was opened, water gushed through the bow-cap and torpedo tube, and the vessel dipped and went down by the head.

BUILDERS' RESPONSIBILITY

Under the contract for building the submarine Cammell Laird were bound to paint the inside of the torpedo tubes. The work was carried out under a sub-contract by Walles Dove Bitumastic Ltd., but the hole in the test-cock of No. 5 torpedo tube was blocked by being completely coated over.

In fact two out of the six forward torpedo tubes of the submarine were out of order.

In no sense were Lt. Woods and Hambrook overseers or responsible for seeing that the work done in the ship complied with the contract. They were attached to the ship for instruction.

Neither could have been expected to be on guard against what happened in this case when the whole of the hole in the test-cock was completely blocked by being enamelled over before the Thetis sailed.

"Lt. Woods and Ldg. Seaman Hambrook," added the Judge, "were in the end, misled by the state of the test-cock. So far as the case against Lt. Woods and Mrs. Hambrook is concerned, there has not been established to my satisfaction the failure of any duty by Lt. Woods and Ldg. Seaman Hambrook to take reasonable care.

"SLOVENLY PIECE OF WORK."

"The man of the Bitumastic company who did this painting did a slovenly piece of work. Two of these holes were obstructed, and a cursory inspection would have shown them to have been blocked."

On behalf of the Bitumastic company, it was said that they were humble painters. This argument was not available to Cammell Laird. In fact, their master painter inspected the work and should have been in a position to notice the blocked hole.

His lordship thought that the sub-contract did not absolve Cammell Laird from seeing that the work was properly done.

They sent none of their highly qualified engineering staff to see that the painting was so done as to leave the safety devices on the rear doors of the torpedo tubes in order.

The Bitumastic company had turned what was a harmless thing into a dangerous thing, but he did not consider that they owed any duty to Mr. Duncan or Mr. Craven in which they could be said to have failed.

Concluding, Mr. Justice Wrottesley said: "In my view each of the plaintiffs succeeds in establishing the liability of Cammell Laird for the loss of their wage-earners, on the ground of negligence.

"They failed to discover the defect in the test-cock of No. 5 torpedo tube, and this they would have detected if they had exercised proper care. As against the other defendants, the claim against each of them fails."

His lordship entered judgment for Mrs. Duncan and Mrs. Craven against Cammell Laird and Co., with costs. Judgment was entered for the remaining defendants, with costs against Cammell Laird. A stay of execution was granted, pending consideration of the question of an appeal.

- Aftermath of a disaster

In the High Court of Justice,

KING'S BENCH DIVISION.

(Writ issued the 28th day of November 1939).

Between

VICTORIA SUMMERS (Widow)
(Administratrix of George Albert Summers, Deceased)
Plaintiff,

—— AND ——

CAMMELL LAIRD & CO. LIMITED, LIEUTENANT FREDERICK GREVILLE WOODS, Royal Navy, SYBIL BOLUS (Widow) as Executrix of Lieutenant-Commander G   H   Bolus, late of the Royal Navy, Deceased, and MATILDA ANN HAMBROOK as Administratrix of Leading-Seaman Walter Leslie Hambrook, late of the Royal Navy, Deceased
Defendants.

Statement of Claim

1. The Plaintiff, as Administratrix of George Albert Summers, (hereinafter called "the Deceased") brings this Action pursuant to the Fatal Accidents Acts 1846 to 1908 for the benefit of herself, Wife, and Agnes May, Elizabeth and William Thomas children of the said Deceased, who have suffered damage by reason of the negligence of the first two Defendants and the said Lieutenant-Commander Bolus and Leading-Seaman Hambrook or some or one of them in the management and/or control of a submarine named Thetis (hereinafter referred to as "Thetis"), the property of the First Defendants who were the builders thereof, whereby "Thetis" on or about the 1st June, 1939, in Liverpool Bay, whilst carrying out diving trials preparatory to her being taken over by the Admiralty, dived and failed to come to the surface until the said Deceased, an employee of the First Defendants, was killed by drowning or asphyxiation or otherwise in the said submarine. The Plaintiff further claims damages, suffered by the estate of the said Deceased, whose death was caused as aforesaid under the provisions of the Law Reform (Miscellaneous Provisions) Act, 1934. Or alternatively as against the First Defendants for damages for breach of contract.

The writ issued on behalf of Victoria 'May' Summers in November 1939

PARTICULARS of NEGLIGENCE alleged against the Defendants, save that particulars under (G), (J) and (K) will not be relied upon as against the Defendant Matilda Ann Hambrook.

(A) Failing to take any or any proper care to ensure that the equipment and mechanism provided by the First Defendants in "Thetis" should be in a safe and proper condition to enable "Thetis" to undergo her diving trials.

(B) Failing to observe, or, if observed, to take any or any proper steps to ensure that No. 5 bow cap and/or its operating mechanism was, preparatory to, or in the act of, diving, in such a condition or position that the sea water could not enter No. 5 torpedo tube.

(C) Failing to take any or any proper steps preparatory to or in the act of, diving to ensure that No. 25 bulkhead door was in such a condition as to be, when fastened by the apparatus provided, watertight.

(D) Failing to observe or, if observed, to ensure that the test cock on the rear door of No. 5 tube was clear and fit for the purpose of testing whether or not water from the sea had entered or was entering the said tube.

(E) Failing to observe, or, if observed, to remove and replace by appropriately stopping the aperture a 1" thread cock on the starboard side of No. 25 bulkhead and/or causing or permitting the said cock to be in an open position, thereby allowing water to flow from forward of No. 25 bulkhead into the torpedo stowage compartment.

(F) Failing adequately to trim "Thetis" before entering upon the said trials.

(G) Failing, before "Thetis" was caused or permitted to dive, to ensure that the said Deceased was trained and familiar with the Davis Submarine Escape Apparatus.

(H) Failing to ascertain, or, if ascertained, to ensure that the A.I.V. vent was fully shut before "Thetis" dived.

(I) Failing, after "Thetis" had come to rest on the bottom of the sea, to take any or any proper and/or sufficient steps to cause "Thetis" to come to the surface by reversing the telemotor system, or otherwise.

(J) Failing, preparatory to diving, to arrange for surface craft to be in such a position as to mark the course and position of "Thetis" after diving and to have ready for action all necessary gear to cause "Thetis" to be brought to the surface in the event of her being unable to do so under her own power.

(K) Failing to arrange, before diving, any sufficient or proper means of communication with surface craft.

- Aftermath of a disaster

2. The said Deceased, as an employee, namely, an Electrician of the First Defendants, in the course of his said employment was on board "Thetis" as the servant of the First Defendants. The First Defendants accordingly at Common Law or by reason of the said Deceased's contract of employment owed to the said Deceased a duty to ensure that the equipment and mechanism provided and installed by the First Defendants in "Thetis" should be safe and in a fit and proper condition to undergo the diving trials for which "Thetis" was submitted by the First Defendants.

3. In breach of their aforesaid duty the First Defendants in addition to the Particulars of Negligence specified in Paragraphs 1 and 2 hereof, failed to ensure that the equipment and mechanism provided and/or installed by them was safe and in a fit and proper condition to undergo the diving trials for which "Thetis" was submitted by them. Further particulars of negligence or breach of contract against the First Defendants cannot be given till after discovery.

4. Further, the Second Defendant was the prospective Torpedo Officer on "Thetis" if and when she had completed her trials and been accepted by the Admiralty. At all material times it became and was the duty of the Second Defendant, *inter alia*, to take every step appropriate to ensure that the mechanism and equipment of No. 5 tube was in proper working order so as to prevent sea water from entering No. 5 tube or if such water had entered No. 5 tube, to prevent its entering into the torpedo compartment of "Thetis".

5. In addition to the Particulars of Negligence set out in Paragraph 1 hereof and in breach of his aforesaid duty, the Second Defendant :—

(A) Failed to apply adequate tests to ascertain if sea water had entered No. 5 tube before he opened the rear door of No. 5 tube by which action the sea water entered the torpedo compartment of "Thetis" and flooded it.

(B) Failed to warn his Captain, Lieutenant-Commander Bolus, and/or the appropriate employee of the First Defendants on board "Thetis" that he had not applied the appropriate tests for water in No. 5 tube before any steps were taken to put "Thetis" into the diving position.

(C) Failed to warn his said Captain and/or the appropriate employee of the First Defendants on board "Thetis" that the test cock on the rear door of No. 5 tube was blocked.

(D) Failed to use the Rimer provided upon the aforesaid test cock and failed to warn his Captain and/or the appropriate employee of the First Defendants on board "Thetis" as aforesaid of his neglect to do so. Further particulars of negligence against the Second Defendant cannot be given till after discovery.

6. The Third Defendant is sued as Executrix of her husband, Lieutenant-Commander Bolus Captain of "Thetis" who, in addition to the negligence set out in Paragraph 1 hereof, was further negligent in :—

(A) Failing to exercise proper supervision and/or control of the officers and men of the Royal Navy on board "Thetis" at the material time, including the Second Defendant and Leading-Seaman Hambrook, to ensure that No. 5 bow tube, its equipment and mechanism, were in a fit condition to enable "Thetis" to dive without sea water entering "Thetis" by the said bow tube.

(B) Causing or permitting "Thetis" to dive without taking proper care to ascertain the true condition of No. 5 tube and whether "Thetis" was in a fit state to submerge in the circumstances.

7. At all material times the First and the Second Defendants and the said Lieutenant-Commander Bolus, Deceased, and the said Leading-Seaman Hambrook, Deceased, were engaged in a common purpose in taking "Thetis" to sea to carry out and in carrying out her diving trials and the Plaintiff will contend in the premises that the First and Second Defendants, and the said Lieutenant-Commander Bolus and the said Leading-Seaman Hambrook, and each of them was acting as agent for each other in carrying out the said purpose.

8. By reason of the said breaches of duty on behalf of the Defendants and each of them, or alternatively as to the First Defendants, by reason of their breach of contract as alleged in Paragraph 1 hereof, the Plaintiff, as Administratrix of the said Deceased, has suffered pecuniary loss and the estate of the said Deceased has sustained damage :—

(A) By reason of the pain and suffering endured by the said Deceased before death took place, and

(B) By reason of the said Deceased's loss of expectation of life.

PARTICULARS of SPECIAL DAMAGE.

	£	s.	d.
Clothing destroyed	1	10	0
Personal belongings	5	0	0
Funeral expenses	23	18	0
	£30	8	0

- Aftermath of a disaster

PARTICULARS pursuant to the Fatal Accidents Acts, 1846 to 1908 are as follows :—

Names of the persons on whose behalf the action is brought :—

Victoria Summers, age 30, Widow of the Deceased.

Agnes May, age 7 years, his daughter.

Elizabeth, age 5 years, his daughter.

William Thomas, age 1 year, 2 months, his son.

The nature of the claim in respect of which damages are sought :—

The said George Albert Summers was an Electrician, in the employ of Cammell Laird Co., Limited, 30 years of age, a healthy man earning £4 18s. 6d. per week, and was the sole support of his wife and children and by his death they have lost all means of support and living.

THE PLAINTIFF CLAIMS damages.

HERBERT MALONE.

DELIVERED this 24th day of January, 1940, by ROWLEY, ASHWORTH & CO., 10 Kennedy Street, Manchester 2, Solicitors for the Plaintiff.

EVILL & COLEMAN,
SOLICITORS
TELEPHONE TEMPLE BAR

18-20 York Buildings,
Adelphi,
London, W.C.2

9th August 1944.

OUR REF: E.

YOUR REF:

ALSO AT 39, ETON AVENUE, HAMPSTEAD, N.W.3.
TEL. PRIMROSE 4461.

Mrs. M.M.J. Craven,
231, Lansdowne Road,
Birkenhead, Ches.

Dear Madam,

re H.M.S. Thetis.

We have now received a letter from the Treasury Solicitor to the effect that Lieut. Woods intends to appeal to the House of Lords. We shall have to cross-appeal in respect of the acquittal of Cammell Laird & Co. Ltd., the Administratrix of Leading Seaman Hambrook and Wailes Dove Bitumastic Limited in order to preserve your rights and to enable the House of Lords to deal fully with all the facts of this complicated test case.

Yours faithfully,

Letter to Mrs. Mabel Craven almost five years after the writs were issued indicating that the battle for damages was fast becoming a losing one.

What then of Navy personnel and their relatives after the disaster? They too had to suffer the burden of burial costs should they wish their loved ones home but surely they would have some better form of support and assistance than that 'received' by the Cammell Laird relatives?

None of the naval relatives were easy to find. However after many months, many miles travelled and very big phone bills they told me their stories.

The story of Peter Wells and his brother Jim, the two sons of Stoker Petty Officer J.W. Wells, and their mother is in itself a very sad tale which would make another book.[7] One example: on submission to the Admiralty of satisfactory annual School Reports for the boys their Lordships awarded 'contributions towards expenses' incurred by attending their respective schools, the last recorded payment being in 1952. The sums involved amounted to some 25% of annual school fees, less than £3.00 per year.[8]

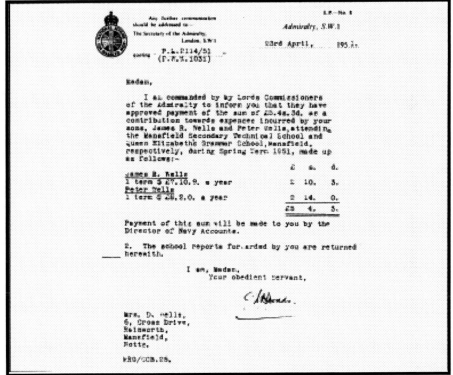

The same two year old son of Commander P.E.J Ryan mentioned in the *Daily Herald* report of 1939 incredibly went on to become a submarine commander in the Royal Navy after the war and Commander D.P.B 'Paddy' Ryan OBE

- Aftermath of a disaster

RN (Rt.) contacted me. Paddy wrote to me after reading an appeal for relatives or information which was kindly printed by Mr. Ray Gritt, the editor of the *SOCA* (Submarine Old Comrades Association) *News,* March 1998 Edition. He confirmed that his mother had to send his school reports off 'to make sure I was worth it' in order for her to get some help with his school expenses.[9]

This assistance did not appear to be a great deal and was hard won but contrast the treatment of some Naval relatives with that of Victoria 'May' Levelle (formerly Summers) when asking for assistance for her own son's learning, as an apprentice Joiner in Cammell Laird's shipyard.

Harry Dillon-Shallard, son of Chief Stoker H.J. Dillon-Shallard remembers as a seven year old boy living and going to school in Birkenhead, visits to Birkenhead Park, Bidston Hill and the seaside at New Brighton...he also remembers that 'it would have been nice to have a dad'.

The arrangements for the so called 'Officer Class' seemed to be the most difficult section of all to get a handle upon. Could this be because they effectively closed ranks and kept themselves to themselves? What was their own perspective on the events of 1939 and afterwards? Many months after he had first contacted me I sat down in the Somerset home of the son of Lieut. P.E.J. Ryan, lost on *Thetis*. His views are here too.

'Paddy' Ryan OBE, is a third generation submarine Officer who, though retired, is still involved with the Royal Navy, ironically, and some may say chillingly, working upon submarine rescue systems. Continuing this long tradition, Paddy's son Patrick recently joined the Royal Navy and may well become a unique fourth generation submariner.

Unfortunately, and perhaps understandably, Mrs. Gladys Eva Batten did not want to 'bring the whole thing up again' so no interview was possible, however Roy Batten, the son of Gladys and Leading Signalman Francis Brinley Batten, was very happy to help and able to supply the documents relative to his mothers payments from the *Thetis* Fund as well as some photographs.

Francis Batten was a native of Treforest in South Wales and his younger brother Glyn was also serving in the Royal Navy. Sadly Glyn had been sent to the China station six months before *Thetis* was lost. In the *South Wales Echo* of June 10th 1939, a distraught Gladys Batten said that she 'had wanted to see the both of them in their uniforms... a most cruel death... to think of my poor boy down there...the only signalman on *Thetis*.'

Also from South Wales, Ely, Near Cardiff, was Ldg. Telegraphist Bill Allen. His widow Mary had a one year old son named after his father and was just two months pregnant. Given the shock Mary Allen must have suffered it could be considered a surprise that this pregnancy went to term. But it did...and Mary and Bill's daughter Cynthia, and their son Bill were kind enough to talk to me. Cynthia told me that her mother had always said to her that she was 'the last bit of love I ever had from your dad.'

When I met them we were all surprised to find that they were actually mentioned by name in the minutes of the trustees of the Fund back in 1952. Widowed Mary Allen was granted 'a compassionate grant' of £16.00 for 'a raincoat, tunic, blazer, two blouses and shoes' for Cynthia as she was 'big for her age' and 'required clothing normally used by a girl of 15 or 16'. Although the source of some 'mickey-taking' among the Allen family today Cynthia, no longer 'big', takes it in good heart. Is it not though incredible that such highly personal details are recorded in such minutiae? Such was the obsession with holding on to the purse strings... to ensure that the people who really needed help had to jump through hoops to try and get it.

Perhaps most heart-rending of all was Mrs. Edith Bleakley (nee Crombleholme), from Blackburn, Lancashire. Edith was 17 years old in 1939 when her elder brother Able Seamen Stanley Crombleholme was the youngest navy man lost aboard *Thetis*. Stan was just a few months short of his 21st birthday, his coming of age. Edith told me that she'd 'been saving sixpence a week in a jar for Stan's 21st birthday present...instead I spent it on red roses in the shape of an anchor to take out on the *Hebe* and cast over the place where we lost Stan.'[10]

Edith still goes to Holyhead every year on the 1st of June, the anniversary of the tragedy, to remember her brother Stan.

The Royal Naval Benevolent Trust

Patrons: Her Majesty The Queen and His Royal Highness The Prince of Wales

CASTAWAY HOUSE, 311 TWYFORD AVENUE, PORTSMOUTH, PO2 8PE

Tel: (01705) 690112 (Administration), (01705) 690296 & 725841 (Grants). Fax: (01705) 660852

FUND: THETIS DISASTER RELIEF FUND

REF NO: 99/11/01 (18851) 1 May 1998

NAME:

Mrs G E Batten

GRANT: £9.62

PERIOD: One Month ending 31 May 1998

THE ROYAL NAVAL
BENEVOLENT TRUST
CELEBRATING 75 YEARS

Mrs. Gladys Batten's monthly letter from the RNBT with her 'relief allowance', and (inset) her husband, Signalman Francis Brinley Batten.

Stoker P.O Jim Wells

Peter Wells

Peter Wells. DOB 6.2.1938. Son of Stoker Petty Officer Jim Wells.

My father was James William Wells, Stoker Petty Officer on *Thetis*. He was 33 years old at the time when *Thetis* happened.

I was quite young actually when I realised what had happened to father. I had a strange upbringing because when my father died or was killed, after various events I ended up being adopted by my grandfather who married my mother. In those days, not like it is now, I was born out of wedlock, my father had been married before he met my mother...they never divorced.

So my mother and my father weren't married, when the *Thetis* went down... So there was a stigma, I had a brother who was older than me, so there was a stigma of being born a bastard was not like it is today were everything is done to help you. In those days everything was against you...So by whatever rhyme or reason I don't know what went on, my mother married my grandfather.

I remember my grandad telling me, when I was still a boy, rather than a teenager, why he had married my mother which was to give us a name that was acceptable. It sounds a laudable idea but when they married we had to go and live in a small mining village in the Midlands, Rainworth near Mansfield, where prejudices and everything else were as they were in small villages... it was good God that woman has come here with her two children, and she isn't

- Aftermath of a disaster

married, then she marries this old man...this is ridiculous.

So he gave us the name...and I suppose – depends how cynical you get about it all...He may have thought he was doing it for all the best reasons, but obviously when they got married my grandmother had already died some years before. There was also, I suppose, in his mind that here was a chance of getting somebody to look after him through his old age and have young children with him as well, as he was very good to us in many ways.

That was how it all came about, and that is how my brother and I were brought up in that atmosphere. So one always felt, well I did anyway, that you were different. You weren't like the other boys in the village...You weren't like the other girls... You were somehow different... There was a perception in my mind that I was different... Not from anything I could put my finger on... I couldn't say any particular item or occasion that happened but I knew very early what had happened. My grandfather made it known what had happened. Despite all the things that had gone on before.

Mother was left alone with my brother and me, and seven months pregnant. She had a girl two months later....Not being there at the time, if you know what I mean, one assumes that decisions were made that we would live with grandfather, in this three-bedroomed colliery house but also at home was the youngest son of my grandfather, my father's youngest brother. So he lived at home, so that meant there was grandfather, mother, uncle, and brother all living in this house.

I assume my mother was in a state of some shock and distress, and an aunt, my father's sister, who had had a boy, and couldn't have any more children, was desperate for a girl, and I've since found out in recent years, was very very close to my father. So for whatever reason she adopted that little girl. She went away and she was brought up as the daughter of my father's sister, and her husband.

We went there after the disaster to live in this village, when I was 12 my mother went into hospital...And really she never came out. So when I was 14 she died, but as part of my life and Jim's life, she had gone at 12, when I was 12 years old. So she never really said anything much about it at all. Never really talked about it. Never talked a lot about anything. Thinking back, she was very quiet.

Mother was originally from Barrow-in-Furness. It is interesting because I'm not quite sure where they met, but my mother's family in Barrow, knew my father. So it must have been up there with the Navy on something where they met…So that is where they must have met…she was a shipyard worker's daughter in Barrow… he was a Turner…her mother died very young and she was bringing up 5 of them…a real life of drudgery from what aunties have told me since. With a belligerent father who wasn't the nicest man in the world I don't think, if you believe them...so I would imagine when this big, 6'4" stoker came strolling down the street in his Navy uniform making eyes…My mother was only 5 foot tall…took size 2 shoes and she was tiny. So you can imagine her with this big, good looking, dark haired guy and off they went. I assume she just went with him and left.

As far as I am aware we had no help, because I would assume that his first wife would have got anything that was going. I may be wrong I don't know but I can't ever remember seeing anything or being told of anything until my brother missed the 11+ because he was ill and he took what was 13+ in those days. I took 11+ in the same year. I passed for Grammar School and he was for the Technical College. Somebody must have suggested or decided to write to the Admiralty and say look these are two lads who are a Navy man's sons, going to school and got big bills, do you think you could help? And there was some help through various terms at school were they paid towards school uniforms and things like that. So we had an acknowledgement of who we were. But that was all, and I suppose at that time to get £5 or £6 towards a blazer was very handy…Because they never had any money… Grandfather worked at the pit but he retired at 65. There was never any money in the house… I suppose it was something. But it was all very formal.

With my mother dying when I was 14 there were just 4 men left in the house – my grandfather, my uncle, my brother and me. That was how I lived for 7 years…No female in the house.

I think as you get older you do begin to think about it. When you are young you don't care you are getting on with your life and doing things but when you get older and you start, suppose get nostalgic, and think what the hell did happen at that time. And then I got the book. The first copy of *The Admiralty Regrets*. I read that and I thought that was it. That is what happened it was an accident and somebody did something wrong, and the War came, and then I suppose I was fairly content with that for a while. But one always wonders, and you'd see programmes on television, disaster things now and

- Aftermath of a disaster

again, and I know they showed the *Thetis* once, and then you begin to think I wonder what this guy was really like. And one of the biggest problems was that when all this happened and my sister was adopted, there was a total estrangement between my father's side of the family and my mother, and my grandfather as well virtually because he sided with her.

So the biggest regret is that I never knew my father's family…and by the time I got to know them, they were all dying. So I never got a real chance to talk to them. I have one uncle and aunt still alive now, and he'll talk about it. But of course he went off to the Navy when he was a young man. He was the next eldest in the family, George is the one who is left alive, and he was way down. All he remembers of my father is this guy who came home every so often in his uniform and stayed for a few days and went back to sea. There was no real growing up because he'd gone and another one went in the army the same thing. They all went away from home. So to get a real picture of him is difficult. But I know he was a keen sportsman. He played football at a fairly good level. He swam and he loved life in the Navy from what they tell me. He was in the China Station for several years before he went into submarines.

The final responsibility to my mind lies with the people who built the machine, Cammell Laird's, because of their procedures failing to carry out proper checks before the ship was launched…and the Admiralty for being slow in reacting to the disaster. I still believe that they could have done something and nothing will change that. But you get the old feeling about it that they really didn't want to do anything to damage that vessel or to really put themselves out. It was like a state of inertia settled on them all… Just didn't seem to know what to do, when to do it, how to do it. It was pathetic really.

There was a lot of money collected in today's terms, a lot of money. It is very difficult to find out where that money went, it seems to me, who did get it? We've only talked to a few people. But somebody knows where it went, somebody must have the details and it should be made public of where that money went. Somebody must know where it went. Whether it is in pension payments or whatever. And they should be open and honest and say that is where it went, and then everybody will be happy. The Navy people were looked after, the civilians, I don't know… I couldn't say…If they were married they were looked after… They weren't looked after if they weren't married!

Chief Stoker Harold 'Jack' Dillon-Shallard

Harry Dillon-Shallard

Harry Dillon-Shallard - DOB 29.1.1932.
Son of Chief Stoker H.J. Dillon-Shallard

I was born in Arunel Street Portsmouth in 1932. My father was in the Navy, Harold John Dillon-Shallard. Chief Petty Officer, Stoker in the Royal Navy. My dad went down on the *Thetis* in 1939. We didn't live in the north then. We lived in Portsmouth. My father was on commissions before that to Malta and China and places like that. When he came back in 1939, he got assigned to the *Thetis* which was being built at Cammell Lairds and he went to the ship there.

I visited Birkenhead for short stays, I remember now... I lived in No 1 Cole Street...I went to the school opposite - Cole Street Primary School...I remember the playground was on the roof of the school, and I remember going there for a short time, it must have been three months or so, and they thought I better go to school. I remember going on picnics when my father was off. We went on picnics to Bidston Hill...there is a windmill up there...going to New Brighton on the sands, where the tide went way out. You could walk out quite a long way to the sea. I think there was a fairground there as well. I remember coming back and there was a chap in the woods near Bidston Hill, and he made me a bow and arrow out of a branch of a tree. I remember my father playing games with this. Little things like that... and

Birkenhead Park. I remember that my father took us over, my brother and myself, over into the Park there, and there was some cannon guns, and he sat us on these cannon guns. I don't know if they are still there.

They may have been taken away by now…they were just inside the gate.

We were back living in Portsmouth at the time when it happened. My mother had stayed in Birkenhead with my father. My grandmother was looking after me. Mother went up to the boat because they were launching it and everything, taking it out on trials. I stayed with my grandmother at Raymond Road, Porchester, and then we had the news come through that a ship had foundered and they couldn't get it up.

A friend of my mother's told my grandmother the news as my mother was up in Birkenhead. So a friend rang to say that this thing had happened and I mean it was on the news anyway…on the radio that the boat had gone down and they were trying to get it up…attempting to get it up. This went on for quite a while and then the news came through that they couldn't get up at all. Three or four had survived … I knew it was dad's ship….It is a funny thing you know, the afternoon that it happened, I was in the garden with my grandfather, and I stuck a pitch-fork through my big toe! And it happened at the same time as the news came through that the boat had gone down…. I knew something had happened because it was all going on and my grandmother was crying, and you sense these things even if are only a young lad.

Then my grandmother went up there, and I went to stay with an auntie in Portsmouth while my grandmother travelled up to Birkenhead to bring my mother back from the north. When my mother came back she broke the news to me, which is awkward to do, to break the news to a 7 year old boy that his father wasn't coming home any more… that he had gone to heaven, and all that sort of thing, and that I was to be a good boy …it was mother who broke the news to me.

We felt a little bit deprived I suppose, really. Especially when other children had their dads, we didn't. We had to make our own amusement. We never got into trouble, I mean, we were like any young boys who went scrumping in the old orchard and then get chased. Used to do little naughty things. We weren't criminals or anything like that. But other children had dads and we often felt wouldn't it have been nice to have a dad.

My mother didn't have her own house at that time, and we moved to a rented house in Gosport, Eastbourne Avenue. That was in 1940. We stayed with my grandmother till 1940. Then we moved to Eastbourne Avenue, Gosport. I went to the local school there which was about half a mile up the road, and I remember the aircraft from the local Grange Airfield coming over, circling round, they were two winged Tiger Moths, they were yellow, training planes.

On the 10th of January 1941, we had a big air raid on Portsmouth....a land-mine fell in the middle of the Eastbourne Avenue estate. Blew a lot of the houses away, including ours as well. They were blown right through. All our furniture was damaged, and I had an auntie in Harrogate, Yorkshire, and she said to my mother, it is getting too dangerous to stay down there in Portsmouth with all the bombing, you better come up here. Mother salvaged what she could of the furniture and put it in store in Gosport. We arrived up in Harrogate and about a month after we arrived there, she had a letter that the store had been bombed in Gosport and we'd lost all our furniture. On top of losing her husband, she lost all her home as well.

She had a Naval Widow's Pension which wasn't very much in those days. I don't know if it was around £1 10/- a week, something like that. I think there was a £1 a week from the *Thetis* Fund. I think that was all. I know she had a part time job cleaning, that sort of thing. So we must have been in need of some money for her to do that. Because she hadn't been used to going out before doing that sort of thing. Needing the extra cash I suppose she thought she had to.

When we were in Harrogate, the Admiralty paid for us to go to Harrogate College, a private school. I think the fees were £6 a term or something like that, they weren't very high, although I suppose in those days it was a lot of money.

She always said that the Navy didn't do very much for her. She asked once for a holiday, her nerves were bad, about 1948 or thereabouts. She wrote to the Naval Benevolent Trust and asked them could they provide a holiday as she felt very low. They wrote a letter back to her and said if she contacted the Salvation Army she might get some help from them. That is what they said to her. As the years went on she remarried and as more time went by, I think she had given up on any help because she had this letter that said there wasn't any help for a holiday and things like that. I think in the end she just gave up.

Because it was such a long time ago and I thought nothing will happen now after all this time in the end I got on with my own life...but we always

- Aftermath of a disaster

wondered where all the money went to. Because there was quite a bit collected at that time.

Often I think about my dad, I've got a photograph up in my bedroom, I often think of him. What it could have been like if he'd been alive. He'd probably be dead now because he would have been 90 or more now if he'd lived.

I think it was naivety on the Admiralty's part. I don't know whether you'd put it down to negligence or naivety really. But what I've read into it the left hand didn't know what the right hand was doing, half the time. That is what I think. They didn't have the equipment, they didn't have the equipment on hand. If it had been today, they would have been there taking the back off the submarine, when it was out of the water and got everybody out. But everything was so slow.

It's hard to say really... I think they should have had a proper check on the torpedo tubes, the bleeder valves on the torpedo tubes. All that sort of thing should have been checked beforehand. They said they were all blocked up with paint or something. They registered that they were closed, but they were open. Lieutenant Woods he went down, he was in the forward torpedo section, to open the torpedoes, and they registered closed...and when he opened up all the water came in.

I suppose mother had a pretty sad life. But she had a happy life when she got married again. She didn't marry a wealthy man, but, she was happy at the end of her life. Which was the main thing. Of course, she never forgot dad. She always had his photographs around. Her second husband, he understood.

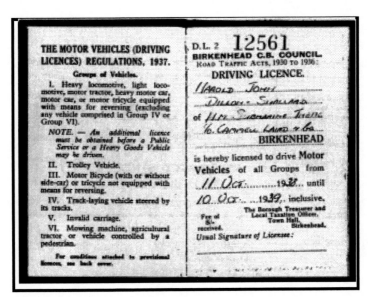

Driving Licence issued by Birkenhead County Borough Council to Harry Dillon- Shallard, valid for one year from October 1938 to October 1939. His address is given as HM Submarine *Thetis* c/o Cammell Laird & Co.

Mrs. Mabel ' Billie' Dillon- Shallard.

- Aftermath of a disaster

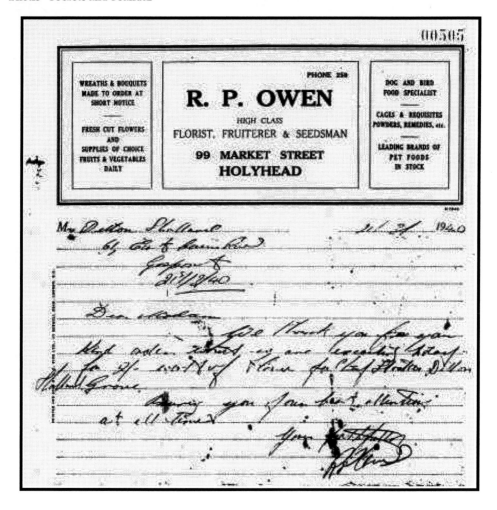

Receipt from Holyhead Florist reads:
Mrs. Dillon-Shallard, Gosport 21/3/40.
Dear Madam, we thank you for your kind order which we are executing today for 2/-
(two shillings) worth of flowers for Chief Stoker Dillon - Shallard's Grave.
Assuring you of our best attention at all times...

Lt. P.E.J. Ryan   Commdr. D.P.B. 'Paddy Ryan OBE

Commdr. D.P.B 'Paddy' Ryan OBE, RN Rt., son of Lt. P.E.J. Ryan.

I was born in 1937, April, two years before the *Thetis*. I retired from the Navy in 1990, having spent my entire service life, virtually in or with, submarines. Someone very kindly gave me an OBE towards the end of my time in the Navy. My father's name was Patrick Edward James Ryan, and he was the First Lieutenant of *Trident,* which was the second of the building line at Cammell Lairds.

He was aboard *Thetis* as an observer, with several other officers from *Trident.* I don't know exactly how many officers they were carrying that day, but they had their own ship's complement of officers, and I think about seven others from *Trident* and from various staffs.

Home for us was somewhere on the Wirral. Hoylake, or Neston, if I remember rightly. But at that stage, one's memory doesn't go back that far. In digs, like so many other families, surrounded by ships building.
At the age of two I didn't have any real comprehension of what was going on...
Although funnily enough, I have a recollection of pushing a wooden train along tracks in the grass, but whether I really do remember it or I do think I do.... I don't know.

Afterwards I think we came back down here to Somerset, then War

- Aftermath of a disaster

was declared, some 4 months afterwards, and we moved actually to Herefordshire for a couple of years, three years I think, really just to get away. My mother wanted a bit of peace and quiet, and was lent a small cottage which was part of a prep. school, and all the staff had gone off, and she got free accommodation, near Malvern…I'd probably be about 6 years old when I realised the situation… one's got to remember in the War there were an awful lot of people in very much the same circumstances. One certainly wasn't unique, so I don't know, I suppose because one had grown up without a father, and I was an only child, it just seemed to me as a young lad, that was the way the world went.

I think financially it was an enormous struggle on a Naval pension. It is interesting how times have changed, that there was petrol rationing, and as a result I started as a boarder, albeit a weekly boarder, at the age of 6, for the simple reason that it was the only way one could get round with the petrol coupons. In fact, I boarded about 4 miles away from here, and then went on to the prep. school, again just the other side of Taunton, boarding again.

One doesn't know the strictures and the privations that my mother went through. But I know they were very considerable. I know that at the end of each term, my school report had to be sent off to somebody, I know not whom, to see that a) prove I'd actually been to school, b) show that the money that was being given to my mother, was actually being well spent. Whether it was or not I don't know. This was the help for the school fees. Who that came from I really don't remember, but I seem to remember it was King George's Fund for Sailors, but I may be wrong…it's not the sort of fact one would know. I also know that my prep. school gave her an extremely generous reduced rate on my education, but in those days what were school fees? Minuscule to what they are now.

I know that my first terms school fees at Public School, were £85.00 a term. That included buying all one's books and my last ones were £125.00 and that included selling all the books again. I've still got a child at school and I'm looking at £4,500 a term. So that gives you a feel for inflation. Then I went on to Marlborough…when I was 13. From there I went straight to Dartmouth…as I went straight to Dartmouth, I didn't go to University, and I think at this stage, my mind was already set on going into submarines. I think some families become solicitors, and some become Naval Officers and some become submariners. I went into the submarine circuit.

It seemed to me to be rather fun. As a teenager, I'd been taken to sea in a submarine for a couple of days, which I found absolutely fascinating. I suspect, an awful lot of my mother's friends were contemporaries of my father's and were Naval Officers, they may have retired after the War, and one got to know quite a lot of people in the Navy, that way. It seemed to me a lifestyle which I rather enjoyed or would enjoy. After 35 years of it, how right I was!

Obviously mother had major reservations when I mentioned going into submarines... but my grandfather was also a submariner. He was lost in the First World War...as Captain of a B-Class submarine, and I think probably mined in about 1916.

Mother never remarried so she got her Naval pension, a War Widow's pension... as far as I'm aware the War pensions actually started on 1st June, so they did actually include *Thetis*. How much better they were than peace time pensions, I have no idea. I'm sure by good research you can find out. Then she got something, how much, I really have no idea. I don't think I can even go back to her bank statements, even if I've got them. They may be somewhere in a dusty box somewhere. A cheque arrived, once a month or once a quarter, or once a year. I don't know.

I do know I was subsidised over and above, but I think only because I went to boarding school. I think if one had gone to the local primary school and secondary school, whatever they were called in those days, probably I wouldn't have got any subsidies because it was free education anyway. But it certainly didn't pay all the fees, not by any means. I know she dipped into her pocket and my grandmother helped out, I think, not that she had very many beads to rub together. I think the family all contributed to help out... I certainly didn't get a scholarship to Marlborough...she might have got a slight reduction as a Naval widow. I really don't know...and there is no way I can check.

I think if you go back in history that was probably not purely and simply because of finance, I think by and large, in those days, that sort of society went to boarding school. The middle classes went to boarding school and that was the natural pattern. It continues in a more affluent society now that the affluence is much wider spread, more people do. It is very interesting, I've a daughter still at boarding school, looking at the cross-selection of parents, it is certainly not all just middle class, by any means. That's a very good thing. But I think anybody who is wanting to do the best for their children, even if they are going to have to make a financial sacrifice, well I've chosen the

- Aftermath of a disaster

boarding school route for my family. I believe the education is better...and I make a very big financial sacrifice for doing so.

I only really realised what had happened to father, in technical detail so to speak, when I was about 20 years of age, again it was not a subject which was terribly tactful to discuss at home,. I suppose that was the first time I really went into it in any depth. I was 22 when I joined the submarines. I suppose in the submarine service there was the opportunity to listen to other people who were older than me, and hear a little bit more about it...I had some very clear instructions in any submarine which I was in even as a young officer, about opening torpedo tube rear doors. And I think people, knowing that my father had been lost on *Thetis* actually respected those wishes ... I do remember actually having a slight scene with one officer about my ideas, who said he thought it was a waste of time,... I remember telling him precisely what I thought about that one...what the procedures were, what I wanted done, and that was the end of the argument and he complied with, not my orders, but my request and my feelings.

I think again thereafter, I was a fairly cautious submariner from a point of view of safety, and its a theme I carried on throughout my life. I'm a keen sailor and I believe I'm an extremely safe sailor. It is not the sort of thing you can be too cavalier about when you are at sea. You can be pretty cavalier, fairly irresponsible in harbour, but you've got a lot of people's lives. Everyone is in it together, I mean the chef can sink the boat, the Captain can sink the boat. And anybody in-between can do it. The lovely thing about it is that you do have trust, and everybody trusts everybody else. Would it were the same in the rest of the world.

I think I've served in nine different submarines, perhaps it is ten and I've actually commanded four which is more than a lot of people. I've always gone for jobs at sea or jobs on the waterfront and tried to avoid, as much as I can, the dreary business of Whitehall and the Ministry of Defence...I'm very much still involved doing the submarine rescue thing. I think if you've got background that I fairly uniquely have, you've got to try to make life safer, for submariners, doesn't matter what nationality they are, and I suppose that has been rather my crusade, certainly since I've retired. And it provides me with a bit of employment, and something to get up in the morning for, which is nice. Otherwise one becomes a vegetable.

I think one of the things that I've learnt through my submarine career that you must learn by other people's mistakes. We lost only one sub in 1905 because it didn't have a lower conning tower lid. We put clips on the rear doors of torpedo tubes after the *Thetis*. And every time there has been a major accident, a major peace time accident, and it has been possible to analyse it, and you have to exclude war time accidents because that is a different category all together, we've learnt by our mistakes. The day you don't do that is real folly. One of the things I think that nuclear power brought into the submarine system, was a very much tighter control of procedures, much better testing and tuning and generally working out how things work and how they didn't work and why they should and why they won't.

If you go back to *Thetis*, the incredible system, and I suppose again it was the rush leading up to the Second World War, which then seemed pretty inevitable, that people were short-cutting, but to build a system by which 5 levers worked in one direction, and one lever worked cack-handedly, nowadays it seems totally and utterly inexcusable. Now whether that was a design fault, or a ship fitting fault, or just lack of 'nous', how do we tell 60 years on?

But somewhere in the combination between those three things, design, ship fitting or 'nous' must lie the error. The fact that in those days people didn't actually sit down and test everything before they went to sea, and people just switched the submarine on, and got into it, and went to sea, and hoped it would work! It was really foolhardy.

Nowadays, the testing of the tubing and the checking ... you wouldn't get into an aeroplane by kicking the tyres, light the fires and off we go. There is a huge, great procedure to ensure the whole thing is safe and ready to fly. We've come to expect that nowadays, and aren't we lucky? And I think that is one of the things that perhaps, slowly came out from *Thetis* except there was this awful six years of war when people didn't have time to do very much, apart from fight the war and win the damn thing. Nuclear power, certainly brought in much better procedures and safety. You then continue on from the *Thetis* accident, again procedures have got much better but you read in the book, and I can only presume it is true, where the boy with the telegram got a puncture in his bicycle, as he pedalled from Gosport round to Fort Blockhouse. But we've now got used to modern communications. E-mail, instant communication. Television, men walking about on the moon. But 60 years have passed and that was probably about the norm in those days... now we look back at these things, it seems so pedestrian the whole thing. But it was the normal way of doing business in those days.

Somebody had actually thought it through, there was a test cock in the back of the torpedo tube and that should have been a perfectly sensible way of doing it before you open the torpedo tube, you open the test cock and see if any water comes out. By pure chance, somebody had painted over that, and the water didn't come out. That was yet another cog in the whole chain of disasters which should have been bowled out before. Whether it should have been bowled out by the shipbuilder, whether it should have been bowled out by the ship's staff, the overseers or any of the other parties...What I do know is that would not be possible now, without a genuine human error. Because the procedures are tighter now and the thinking through and the logic people employ to make sure things are safer, would bowl that out now. Yes, of course, there is always the chance that something will slip through the loop, but...

Was there a rimer?...Wasn't it used?...In which case it became a human error. It became a drill error not to put the rimer through. Perhaps they put the rimer in, perhaps it didn't go all the way...so that was straight human error, drill error. But we don't know whether the chap actually opened the test cock and no water came through...the submarine was obviously, blatantly out of trim. That too was human error. But if any professional submariners dive with their submarine out of trim, the answer is to do it light, and not heavy, and the boat was obviously desperately light. Again it was a new class of submarine and people probably didn't actually look at the draught marks or hadn't worked out what it should look like or something like that. So they were into a casualty mode of trying to find out where the water was, and again modern procedures will make sure that happens very much better. It is very easy to cast aspersions at people in those days, but I don't know how much of rush they were to actually make sailing, on the tide of the 1st June 1939.

The more one looks into it the more there were mistakes made by an awful lot of people. Whether one should try and apportion blame or not, I don't know. It's the same with any accident, seldom is it one person that makes it, unless it's the Captain of an airplane...who just screws it up.

There was I think a rush to war...and the moment it rushes, we all do it, it is human nature, there are short-cuts...people try to short-cut it. I think in those days, the submarine service was rather more cavalier than it is now.

I don't think much of the wisdom of taking 103 people to sea in a submarine which was designed for 55 or thereabouts…one of the things that came out of the *Thetis* report which is still absolutely sacrosanct now is the maximum number of people on board. Sixty years later it is one of the major constraints on contractor sea trials…particularly contractor sea trials when you've always got ship builder's men, trials people all sorts of other people, caterers, pilots etc.

Like any tragedy you have to learn from your experience. I think we have. I know we have. That I'm certain of. Because even with my specific interest in *Thetis*, I can see the submarine service still continue to use those lessons…I don't think the modern generation of submariner would say, ah! we do that because of *Thetis*.

Actually the *Thetis* clip, well it was known as the *Thetis* clip, its official name was the safety swing bolt, or something, has now been designed out with a rather more practical system which, when I first met it, when I was building a nuclear submarine, I slightly wrinkled my nose and thought I'm not sure I like that one quite so much. But having seen it in operation, it gives just as safe, probably was safer, but it didn't quite have the same sort of 'built like a brick shithouse' look as the *Thetis* clip, I looked at it and thought, is that safe?

But you know, design moves on, and things get better. Cars used to have running boards, now they don't. Things have evolved. So long as it is evolution and not revolution, it is good news.

My mother was a great friend of Sybil Bolus, that was. And though Sybil remarried, they stayed life-long friends, I know that Sybil Hammond died about 3 or 4 months before my mother and my mother was actually extremely upset. I'm not sure in hindsight that it may not have hastened her own death, in actual fact. They were very good friends, I think in tragedy like that, you are brought very closely together. I did actually meet Sam Bolus' son, Martin, who I had met a very long time ago… I'm not even sure if I was a small boy in shorts… I may have been at his wedding…but I haven't met him for years now… we exchanged Christmas cards for a couple of years but now I've lost touch with him again.

As far as the *Thetis* Fund goes I think anybody who runs anything like that, you don't want the money to run out because if you've still got recipients and suddenly the coffers are empty, that is a very difficult one… anyone running

- Aftermath of a disaster

a fund like that, they don't actually know what the interest rates are going to be. You've still got something in the pot and it is still going to generate some interest. How far do you let it run down? The difficulty is to balance the amount of money left against the number of people drawing from it. This is what actuaries are all about. If it ran out and you still have 60 widows and the pot was empty, where do you get the money from? Do you pinch it from some other fund?

Mother had been married for four years. Obviously extremely happy. I feel that she probably never met anybody who she thought would replace her Pat. But as I said before, whether or not on tape, so many of her contemporaries, or my father's contemporaries, were lost in the War. Though I think she certainly didn't want to remarry quite soon, and again I think the moral code this is, by remarrying after death was different to what it is now. If she then considered it, she would probably have married another submariner. It could have happened twice.

By the end of the War, six years had passed, her lifestyle had changed, perhaps it was then too late. So she never did remarry. Set her life really on what is unkindly called 'good works'. If there was a charitable organisation wanted somebody to help run it, my mama got involved. Whether it was the Red Cross, or whatever it was.

She gave her life to those sort of things. Governor of the local school, local magistrate. I would say to her all the things you do you do them all voluntarily, if you'd actually sat down and done something which paid you with your intelligence, she was a very well read woman, you wouldn't have had all these troubles. But she never got around to doing that. She was just too charitable, I think. That may be, because she had been very well looked after by charity. By the *Thetis* Fund. This may be a thread which I've put whilst I've been talking to you all along, I've been lucky enough to benefit, indirectly, by other people's generosity, and charity and I feel that it's this business of always trying to find out where things have gone wrong I personally find unattractive. But that is my rather old-fashioned view point of that.

I think when you sit down and listen to the tape, you'll find all along, I'm always trying to look at it from how the system worked at the time, as opposed to the awful thing of it's my right. I think this is one of the sad things about society nowadays that everything is their right, my right, your right, our right. And you then try to get people actually to be generous as well, and it is all bloody take and very little give. This is a sad reflection on society as it is at the moment. I've been very lucky, in hindsight, that said as one has progressed and made some money either by employment in the Navy or what else, I would hope that one is still fairly generous, if there is a submarine accident, thank God we haven't had any for a long time, the last one I can think of was *Thresher*. My cheque was in the post fairly fast…If the money has not been fully distributed or there is a glitch in the system somewhere, it is history... It was not done with any malevolence.

- Aftermath of a disaster

I had seen a video recording of the 50th anniversary service held at Holyhead in 1989 to honour the *Thetis* dead. There was a woman with a very strong Welsh accent being interviewed who condemned the Navy in no uncertain terms, accusing them of *'letting those men down and letting the country down'*. I had wondered who she was until her son Bill Allen contacted me about an error in the spelling of his fathers name in *'The Admiralty Regrets'* book. The woman on the film was Mary Allen of Amroth Road, Cardiff... the widow of Ldg. Telegraphist William Earnest Allen. Their son and daughter recalled their childhood after *Thetis*.

Bill Allen. DOB 16.3.1938   Cynthia Daly (nee Allen).DOB 12.1.1940

My father was William Ernest Allen, Leading Telegraphist on the *Thetis*, I was one year old when it happened...my mother was two months pregnant with my sister Cynthia...I suppose thinking about it now she was lucky to go the full term after such a shock.

I didn't really realise that Dad wasn't coming home until I was about five years old. I was told in school by a bully boy that his dad was coming home on leave from the War and that your dad wouldn't be coming home because he was dead. He died on a submarine. Up until then my mother always led me to believe that my dad was coming home in a little yacht for me...I mean I'm just a little five year old kid.

I went home... I was very upset at the fact that I was told about my dad. I asked my mother straight away what was true...and she broke down in tears and told me exactly what had happened...but I was still very young... obviously at that age you don't comprehend the seriousness of the whole thing... my sister was just a little girl then too.

Once you've realised and you've had the impact of knowing you haven't got a father and you see other kids with their mum and dad you start to wonder why and then by the time I got to the age of ten I started getting interested in how it happened, and why it happened and so on and so forth...mother always told me when I was at an age were I could understand what she was talking about that she felt it was sheer neglect and murder...she classed it as the Admiralty had murdered the people on the *Thetis*... that was her attitude.

Even when we were teenagers ... there's 18 months between my sister and myself...mother had been a widow for 15 years, during that 15 years it was a hard struggle. There was no help at all from any outside influence...I think she had a small Navy pension but it never amounted to a heck of a lot... But I can't recall any help...because I know my mother went to work, and it was a struggle for her. For all of us.

When I reached the age of eleven, I was about 10½ actually when I had information from the Navy to say that there was an opportunity for me to go to RHS (Royal Hospital School) in Ipswich, Holbrook near Ipswich. I went there passed the entrance examination and stayed there till I was 13½...it was a sort of naval college with a naval sort of influence.

I remember an aunt of mine giving me a book called *"The Admiralty Regrets"* and I had been reading that... I've always been interested in trying to find out about various things, what happened, how it happened...talking to various different people, total strangers before I mentioned the *Thetis*...but as soon as I mention that my dad was on the *Thetis* they were quite surprised...I believe there were three crew members who came from South Wales...One was from Pontypridd... and I think another was brought home and buried in the cemetery in Cardiff...but my dad was buried with his crew, in Holyhead...it was because my grandfather suggested to my mother...my mother wanted him to come home... but my grandfather suggested that it would be better for him to be buried with his crewmates.

Cynthia: I think when I was probably about 5 or 6 years old when I realised I was different...I used to get a lot of information from my brother,

- Aftermath of a disaster

he used to tell me different things. But when I really thought about him missing was when you hear your friends in school and they say 'well we've been down to Barry Island with mum and dad'... and then if any of our bicycles needed anything done we always used to have to ask the neighbour to fix them...because there was no man there to do any of these things. All sorts of little things like that.

It was really hard for mum and all of us...my mother used to work in a place called Chivers and she used to have to leave the house at five o'clock in the morning. Then she worked in the Ammunition Factory for a while and on the Railway. We always had different people looking after us... It was as though we were farmed out... There were lots of times. It was as like my mother had to be father and mother. She used to say to us when we used to get naughty, ...she couldn't say wait until your father gets home, he'll get you sorted out... what she used to often say was 'well the thing is I've always had to be mum and dad to you two'.

I used to ask my mother different questions about what had happened and she'd say it was Churchill's fault...she always told me it was Churchill's fault... she said it was pure negligence on their part... then she did say that they'd surfaced, there were tugs trying to get her up and apparently they brought her up twice and it had gone back down! I'd heard different things.

Once a month I remember she would take us into the main Cardiff Centre and that day would be like a Christmas Day...we'd go to the pictures twice and then we'd have something to eat in Marks and Spencer's restaurant. That was the day she used to buy either shoes for my brother, or myself, or whatever it was we needed as far as clothes were concerned...it was a big day out... then for the next month we'd be scraping again.

She did eventually remarry and I suppose her pension stopped then... and what little she got for us stopped as soon as we started work.. I was 14 then.

My mother used to show us dad's picture and tell us this was your dad... even after she remarried... Oh yes, it had the pride of place over the mantelpiece... the central place over the fire... I think that is why the second marriage didn't prove to be very successful, to be frank... because of that fact... she never ever forgot him...even after her divorce she reverted to the name of Allen and even on her headstone now it is Mary, Mary Verdun Allen.

Bill: Every night she used to ask us to kiss the photograph.

Cynthia: That's right, before we went to bed.

Bill: You know, I take my hat off to the fact that you've got all this information together, collated a lot of it, but I sometimes wonder why wasn't this available to other people...such as myself. I've attempted various different ways, different channels, to try and get this information, but I've always come up against a blocked or shut door... and I haven't been able to get an answer to my questions.

Cynthia: They don't seem to realise that being neglectful like this they have actually changed the lives of hundreds of other people. I mean... my brother and myself, well we wouldn't be sitting here today, our lives may have been totally different if we'd have had that father back, as we should have had...good god my mother was even told to sell her wedding ring to buy myself a uniform to go to school! When I was eleven I had to go to a girls' school, Windsor Clive Secondary Modern School for Girls...you had to be dressed in their uniform... My mother just didn't have the money to buy it. So she went along somewhere, don't ask me where, and she took me with her and she said I need help to buy a school uniform for my daughter, and she was told politely sorry we can't help you... sell your wedding ring.

I mean my brother and myself we grew up in our important years not knowing what it was like to have a father... so we only had half of the family.

My mother always used to say to me 'you were the last bit of love I had from your dad'.

- Aftermath of a disaster

Widowed Mrs. Mary Allen and her children.

Mrs. Mary Allen, with the look of a determined woman, outside the law courts in London during the *Thetis* Enquiry.

Leading Telegraphist Bill Allen and his wife Mary on their wedding day.

- Aftermath of a disaster

Able Seaman Stan Crombleholme   Edith Bleakley (nee Crombleholme)

Edith Bleakley (nee Cromblehome) - DOB 7.10.1921.
Sister of Able Seaman Stanley Cromblehome.

Stanley did his training as an Electrical Engineer at, McCall's in Blackburn. He was a Troop Leader with the Scouts, did everybody a good turn if he could...popular with the girls too. He never finished his apprenticeship...when he was only 17½ he went in the Navy as he had an uncle in the Navy and I think from an early age every time his uncle came home on leave, Stan thought I'm going to be a sailor when I grow up, and I think it was always with him, he always wanted to go in the Navy.

He went down to Plymouth to HMS *Drake*, the training ship there. He went out to Bermuda...He ended up on submarines for more money. Extra pay for my mother. Half a crown a day extra ... what bit he could for mother and me.

When he was assigned to the *Thetis*, he went to Birkenhead, and went in private digs for about 3 or 4 weeks, as there were two dives before that final one. So he used to come home every weekend then.

The last time I saw Stan was the day before on the Wednesday...he'd been home for the Whit weekend ...he went back on the Wednesday and took the trial dive on the Thursday 1st June. He told us about the dive because they'd had two before. He said everything will be all right mum... he was confident... see you Saturday he said... Then he was lost on the *Thetis*. ..Saturday we got the telegram to say there was no hope left.

He was a torpedo man. Just 20 years old...I was 18... he would have been 21 in September that year. I believe he was in the control room, and I understand from Walter Arnold, Derek's dad, ...I spoke to him at the memorial service at the time, and he said that if everyone had come out as they should have done, Stan would have been next up. How it happened a civilian got panicky I believe. A Naval man and a civilian were to come up together I believe...according to Stoker Arnold then. I don't know what has been proved since but he got panicky did this civilian and he stopped any more from coming up...he said, according to what he told me, Stan would have been next with a civilian after that, from the control room. The control room was close to the escape hatch.

I remember when the Police came to the house to tell us...the local police station was just around the corner and they came back every hour and they were never away that night. No news, no news. That was on the Thursday and it was the Saturday when we got the final telegram to say that all hope was lost. No hope of saving any more lives. Mother was terrible... she was 49 at the time.

The week after we had that memorial service at sea, that was on the *Hebe* the minesweeper. I remember we had to throw our wreaths on the water and the position of it was marked by a buoy. That were worst thing to me, it was so upsetting. My mother didn't know anything she just collapsed and they took her down into the sick bay and that was it.

The Vicar at our own little Church made a little bit of a collection among parishioners, now what that was I don't know but it was very little in them times, because everybody was hard up... I don't know how much it was.

My mother did work in the mill but she had been ill and had been off work. She did some cleaning, that's all, after that. She got a bit of a pension from the Admiralty...I don't know whether it was half a crown a week or not. But I couldn't swear to it. But it was less than 10 shillings. Not a lot. It came in a sort of pension book...at the Post Office. She got that up to the day she died.

She got something, not very much, from the *Thetis* Fund...but I haven't

- Aftermath of a disaster

a clue how much... more went to the wives of people, not dependants.
Times were hard then .. we weren't living in the lap of luxury... I was earning
10 shillings a week...brought home 8 shillings and 8d...as they took a national
insurance stamp out of the earnings.

I never really talked about money with mum...I always knew we were
hard up...put it like that. We had nothing...that's why Stan went into
submarines, to give her the extra money.

I'd been saving sixpence a week in a jar for Stan's 21st birthday
present...instead I spent it on red roses in the shape of an anchor to take out
on the *Hebe*. I don't remember how much it cost.
Stan is buried in Holyhead... unidentified body. His watch was found on the
control room floor, we got that back. We knew it was his. The inscription says
presented to Stan from the Tomahawks, The Scout group of St Thomas'
Church Blackburn gave it to him when he was going in the Navy.

Stan's old boss from Macall's took us in his car to Holyhead for the
ceremony with Stan's friend, my mum and me. The navy never offered us any
help until we went to the funeral, then they gave us a rail pass...and it provided
us with Bed and Breakfast and a meal. I remember that as it was Station
Hotel at Holyhead where we stayed. My mother and me and another friend
who died at Arnhem. I remember we got a voucher to go on the train.
There was no big monument there then when they had the funeral...nothing
there. They just put a small one on and it was after the War when they put the
big one up.

I don't know where the fund money ended up, because everything
stopped when my mother died, you see. I couldn't claim anything... Mother
was more upset than angry...I think they all were. She didn't feel like we were
treated as we should have been.

Perhaps I shouldn't say it but I think the Admiralty was responsible for
the whole thing. Because if I remember rightly, there was someone in Scotland
volunteered to burn through with acetylene equipment into the stern that was
sticking up, and they turned it down as it was a new submarine, so I think
really they must have been thinking about the money, mustn't they? Not the
lives inside. Thinking about the ship itself, a new submarine, it was worth a
lot of money. They said over and over again it should never have happened,
but I think something could have been done. They were hearing knocking for
hours and hours after. They knew most of them were alive.

I'm still upset about it. Stan was my only brother. He was the youngest navy man aboard. Don't you think the amount of people on board was a bad thing...it shouldn't have been allowed, should it?

I remember Stoker Arnold that day at the service, he said we must meet again, I've a lot to tell you, but this isn't the time...and I never met him again.

Edith holding a photograph of her lost brother Stan. Stan was the youngest navy man aboard *Thetis*.

- Aftermath of a disaster

Stan Crombleholme was not the only son of Lancashire lost on *Thetis*. I had heard that an Officer had also originated from the area and after an appeal via BBC Radio Lancashire, Miles Leadbetter, a driving instructor from Clitheroe Lancs. made contact and not only supplied the details ...he took the photograph of the window that is printed here.

Lieut.- Commander Richard Newstead Garnett was in command of HMS *Taku,* also building at Cammell Laird, and was aboard *Thetis* to 'get the feel of her'. He came from a Lancashire family who were the local mill owners and built most of the village of Low Moor and also the church at St.Pauls. The Parish Church of St.Paul is in Edisford Road, Low Moor, in the Diocese of Blackburn. The mill was used during the war as a training battalion for the Royal Engineers and there is a chapel in the church dedicated to them. Above the church altar is a magnificent stained glass window with a strong maritime theme, to the memory of Richard Garnett.

The inscription reads:-
To the Glory of God and in loving memory of Richard Newstead Garnett, Lieutenant Commander RN - in command of HMS Taku - lost in Thetis, June 2nd 1939. Third son of Newstead and Caroline Garnett. Dulce et Decorum est pro patria mori.'

The perspectives of the 'officer class' are clearly very different from those evidenced by the views of those like Edith Bleakley, a ratings sister from Blackburn.

There is little bitterness evidenced from Paddy Ryan despite losing his father at a very early age. His is a more reasoned positive approach toward 'the growth of knowledge' and 'learning from mistakes' as well as fierce loyalty to the Royal Navy and in particular submariners. He was also clearly reluctant to look at the past from the perspective of a society that has changed since the 1930's and 40's...as he said... *'this business of always trying to find out where things have gone wrong I personally find unattractive'.*

Paddy certainly was lucky, and is positively and genuinely grateful for the help he and his mother received, however he was from the 'Officer class' and indeed continued to be so throughout his own career, after Marlborough and Dartmouth. I have no wish to demean the efforts of men like Paddy Ryan and their role in their country's service. These are all talented, brave and extraordinary men, but the whole *Thetis* affair is steeped in the prevailing class attitudes and social perspectives of the day and I feel that perhaps Paddy's responses provide a reflective glimpse of how thing were and perhaps how things still are viewed from the 'upper decks'.

By this time the clear and common thread from the relatives of working class or 'lower deck' victims, was of harsh and insensitive treatment which, bluntly, could have been alleviated by one thing. Money. Money was the key and all of those people who I had spoken to were convinced that somewhere there was a large pot of money from the public and private donations to the Thetis Disaster / Memorial Fund. The fund had been set up by the Lord Mayor of London, Sir Frank Bowater and within two days the fund stood at £115,000[11]. The Fund was notified that the Navy had decided to have three classes of dependants: officers, chiefs and petty officers, and ratings. It was agreed to divide up the civilian casualties in the same way.[12]

At this point there were side issues of blame and/or responsibility. I was still very busy talking to and recording relatives and so had to choose which strand to follow, the stories of relatives, the legal scenario, or the money. I decided to look for the money and what a chase this was.

It started with another contact from the radio phone-in, a retired employee of Martins Bank (now Barclays) in Liverpool, who wished to remain anonymous.

He remembered taking donations to the *Thetis* Memorial Fund as recently as the early 1960's ! An approach to Mr. Ian Kinvig, Barclays PR man in Liverpool HQ, started the ball rolling but it was not long before he was 'unable to speak any further on the matter' and referred me to Barclays press department at London HQ. Two women worked there, Asmita Kapadia and Jane Vidler. They returned my calls and instituted a search for the account/s.

In an effort to add weight to my request in November 1997 I wrote to Mr. Frank Field, MP for Birkenhead.[13] As the then minister for Social Security and with a reputation for direct speaking I felt sure that he would support my requests for information from the bank. After all he had written a foreword to my first book on the subject of Cammell Laird back in 1991. I was more than a little surprised when he replied to my letter unable to offer me assistance as I was not in his constituency of Birkenhead!

What Field did say was that he would pass a copy of my letter to my own MP, Ben Chapman, and liaise with him over developments.[14] Chapman's 'researcher' John McCardle made contact with me after reading my letter. This letter asked very specific questions and had very specific requests for information and assistance. McCardle rang me and asked me 'what exactly is it you want us to do'? Reiterating my suggestion of a letter to the bank in support of my request he eventually got around to doing so by mid December 1997. He never did come back to me to ask how things were progressing. This was the sum total of support received from my elected representatives who I now realise have very little actual power and display little or no interest in causes which are not obvious vote winners. I never actually spoke with or met any MP on the subject of *Thetis*.

With or without the support of MPs, Barclays Bank Press office in London eventually responded in writing in January 1998.[15] They confirmed that the account was originally opened at the Liverpool Heywoods branch of Martins bank which subsequently became Barclays Heywoods when Barclays took over Martins in the 1960's. This branch went through further metamorphoses until becoming Barclays Liverpool City Business centre. No trace of the account has been found there and 'we must assume the account was, at some time, closed or transferred'.[16] A dead duck.

Concurrent with the above enquiries I wrote to The Royal Naval Benevolent Trust on behalf of May Levelle (formally Summers) asking for some assistance for her, as a *Thetis* widow in 1939.[17] In essence the reply was sadly 'try the social security' but what **was** in the reply was a reference to the fund being:-

'*...an annuity insurance administered by an Insurance company*'*! and 'whose payments to the four remaining widows of servicemen who lost their lives in the Thetis are paid through the RNBT... As I understand the Thetis fund, it is for those serving men who were lost on board the submarine and not for the civilian contractors concerned*'.[18]

At last here was an organisation that actually owned up to an association with the fund and indeed were one of the Trustees of the Fund. Here too was an organisation who thought that the fund was **for navy only**! Many telephone calls later, to and from Commander Jeremy Owens RN, Chief Executive of the RNBT, his written reply in April 1998[19] revealed the following details:-

a)   The Right Honourable Sir Frank Henry Bowater made an appeal to the Empire for funds to provide relief to dependants of those who lost their lives.

b)   A Trust Deed dated 1 November 1939 between the above named and the then Governor of the Bank of England- Montague Collet Norman.

c)   The Fund was administered by a body of trustees (The Thetis Executive Committee) which included '*amongst others*' (my italics) The Lord Mayors of London, Liverpool, Plymouth and Portsmouth and the Mayors of Westminster, Birkenhead, Chatham and Gillingham.

d)   Four Agencies were appointed to distribute the £150,000* donated to the fund, these were: RNBT (for RN Ratings), Central Bureau of Naval Officers Charities (for RN Officers), Civil Service Benevolent Fund (for Civil Servants), and Cammell Laird (for civilian workers)

e)   The Thetis Executive Committee (see c) determined the allowance to be received by each dependent.

f)   In 1964 an annuity was purchased for the remaining dependants and the RNBT continues to receive cheques from the company for distribution to the three surviving widows of ratings.

g)   The Insurance company concerned is currently General Accident Linked Life Assurance Ltd. (Scheme No 892).

h)   The names of two of the three surviving annuitants were included in the letter. Mrs. E.G. Smithers (widow of Petty Officer C. Smithers) of Woking and Mrs. Batten (widow of leading signalman F. Batten) of Pontypridd.

* Other figures used are £151,000 and even £250,000.[20]

In the days following the disaster people all over the country and overseas were asked to give to the fund and they did. Football grounds, cinemas and dance halls throughout the land filled tins and buckets with money. What your shilling, two-bob or half crown did **not** do was to specify that officers should get more of it than men, or that the ordinary workmen should be treated differently from naval personnel. Here was yet more outrageous social control by 'the establishment'! The money donated was for the families of those left behind, to help and support them. Regardless of class, station or circumstances, a family is a family. Children need feeding and widows need sustenance.

When the Fund was set up in November 1939 there were some 105 adult dependants as a result of the *Thetis* tragedy. Some were dependent mothers and fathers and even a foster father, but the vast bulk of the relatives were widows and children. There were some 48 actual 'families' with widows and children and some 22 childless widows. Why was the fund not shared equitably between all the families with an amount that could actually make a difference to what was left of their lives, instead of the drip feed of almost useless sums? It would have been a fairly simple task to apportion shares on the basis of number of children and adult dependants? Such a share out would provide, assuming a straight forward average between families, some £1000 to each family, a very considerable sum in 1939, and could have provided those families with houses, clothes, educational opportunities, or savings for a rainy day. Such a 'share system' for both widows with children and those without would still only have amounted to just under half of the funds collected leaving a residue of more than enough for the other 35 adult dependants and a possible 'emergency relief fund' could then have been maintained for unforeseen circumstances.

Such ideas were never even considered because the establishment worthies and the Royal Navy took charge just as they had in Liverpool Bay and they did things 'the navy way'. They had their hands on the money but did **not** have any grip upon the reality of the suffering of those left behind. Those that sat in judgement were the same as Judge Burgess who sat in the Birkenhead County Court. They made social judgements of character and need according to their own social mores and upon the strictly defined lines of class as advised by the Navy and indeed aided and abetted by Cammell Laird representatives, which consequently deprived those left behind of any semblance of dignity or viable financial assistance. The initial list of those who put themselves forward was:-

THETIS DISASTER FUND COUNCIL

The Archbishop or Canterbury
The Cardinal Archbishop of Westminster
Rev. S. M. Berry
Rev. P. T. Thomson
Rev. Dr. Bond
Lord Mayor of Liverpool
Lord Mayor of Plymouth
Lord Mayor of Portsmouth
Lord Provost of Edinburgh
Lord Provost of Glasgow
Mayor of City of Westminster
Mayor of Birkenhead
Mayor of Chatham
Mayor of Gillingham
Mayor of Gosport
Mayor of Rochester
Earl of Derby, K.G.
Sir Alan Garrett Anderson, G.B.E., M.P.
Sir George Truscott Bt.
Sir Stanley Goodall, K.C.B.. O.B.E.
Admiral Sir William M. James, K.C.B. (C-in-C Portsmouth)
Admiral Sir Martin Dunbar-Nasmith, V.C, K.C.B ((C-in-C Plymouth)
Vice-Admiral Sir H. J. Studholme Brownrigg, K.B.E., C.B., D.S.O. (C- in-C
The Nore)
Rear-Admiral H.D.P. Pridham- Wippell, C.V.O.(Director of Personal
Services, the Admiralty).
Rear-Admiral B. C, Watson. C.B., D.S.O.
Vice-Admiral G. O. Stephenson (Royal Naval BenevolentTrust).
Captain Bosanquet, C.V.O., R.N. Retired (Central Bureau of Naval
Officers' Charities)
Commander J. R. Poland R.N.
Chairman of the Port of London Authority (Lord Ritchie of Dundee)
Chairman of Lloyds (Mr. S. J. Aubrey)
The Deputy Master of Trinity House (Captain A.R.H.Morrell)
The Public Trustee (Sir Ernest Fass, K.C.M.G., C.B., O.B.E.)

Mr. G. M. Booth (Director of the Bank of England)
Lord Wardington
Mr. Colin F. Campbell
Mr. Edwin Fisher
Hon. Rupert Beckett
Rt. Hon. Reginald McKenna
The Lord Lieutenant of the County of London (The Marquess of Crewe,K.G.)
Mr. H. Eborall, M.B.E. (Civil Service Benevolent Fund)
Mr. Sidney Woodward (Messrs. Cammell Laird & Co. Ltd.)
Mr. J. Reid Young (Messrs. Vickers-Armstrongs Ltd.)
Mr. James Steele (Messrs. Scott's Shipbuilding & Engineering Co. Ltd.)*

\-

* Source: Bank of England Archives.

Was Commander J. R. Poland R.N. the father of the officer W. Poland lost on *Thetis*? No relatives or representatives of any of the 'working class' familes were invited ! Why not ? Conspicuous by their absence are any Trade Union representatives. Were any of the above even the elected MPs for Birkenhead?

The next step was to try and find those very rare ladies indeed, living *Thetis* widows who had not remarried and were still in receipt of 'grants' from the *Thetis* Fund directly from the annuities purchased in the middle 1960's. The names of two of the three surviving annuitants had been provided by the RNBT, Mrs. E.G. Smithers (widow of Petty Officer C.E. 'Ces' Smithers) of Woking and Mrs. Batten (widow of leading signalman F. Batten) of Pontypridd.

After enquiries and investigation contact was made with these remaining ladies and they confirmed that they still receive the princely sum of £9.62 per month (£2.22 per week) from the fund, and in the case of Edie Smithers, **less £1.06 tax!** Mrs. Smithers was nearly 88 years old and was a little unsure initially about the amount she received but then recalled, 'I know that I have to add £1.44 to it to make it up to £10.00 to buy my TV licence stamp'.[24] As Edie put it 'people thought...because they'd collected ... what the majority of people thought was that the money was for the families of the 99 people who went down, and they thought that it was being distributed between the people, but it wasn't'.

It wasn't being distributed to the people because it was now in the hands of those 'worthies' who thought that they knew best.

In 2000 Edie Smithers was a grand old lady of 88 years old. Her constant reminder of 'her Ces' is her almost 60 year old daughter Janet. Edie was carrying Janet when she and 'Ces' lived in Seymour Street, Tranmere, Birkenhead in 1939.

P.O. C.E 'Ces' Smithers   Edie Smithers

Edie Smithers DOB 27.5.1911.
Widow of Petty Officer C.E. 'Ces' Smithers

I was married on 17 December 1938, I was 27 years old. My husband was the same age. His name was Cecil Ernest Smithers he was born 12 August 1911. I was just a couple of months older than him. I'd known Cecil for donkeys years - when I went to school, then we lost track, then we met up again, I knew his brother who used to do the bakers round, he was a baker. When Ces was home, he used to come around with his brother, and we used to have a chat.

Then one day I met his mother through the fields, by Horsell Park, and she said your little boy's coming home at the weekend. So I laughed, and said 'My little boy?' She said, 'Yes, shall I tell him to come and see you?' I said 'You can if you like,' just like that. We met up again and had a chat, went out together again, then of course he went to China for two years.

When we got married he was Leading Seaman, but he had already passed

- Aftermath of a disaster

his Petty Officer's exams, and he was made up, sort of thing, in between us going up to Birkenhead. We went down to meet him at Southampton on the 10th December, and we were married on the 17th. We arranged all that through the post... We lived at home until he went up to Birkenhead, as we knew he was going up to Birkenhead at the end January. I went up with him and we had rooms in Seymour Street, Tranmere....The people we lived with they had the shop, Mrs. Davies, and the daughter was Mrs. O'Neill.

He went to Birkenhead to work on that submarine - *Thetis*...they all went up there for to work on that submarine. I didn't really know much about submarines and what he did... I went on one once when he took us down to Portsmouth and we went on a submarine and we went down on that. I know the little hatchways, I stood at the top and I said I can't possibly get down there. I can't get in that little hole. There was two at the bottom, it is marvellous how you do get down those little holes. They were terrible looking things, weren't they?
I knew that he was going to go out on sea trials. He was going to go on diving trials ...that was on Thursday.

I didn't really find out what happened until the next morning, really... because I was expecting him home that night, and that particular night, what I call fog signals, they kept sounding all night long. Those things kept going all night long and when I woke up early and went downstairs and I said to Nellie, that was the daughter, will you ring and see what you can find out, I said, I can't understand what has happened. They'd had heard it on the news the night before but they wouldn't tell me. They wouldn't tell me that they had heard the news. Oddly enough, that afternoon, I'd gone to her sister's for tea and they came and fetched me back, to keep me away from going around the area to get all the news, sort of thing, so that was it.

Well, then they told me and we went down to the Cammell Lairds. She came down with me. They just let us in a place, I wouldn't say they let us right in. But they let us in an office place to find out all details and so on and so forth. But they couldn't tell us much. First they said yes, they'd got the boat up. Then they said some had come off. Then they said no they hadn't. You got an awful lot of if's and but's, as I call it. Then on the Saturday they declared everybody was lost.
I was pregnant with my daughter, Janet... she was born in October. I was half way, about 5½ months.

I stayed in Birkenhead for a week or so as they had the service out in Holyhead. My mother came up. Well, there was a dairy round the back of Davies' shop and his name was Williams, and he took us through the Mersey Tunnel by car to the docks, and we went out on the *Hebe*. I got sunburnt...It was very hot.

There was a Lieutenant, not Woods, who was on there. They brought Woods round to see me in Seymour Street...I can't remember the other man's name, he was ever such a nice man, the other one, and he made him come and see me. Because, Cecil had got him (Woods) out of the flooded area, and he was one who came up. Commander Oram came off first, then Woods, they made him come off. What reason, I don't know. And then I think Shaw came up next... and Arnold, and then for some unknown reason the thing jammed.

Woods just said he was very, very sorry about it all, that if it hadn't been for my husband getting him out of the flooded area...mind you I was in shock, I didn't sort of take a lot of notice of him to be truthful. But the other man he was really very nice... I don't know...up against the other man, Woods...he just wasn't the same type of man. Put it that way... I think this other man, this other Lieutenant, because he said I made him come and see you...he wouldn't have come otherwise, and I think that was why they had to get him out of that flooded area and get him off the boat, because I think if War hadn't been declared he would have been in for the high jump. That's my opinion of it.

Then I came back down south ... I was expecting my daughter. Lived with my mother and father. I didn't intend to. Because that is one thing I don't approve of really is people living with their parents. But it was the lesser of two evils, because they didn't get the boat up until September, and by that time war was declared and it either meant my mother and father who were elderly would have had to have evacuees, it was sort of the lesser of two evils for them and for me too, in a sense.

I had a pension. Widow's pension....I'm not going to tell you this is right, because I think it was a pound for me and two and six ..or maybe five shillings for my daughter. They made an allowance up to when she was 15 years old. There was a small allowance, but I mean, it was 25/- a week for so long. Each year I suppose it went up by about the odd shilling or two a week.

They collected an awful lot of money for those days , of course that is why people thought I was well off... people thought...because they'd collected

... what the majority of people thought was that the money, 99 people went down, and they thought that it was being distributed between the people, but it wasn't.

It worked out, after it was all finalised, which was a few months before I got anything from that, it used to be £7 and some odd amount a month for myself and my daughter, and then the third month it used to be £9 something a month, every third month. Eventually, after a time, I had a letter from them that it had been… No, that it has been ….it was that a certain amount of money had been put somewhere … like an insurance company…and then the interest off that would help me…that was about 1964….I think it would have been more use to me…altogether…it's wrong I think.

I still get it today…from the RNBT…The Royal Navy Benevolent Society… I'll get a letter for you with the amount on. It's £8 something a month because I put that in the Post Office, and then I pay my television licence with it. I know I have to put £1.44 to make it up to £10.00 so it must be £8.56 I get a month.

Candidly I think a lump sum should have been given to the people. Not necessarily all of it, I wouldn't say that, but a small lump sum, so that you could get yourself sorted out. I got no help in buying this house. This was when I was 56 wasn't I when I had to start buying this place. I could have written to them I suppose and asked them, but….

The thing went up to Scotland previous to it going out, and that went up for diving. But they didn't dive did they?….I don't know what was wrong with it. I mean, my husband, he didn't talk about his work, but he did say one day to me, you have really got to face it, my work is dangerous.

I mean all right, the thing went off merrily, as they thought, to dive. It couldn't dive. So there was something wrong with it then. I don't know what was wrong with it because as I say he didn't talk about it.

Even the people we lived with in Birkenhead, they sort of knew a lot about the boats. They used to try and ask him things and he would never say anything, he used to say well, so and so, and so and so…and leave it at that. There seemed to be an awful lot of things that did go wrong in that yard. Not necessarily always with *Thetis* but in the yard itself you heard of different things going wrong.

I quite think that Woods made a mistake….Jack always thought that too, Ethel's husband… He was in the Navy…he was a cousin, she was an

Aslett she was a cousin of the Aslett who was up in Birkenhead…who was also lost on *Thetis*.

I was broken hearted… It took me a heck of a long time to get over it. In fact, when Jan was still a baby… she wasn't even a year old, I more or less collapsed in the town. That was from shock still.

I never married again because I thought a lot of my Ces. You can't think the same of two people twice…not really.

Edie's daughter Janet
aged 3, in 1942.

- Aftermath of a disaster

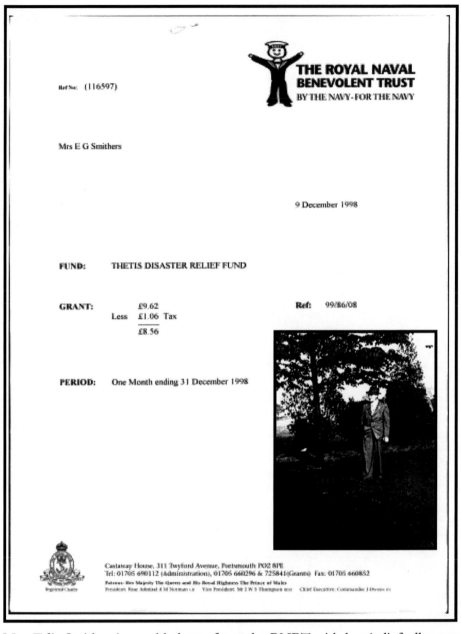

Ref No: (116597)

THE ROYAL NAVAL BENEVOLENT TRUST
BY THE NAVY - FOR THE NAVY

Mrs E G Smithers

9 December 1998

FUND: THETIS DISASTER RELIEF FUND

GRANT: £9.62   **Ref:** 99/86/08
         Less £1.06 Tax
              £8.56

PERIOD: One Month ending 31 December 1998

Castaway House, 311 Twyford Avenue, Portsmouth PO2 8PE
Tel: 01705 690112 (Administration), 01705 660296 & 725841(Grants) Fax: 01705 660852
Patrons: Her Majesty The Queen and His Royal Highness The Prince of Wales
President: Rear Admiral A M Norman CB   Vice President: Mr J W S Thompson RNR   Chief Executive: Commander J Owens RN

Mrs. Edie Smithers' monthly letter from the RNBT with her 'relief allowance'
less tax! (inset) Petty Officer C.E. 'Ces' Smithers in 'civvies'.
Birkenhead Park, 1939.

The list of the so called 'Thetis Council' for the Disaster Fund formed by the Lord Mayor of London, Sir Frank Henry Bowater, reads like the pages of Who's Who. Were they, like Mrs. Dorothy Mack, genuine philanthropists? Or was there something in it for them, perhaps expenses, perhaps a seat on a table with other 'powerbrokers', or perhaps they were, in true aristocratic style, looking for something to do?

In a letter from H.C.B. Myers, the Secretary of the Bank of England to the Governor of the Bank, The Rt. Hon. Montague Collet - Norman P.C., D.S.O., dated 28th June 1940 concerning the appointment of trustees to the fund, Myers states... 'I understand that members of the Big Five have accepted nominations,...what they would like is somebody to represent the Bank.'[21]

The so called 'Big Five' who were eventually to become the Executive Trustees of the fund were : The Royal Navy Benevolent Trust, The Central Bureau of Naval Officers Charities, The Civil Service Benevolent Trust, Cammell Laird & Co. Ltd. and Vickers Armstrong Ltd.

Is it not a startling fact that agents and associations very closely linked with those bodies who were thought by many to be responsible for the whole shocking tragedy, that is the Admiralty, the Navy and shipbuilders Cammell Laird and Vickers, were now given the job of administering and managing the very fund which had been set up to relieve the relatives of those lost by, arguably, their own actions !!! Such a situation could be compared with the crazy notion of the Swiss Banks having the responsibility for the redistribution of the coffers of Holocaust victims to the descendants of Adolf Hitler's regime.

As stated earlier 'the Navy notified the fund that it [the navy] had decided to have three classes of dependants...Officers, Chiefs and petty officers and ratings'[21]. The Central Bureau of Naval Officers Charities is now defunct and the RNBT suggested that their successors may be the Royal Naval Benevolent Society. This organisation itself changed its name once again in 1996 to the Royal Naval Benevolent Society for Officers.[22] My letter of 18th April 1998 to Vice Admiral Sir Anthony Tippet, the Chairman of the RNBSO, asking for information about the fund, produced a response from the RNBSO archivist, Matthew Sheldon, based at the Royal Naval Museum in Portsmouth. They have no records of any payments to *Thetis* dependants. Furthermore the RNSBO confirmed the *'restricted role that the RNBS limited itself to; it did not even help all officers and their dependants, but only commissioned officers i.e. Lieutenants or above... (so) there were only a handful of individuals who could ever come within the RNBS constituency*. [23] A dead end.

Enclosed with the April 1998 letter from the RNBT were the receipts and payments shown in the RNBT's annual accounts for the distribution of funds from the 'Thetis Disaster Relief Fund'. These show donations, 'receipts from other sources', and 'general grants'. 'Receipts from other sources' refers to amounts received from the Thetis Disaster Relief Fund. The RNBT account show minimal interest on these funds therefore the assumption should be that the main 'feeder' fund, the main disaster fund itself, would have accrued any interest. Confusingly the RNBT take money from the Thetis Disaster Relief Fund and then call their work in this area, the distribution of grants, by the same name; that is 'The Thetis Disaster Relief Fund'. The accounts for 1943-44, 1944-45 and 1961-62 are not available. These first two dates can be explained by war, the last one seems strange. This too looked like another blind alley.

From a further letter from the RNBT in July 1998 it was confirmed the Fund had been wound up in November 1964 and the annuities purchased for £60,356 were designed to pay out to the 54 remaining dependants for life. 23 of these were for dependants of RN ratings - 4 Chief Petty Officers, 4 Petty Officers, 6 Leading Rates and 9 Able Rates. Of these 23 annuities, 12 were for widows, 9 were for mothers, 1 for a father and 1 for an unmarried wife. Even the RNBT have not yet been able to track down who handled the remaining annuities for any other relatives still eligible. So even after 25 years of drip feeding almost useless amounts of money to the *Thetis* dependants the Trustees still could not bring themselves to finally distribute the remaining £60,356 that was paid for the annuities between those still left. No children would be left with qualifying status in 1964. Therefore the 54 annuities would be for payment to 54 dependant adults, 23 of whom are listed above.

Why on earth was the money not equitably distributed even at this late date? A minimum of £1000 each could have been granted, almost a year's wages to a working man at the time, and then the fund wound up. But the worthies knew best and no doubt included in the purchasing costs are the inevitable administration fees and commissions charged for such dealings, thus further reducing the amount of money available for growth and ultimately payments to dependants.

There have been other disasters since *Thetis,* some seemingly handled better than others .. examples are another maritime tragedy, the loss of the Penlee Lifeboat in 1981, and the Hillsborough Stadium Tragedy of 1989. In the former just eight families received similar shares of a publicly subscribed fund of over £3 million,[24] whilst those who lost someone in the football disaster at Sheffield also received lump sum payments.[25] The Aberfan disaster in 1966 produced another publicly subscribed fund which is unfortunately still the subject of considerable criticism today over its management and distribution.

In a final attempt to 'get to the money' I wrote to the Governor of the Bank of England, Mr. Eddie George, as the position of the Governor in 1939, the Rt. Hon. Montague - Collet was a signatory to the Trust Deed of the Fund and the responsibilities of same were passed on to his successors. His archivists, Henry Gillett and Sarah Millard, replied to me that *'the fund held its account at the bank...there is little to show where contributions came from... but is more explicit about payments made until the winding up of the fund (with the purchase of the annuities) in 1965. It would not be practical for us to extract information for you, it would be better if you came and consulted the records yourself which you would be welcome to do'.*[26]

So it seemed at the end of a long and arduous trail there was a light at the end of this tunnel. More tunnels went by as I travelled south once more on the London train to visit 'The Old Lady of Threadneedle Street'.

The Bank of England, which probably wields more financial power than any other institution in the world, appears at first to be a relatively small building among the giant skyscrapers of the capital, however not only does it go back a long way it is also very very deep. After passing through very tight security and marvelling at the fact that the 'clerks' still wear the same top hats and long tailcoats of centuries gone by, the lift took me down three floors to the archives.

There, at last, were the files on the fund. The money, those who handled it, the judgements they made, the minutes of their meetings, the letters they wrote and for the first time a comprehensive list of the dependants, who got what, how and why. The Bank only allow access to records under thirty years old in exceptional circumstances. As the papers from the winding up date of 1964 just qualify by a few years I believe that most of this information has never been publicly seen before. The next few pages will show these details.

Set out in a Trust Deed dated 1st November 1939 even this apparently straightforward document for administering the *Thetis* Disaster Relief Fund

- Aftermath of a disaster

almost pushed to one side the non-naval personnel who lost their lives on *Thetis*. The very first paragraph makes clear that emphasis of the fund:

> ... a fund intended to be known as the Thetis Disaster
> Relief Fund for the purpose of making provision for the aid and
> relief of the widows children and other dependants of the Officers
> and Men of the Royal Navy *and other persons* who lost their lives
> in the disaster to HM Submarine Thetis in Liverpool Bay on 1st
> June 1939. (Hereafter ' the victims'.) (My italics)

Even after death the Cammell Laird men, the Vickers men, the caterers, the civil servants and the Mersey Pilot are just **'other persons'**. Perhaps this too was the 'hidden hand' of influence, with the war now really starting in earnest, of 'the Navy way'.

The provisional list of dependants upon the fund, both Navy and 'other persons' is shown here and on the following pages:-

Provisional list of dependants

Name and Address	Relationship to Deceased	Children		Allowance		
		Name	Age, years			
ALLEN, Mary, 85 Amroth Road, Ely, nr. Cardiff	Widow	William Frederick	1	£ s. d. 1 7 8	per week	
ANKERS, Martha Hannah, 19 Derby Street, Barrow	Widow	—	—	1 10 0	do.	
ARMSTRONG, Lillian Emma, 61 Waterpark Road, Prenton, Birkenhead	Widow	—	—	8 6 8	per month	
ASLETT, Mabel Fanny, 91 Prenton Road, East Birkenhead	Widow	—	—	1 10 0	per week	

Name and Address	Relationship to Deceased	Children		Allowance			
		Name	Age, years	£	s.	d.	
BAILEY, Agnes, 49 Duncan Road, Southsea	Mother	—	—	4	3	4	per month
BAILEY, Dorothy May, 130 Woodcote Valley Road, Purley, Surrey	Widow	Doreen Sheila Michael	18 15 12	16	13	4	do.
BAMBRICK, Mary, "Cloneen," Castle Comer, Co. Kilkenny	Widow	Thomas William	2 months	1	7	8	per week
BAMBRICK, William, Bawnree, Old Leighlin, Co. Carlow	Father	—	—		5	0	do.
BATH, Bessie Frances, 24 Meade Road, West Derby, Liverpool 13	Widow	Elsie Margaret	8	1	7	8	do.
BATTEN, Gladys Eva, 19 Oxford Street, Treforest, nr. Pontypridd, Glamorgan	Widow	Roy Brinley	4	1	7	8	do.
BATTEN, Martha Jane, 19 Oxford Street, Treforest, nr. Pontypridd	Mother	—	—		10	0	do.
BEATTIE, Mary Ellen, 4 Clare Street, Lower Tranmere, Birkenhead	Widow	Jean	9	1	17	8	do.
BOLUS, Sybil, Bury Hall Farmhouse, Alverstoke, Hants	Widow	Martyn Howard	9	12	10	0	per month
BRESNEN, Wilhelmina, 3 Stuart Road, Higher Tranmere	Widow	Minnie	17	1	7	8	per week
BROAD, Mary Eileen, 39 Bankville Road, Birkenhead	Widow	Margaret Ann Mary Eileen	1 11 months	1	15	4	do.
BROOKE, Lilian, 37 Southdown Road, Southdown, Bath	Widow	—	—	1	0	0	do.
CHAPMAN, Inez Ruth, White House, Frensham, Surrey	Widow	Felicity Anne	2	10	0	0	per month
CHINN, Vera, 29 Canterbury Road, Rock Ferry, Birkenhead	Widow	—	—	1	0	0	per week
CORNISH, Mary Jane, 35 Brinkley Road, Worcester Park, Surrey	Mother	—	—		10	0	do.
COSTLEY, Ada, 7 Martin Road, Portsmouth	Widow	James William Maurice Alfred	11 5	1	15	4	do.
CRAGG, Sarah Florence, Broadgate, Victoria Road, Ulverston	Widow	—	—	1	10	0	do.
CRAIG, Elizabeth, 69 Whitworth Road, Gosport	Widow	William John	6	1	7	8	do.
CRAVEN, Mabel Mary Jane, 231 Lansdowne Road, Birkenhead	Widow	John	10	1	7	8	do.

- Aftermath of a disaster

Name and Address	Relationship to Deceased	Children		Allowance			
		Name	Age, years	£	s.	d.	
CROMBLEHOLME, Jane, 91 Withers Street, Blackburn, Lancs	Mother	—	—		8	0	per week
CROUT, Gladys Mary, 35 Bramwell Avenue, Prenton, Birkenhead	Widow	—	—	8	6	8	per month
DILLON-SHALLARD, Mabel Marguerite, 7 Raymond Road, Paulsgrove, Cosham, Portsmouth	Widow	Harold Arthur David John	7 5	1	15	4	per week
DUBELLS, Jessie, 31 Strathmore Drive, Crosby, Lancs	Widow	—	—	1	10	0	do.
DUNCAN, Rose, 72 Montrose Terrace, Edinburgh 7	Widow	—	—	1	0	0	do.
DUNCAN, Mrs. 72 Montrose Terrace, Edinburgh 7	Mother	—.	—		5	0	do.
DUNN, Emily Jane, 27 St. Ann's Street, Gilfach, near Bargoed, Glamorgan	Mother	—	—		10	0	do.
ECCLESTON, Ellen, 46 Wycliffe Street, Rock Ferry	Widow	Allan Richard Maureen Agnes	12 5	1	15	4	do.
FEENEY, John James, 194 Boundary Road, Walthamstow, London, E.17	Father	—	—		5	0	do.
FEENEY, Vera, Old Home Cottage, Church Road, Plymstock	Widow	James Ronald	1	1	7	8	do.
FINEY, Lola Patricia, 14 Beach Road, Southsea, Hants	Unmarried wife	—	—	1	0	0	do.
FRANCIS, Ada, Carr Road, Healing, Grimsby, Lincs	Mother	—	—		10	0	do.
FRENCH, Doris, 27 Foster Road, Kempston, Beds	Widow	—	—	1	0	0	do.
GARNETT, Mary Irene, Haddon Heyes, Neston, Cheshire	Widow	—	—	8	6	8	per month
GISBORNE, Mary Amelia, 43 East Way, Greasby, Upton Wirral	Widow	—	—	1	10	0	per week
GLENN, Marie, 9 Warwick Street, Leamington Spa, Warwickshire	Widow	Jan Demetrius Brenda Sheila John Roy	16 14 12	2	13	0	do.
GOAD, Doris Kathleen, 29 Cedar Road, Strood, Kent	Widow	Doris Jeanne Godfrey John Theo Elizabeth Sonja Maria	10 6 4	2	3	0	do.
GRAHAM, Vera Maud, 5 Evans Road, Southsea, Hants	Widow	—	—	1	0	0	do.

Name and Address	Relationship to Deceased	Children		Allowance			
		Name	Age, years	£	s.	d.	
GREEN, Florence Rose, Bell House, Horham, nr. Diss, Norfolk	Mother	—	—		10	0	per week
GRIFFITHS, Rose Jane, 126 Grove Road, Wallasey	Widow	—	—	1	0	0	do.
HAMBROOK, Matilda Ann, 68 Elson Lane, Elson, Gosport	Mother	—	—		7	0	do.
HAMILTON, Mary, 31 Asterfield Avenue, Bebington	Widow	—	—	1	0	0	do.
HAMILTON, W., 87 Larch Road, Birkenhead	Mother	—	—		10	0	do.
HARWOOD, Alice Maud, 20 Alacross Road, South Ealing, London, W.5	Widow	—	—	1	0	0	do.
HAYTER, Elizabeth Dorothy, at Tay Lodge, Kilmacthomas, Co. Waterford	Widow	Eve Ann George Anthony	9 11 months	14	3	4	per month
HILL, Elizabeth, 9 Craigmore Avenue, Stoke Devonport	Mother	—	—	5	0	0	do.
HILL, Ethel Freda, 36 Village Road, Oxton, Birkenhead	Widow	Leslie Adair Fitzgerald Peter Steuart	12 8	16	13	4	do.
HILLS, Gladys Evelyn, 46 Longs Road, Portsmouth	Widow	Evelyn Gladys Albert Edward Leslie Roy	15 14 10	2	3	0	per week
HOLE, Caroline Mabel, 19 Avondale Terrace, Devonport	Widow	Eugene	6 months	1	7	8	do.
HOMER, Edith, 113 Cambridge Road, Wirral	Widow	John Hanley David Arthur Malcolm	9 5 11 months	2	3	0	do.
HOPE, Miss E., 3 Dilston Avenue, Hexham, Northumberland	Daughter	—	—		7	6	do.
HOPE, Kate, The Holme, Elliott Terrace, Wark, Hexham, Northumberland	Step-mother	—	—		10	0	do.
HORNE, Lottie Beatrice, 170 North Road, Plymouth	Widow	—	—	1	10	0	do.
HORSMAN, Ethel May, 22 Rouge Bouillon, St. Helier, Jersey, C.I.	Widow	—	—	1	10	0	do.
HOWELL, Edith, " Esnor," St. Luke's Park, Torquay	Mother	—	—		10	0	do.
HUGHES, Catherine Ellen, 31 Wilton Place, S.W.1	Mother	—	—		10	0	do.

- Aftermath of a disaster

Name and Address	Relationship to Deceased	Children		Allowance			
		Name	Age, years	£	s.	d.	
HUGHES, Doris, 23 Armscot Close, Speke, Liverpool 19	Widow	Margaret Josephine	3	1	7	8	per week
HUNN, Florence Violet, 221 Drayton Bridge, West Ealing, London, W.13	Widow	—	—	8	6	8	per month
IRONS, Charles, 51 Peddie Street, Dundee, N.B.	Foster Father	—	—		7	6	per week
JACKSON, Jessie Jane, 50 Pitville Avenue, Mossley Hill, Liverpool 18	Widow	John James / Peter Charles / Gladys	14 / 9 / 7	2	3	0	do.
JACKSON, Thomas Dr., Woodside, Keswick	Father	—	—	5	0	0	per month
KENDRICK, Dorothy, 41 Milton Avenue, Harlesden, London, N.W.10	Widow	Stanley / Albert / Robert	6 / 4 / 1	2	3	0	per week
KENNEY, Frances Hannah, 11 Westwood Road, West Silvertown, London, E.16	Widow	Sheila Kathleen	1	1	7	8	do.
KENNEY, John, 44 Clyde Road, Silvertown, London, E.16	Father	—	—		10	0	do.
KIPLING, Mary Annie, 50 Rodney Street, Birkenhead	Widow	Mary / Jean / Robert / Evelyn	9 / 8 / 7 / 1	3	0	8	do.
LLOYD, Marie McRae, c/o R. Temple, Esq., 43 Park Street, London, W.1	Widow	New baby	2 months	10	0	0	per month
LONGSTAFF, Grace, 7 Arthur Terrace, Cockton Hill, Bishop Auckland, Co. Durham	Mother	—	—		5	0	per week
LUCK, Jessie Isabella, 4 Warwick Road, Upton Wirral, Cheshire	Mother	—	—		10	0	do.
MATTHEWS, Alfred, 10 Grove Road, Mill End, Rickmansworth, Herts	Father	—	—		5	0	do.
MITCHELL, Bertha Rose, 6 Evans Road, Southsea, Hants	Widow	Frederick Charles	14	1	7	8	do.
MORGANS, Mary Kathleen, 20 Alton Gardens, Prittlewell, Southend-on-Sea, Essex	Widow	—	—	1	0	0	do.
MORTIMER, Alfred Healey, 63 Thomas Street, Craghead, Co. Durham	Father	—	—		5	0	do.
ORMES, Florence Eleanor Asla, c/o Union Jack Hostel, Waterloo Road, London, S.E.1	Widow	Pauline Griswood	9	1	7	8	do.

Name and Address	Relationship to Deceased	Children		Allowance			
		Name	Age, years	£	s.	d.	
ORROCK, Annie, 49 Birchfield Drive, Glasgow, W.4	Mother	—	—		7	6	per week
OWEN, Mrs. C., 202 Bebington Road, Rock Ferry, Cheshire	Mother	—	—		15	0	do.
PAGE, Doris Isabella, 4 Rolleston Drive, Bebington, Cheshire	Widow	John Kenneth	4	1	7	8	do.
PARKINSON, Dorothy, 6 Cross Drive, Rainworth, Mansfield, Notts	Unmarried Wife	James Ronald Peter	3 1	2	3	0	do.
PENNINGTON, Barbara, 17 St. Augustine's Mansions, Vincent Square, S.W.1	Widow	Evelyn Dymoke Barbara	14	12	10	0	per month
PHILLIPS, Miss M., 17 Kinglake Road, Wallasey, Cheshire	Half-sister	—	—		10	0	per week
PRESTIDGE, Mrs. M.A., 2 Ashfield Road, Off Ash Grove, Shotton	Aunt	—	—		10	0	do.
QUINN, Ada, 28 Fairway Crescent, New Ferry	Widow	John L. Margaret A.	4 10 months	1	15	4	do.
READ, Phyllis Eva Grace, 279 Highland Road, Eastney, Southsea, Hants	Widow	John Kenneth	6	1	7	8	do.
ROBINSON, Muriel Bowers, 14 Baytree Road, Tranmere, Birkenhead	Widow	Eileen Muriel Barbara June	14 10	2	5	4	do.
ROGERS, Emmie, 463 Lever Edge Lane, Great Lever, Bolton, Lancs	Mother	—	—		10	0	do.
ROGERSON, Clara Rebecca, 3 Greenway, Greasby, Wirral	Widow	Alan Robert	6 months	10	0	0	per month
RYAN, Rosemary Violet Ridgway, Jackless Cross, North Curry, Taunton, Somerset	Widow	David Patrick Blackwood	2	10	0	0	do.
SCARTH, Edith Irene, 6 Cobden Street, Tranmere, Birkenhead	Widow	Joyce New baby	3 3 months	2	5	4	per week
SMITH, Eleanor Mary, 12 Wilson Road, Wallasey	Widow	Adrienne Cornelia	1 4 months	1	15	4	do.
SMITH, J., Briarfield, Pinetree Grove, Moreton, Cheshire	Mother	—	—		10	0	do.

- Aftermath of a disaster

Name and Address	Relationship to Deceased	Children		Allowance	
		Name	Age, years		
SMITH, Marie Catherine Louise, 1 Hill Street, Tunbridge Wells, Kent	Mother	—	—	£ s. d. 5 0	per week
SMITH, Nora, 21 Treyrela Road, Penzance, Cornwall	Widow	Marie Dorothy Nora Elizabeth Edith	15 11 7 6 9 months	2 18 4	do.
SMITHERS, Edie Grace, 1 South Cottages, Bury Lane, Horsell, Woking, Surrey	Widow	New baby	1 month	1 7 8	do.
SMITHERS, Minnie Mary, Pebble Cottage, Carthorse Lane, Horsell, Surrey	Mother	—	—	5 0	do.
STEVENS, Rosa, 32 Weymouth Terrace, Western Esplanade, Southampton	Mother	—	—	10 0	do.
STOCK, Florence May, 33 First Avenue, Luton, Chatham	Mother	—	—	10 0	do.
SUMMERS, May Victoria, 5 Gillbrook Square, Birkenhead	Widow	Agnes Elizabeth William Thomas	7 5 2	2 3 0	do.
WATKINSON, Marjorie, Hessle Moor, Heswall, Cheshire	Widow	John Leslie Richard Geoffrey	17 14	16 13 4	per month
WATTERSON, Elizabeth Ann, 17 Kinglake Road, Egremont	Widow	Marjorie	12	1 7 8	per week
WELLS, Isabella, 15 Mount Pleasant Westfield Lane, Mansfield, Notts	Widow	—	—	1 0 0	do.
WILSON, Ellen, 230 Oving Road, Chichester, Sussex	Mother	—	—	10 0	do.
YATES, Doris, 6 Ash Grove, Swilly, Plymouth	Widow	Robert Edward Allan Roy	2 5 months	1 15 4	do.
YOULES, Matilda, 109 St. Peter's Street, London, N.	Widow	—	—	1 0 0	do.
YOUNG, Florence, 8 Falmouth Street, Barrow-in-Furness	Widow	Joan Hugh Dale	9 8	2 5 4	do.

In time other names were added to and deleted from this list and they each accepted what was given. Widows until death unless they remarried and children up to the age of 18 years unless they started working, as was commonly the case with working class offspring.

However the social judgements did not end there. Widows and children clearly became victims for the second time in less than 6 months. Children appeared, with some consistency, to be worth 7 shillings and 8 pence each (38p) per week. Widows however were to become £1.00 widows, £1 10s (£1.50) widows or in some cases £2.00 widows or more. How so? Class !

Officers, Admiralty Overseers and Cammell Laird Managers got more than navy ratings and shipyard workers. In another throwback to class ridden payment systems almost all of the higher rate payments were made monthly whilst all the lower rate payments were made weekly !

I apologise in advance for adopting a 'school register' approach and using surnames only. Whilst I do know some Christian names through family contact of some of those lost, in the main I have no knowledge of the first names of those concerned so in an effort to be consistent and fair I will use the surnames as recorded in the archives. For ease of calculation I have assumed each month as having four weeks. I have tried to convert to decimal as best as I can.

For example. Widows of Navy ratings Allen and Batten with one child £1 7s 8d per week (£1.33), widow of Navy rating Dillon-Shallard with two children £1 15s 4d per week (£1.66).

Widows of Admiralty Overseers Aslett, Horne and Horsman, either childless or with children over the age of 18, received £1.10s per week (£1.50) as did the widows of Cammell Laird foremen like Kipling and Robinson. The widows of higher ranking overseers like Bailey and Hill with 3 children and 2 children respectively got a phenomenal £16 13s 4d per month (£16.66) and one of Bailey's children was 18 years old? These widows were worth some £2.10s - £3.00 per week(£2.50-£3.00) as were some Officers widows like those of Lt.Commander Bolus, skipper of *Thetis* with one child, and Commanders Hayter and Pennington.

Once more the 'officer class' was divided within itself with other officers widows like those of Garnett and Lloyd getting some £2.00 per week.

Finally, like the navy ratings, the rest of the £1.00 widows. The bottom of the pile. The widows of those Cammell Laird men like Summers, Beattie,

Craven, Watterson, Homer and the others.

Surprisingly there are inconsistencies even here within the lowest ranking widows. Ships Fitter Scarth was a £1 10s widow... was he a chargehand? Whilst the widowed wives of the Liverpool City Caterers men Bath and Dubells, were treated differently, the childless Dubells received £1 10s per week (£1.50) and Bath with one child the standard £1 7s 8d per week (£1.38). Was one man 'senior' to the other?

It must be said that it is all in all an extraordinarily confusing business...who was senior to whom? Who was worth more than whom? Who had longer service than whom? However perhaps the dominant factor was a question of what we would call today 'lifestyle', how people lived. Did they own their own home via a mortgage or not? Did they have children at a boarding school or not? Did they have a car, a telephone, a refrigerator or not? Or was it more about those who 'did' the work and those who 'didn't' do the work. Did they, as Dahrendorf so succinctly defined matters, 'work', 'not work' or had they 'worked and arrived'? Arrival perhaps being more of an escape than an arrival, an escape from the yoke of 'working' and so have an 'ability' to no longer 'work' but make a living out of 'non-work'? Futhermore it is extremely unlikely that any relatives were aware of the manner of distribution or who got what.

The only certainty in this muggy business of class is that, at the risk of repetition, the British public, butchers, bakers and candlestick makers one and all, threw their pounds, ten shillings, half - crowns, sixpences and pennies into buckets for the families of those lost aboard *Thetis*. That self same donation did **not** have a note or charge attached to it to differentiate between those families on the basis of rank, 'working life' or 'lifestyle'.

The donations to the fund were given, in more than a legal manner, in trust, and that trust was, in my view, betrayed.

To conclude this attempt to look again at the whole *Thetis* affair, I returned to archive research and the question of responsibility for, and compensation after, the *Thetis* disaster. It is known that the official enquiry found no individual responsible. It is known that the families tried to sue for damages in November 1939;[27] against Lieut. Woods, Cammell Laird and even the widow of Captain Bolus and the widowed mother of Seaman Hambrook, to whom Lieut. Woods gave the order to open the No 5 tube.[28] It is known that these actions all failed as a result of the official report not apportioning blame. It is also now known that documents were withheld from the widows 'in the public interest'. What I did not know was that fate was to play a hand in this work just as it did with *Thetis* sixty years ago.

I had some semblance of a plan of action for this work which was to try and visit the Public Record Office in Kew, the Imperial War Museum in Lambeth, London, and the Royal Navy Submarine Museum at Gosport / Fort Blockhouse. The PRO are good enough to supply a list of Bed & Breakfast accommodation close to it. I chose the home of Mr. and Mrs. John Dymond. John is a London GP and his wife Christine runs the B&B. John was interested in the story of *Thetis* so I loaned him a copy of the republished book as he vaguely remembered the events of 1939, whilst I suffered the dry throat and eye strain that is the lot of those who surround themselves with old papers and artificial lighting.

The work at the PRO took some days as did the work at the Imperial War Museum and it became clear to me that I would be unable to get to Gosport / Fort Blockhouse in 1998. However, at the PRO the Admiralty records revealed a personal minute, Number 194, from the First Sea Lord referring to the question of the publication, in 1940, of the Official Tribunal of Enquiry report into the loss of HMS *Thetis*. I quote verbatim :-

'All interest in this tragedy has now been submerged by
the war. I should deprecate any disciplinary action unless
some definite act can be traced to an individual. Indeed I
should be glad if Lieut. Woods' mind could be set at rest. I
think the Second, Fourth and Fifth Sea Lords should look
into the matter and advise what the Admiralty should say and
do. They should also advise on publication.

W.S.C 12.2.40 [29]

The responses from their Lordships are attached to this personal minute. They were to concur with the First Sea Lord, in so much as they considered that publication *'followed logically from the decision to set up a Public Tribunal'.*[30] However this recommendation was not tendered without first giving the option of non-publication to the First Sea Lord. Under the subheading 'Publication of the Report' it reads: *'Any official statement at the time, in Parliament or elsewhere, that the Report of the Tribunal would be published, cannot be traced'.*[31]

Thus before recommending publication of the official report the Second Sea Lord (and the Fourth and Fifth concurred with him) sent a clear hint to

- Aftermath of a disaster

the First Sea Lord that there was a 'get-out' to publication in so much as no one had ever publicly said that it would be published. It was also heartening for this writer to know that even Sea Lord's have trouble tracing records!

The official report was eventually published and its 60 odd pages are essentially a summary of the facts and events leading up to the disaster. It details six main causes of the loss of *Thetis*:-

1) **The blocking of the test cock of No.5 rear door.**
2) **The opening of the rear door to No5 tube when the bow cap was open.**
3) **The failure to effectively close the port water-tight bulkhead door.**
4) **The failure of those aboard *Thetis* to refloat her.**
5) **The failure of assistance from outside.**
6) **The failure of those aboard to escape from *Thetis*.**

No responsibility or blame is attached to any individual or organisation. The phrase '*Indeed I should be glad if Lieut. Woods' mind could be set to rest*', from the First Sea Lords' personal minute clearly signals the intent **not** to blame anyone, in particular Lieut. Woods.

But within these replies from the Second Sea Lord were references to an '*Internal Naval Enquiry*' and its findings conducted immediately after the disaster!

By the inclusion of these notes the responses from the various sea lords would also have the effect of protecting themselves from any accusing fingers in so much as they had told the First Sea Lord, in writing, of (a) the existence of an internal Naval Report and (b) what was said therein; the ball was now clearly in the First Sea Lord's court.

I had never heard of this 'Internal Naval Enquiry' and neither had Warren and Benson as they did not have access to the files at the PRO; these were sealed for 30 years after 1939. Where was this? I couldn't find it in the files at the PRO! Had I missed it? Had they ever even had a copy ? What did it say? I just couldn't find it. The staff at the PRO are as helpful as they can be but they have the files and only the files. If you can't find what you want they can do nothing else for you, you are very much on your own! I resolved to have one more look the next day (my last), that is until a chance conversation later that evening back at my Bed and & Breakfast!

It was only later that night back in the Dymond's home that the initials W.S.C. hit me. **Winston Spencer Churchill**... 1st Sea Lord from

September 1939. Without labouring too much upon the highly unfortunate phraseology of Churchill's minute, (it is hard to believe that someone apparently renowned for his vocabulary and oratory would be so callous as to use a verb like 'submerged'!) Personal minute No. 194 was incontrovertible evidence that Churchill, and all the other Sea Lords, knew about an 'Internal Naval Enquiry', and whatever was contained therein, when they agreed, in early 1940, to publish the 'official' report.

That same evening, the evening before my last day in London and travelling back to Liverpool by train, John Dymond casually remarked how much he was enjoying 'The Admiralty Regrets' and that it was strange that he had never heard of Fort Blockhouse but had now heard it twice in a week, ...once from the book and once as the place he had to go to the next day to sit on the interview panel for military medics, as the head man at Gosport Medical Centre was an old college chum of his!

I couldn't believe my ears! He was going to Blockhouse and coming back the same day and yes he had a spare seat in his car !! What is more he telephoned his chum at Blockhouse and arranged that I could have access to the archives through Commdr. Jeff Tall, the curator of the Submarine Museum, whilst John was busy grilling medics!

This whole work must have been a just cause; I was meant to find the Internal Naval Enquiry report. And I did! There it was, gathering dust as the Museum's mainly volunteer staff struggled to try and catalogue the material that they have, much of which is not yet catalogued and in part unknown... But I knew what I was looking for!

Typewritten and marked **'CONFIDENTIAL'** on every page it is dated 29ᵗʰ June 1939, just weeks after the sinking, and only one week before the start of the official enquiry. More than 20 pages long with many appendices, it was written and signed by Capt. C.B. Barry, Rear-Admiral W.F.Wake-Walker and Vice-Admiral and President of the board of Enquiry, R.H.T.Raikes.[32]

The references from the responses of 'their Lordships' to Churchill's 'Personal minute' No.194 are contained therein:-

Para. 4. We consider that in these circumstances there was no adequate reason for Lieut. Woods opening the rear doors and *he was not justified in doing so without instructions*. (My italics)

Para. 8. The combined test cock and locking bolt on the rear door

of No.5 tube was worked by Lieut. Woods *not entirely correctly* …For some time the instruction given at Fort Blockhouse has been that if neither air nor water comes out the rimer should be used to see if the passage is clear. *There is no evidence to show that this instruction was given when Lieut. Woods passed through the training class and he states that he was not instructed as to the use of the rimer at all.* (my italics)

Para. 9. When the rear door of No.5 tube was opened the water came in very rapidly…we consider that if the situation had been correctly appreciated i.e. that the bow cap was open and immediate action had been taken to operate the telemotor lever to close the bow cap it is possible that this could have been done. Lieut. Woods, however, had it so clearly in his mind that the bow cap must be shut in accordance with all the information he had obtained that this did not at first occur to him.

The Second Sea Lord's response to personal minute No.194 went further:-

In my opinion no discreet or experienced submarine officer would have tested the tube for this purpose and especially under the circumstances of the trial dive, by the rear door. Mr. Grundy, the Admiralty Overseer, who inspected the internal painting of the tube, *is also not free of blame* as he failed to make a thorough and minute inspection…. In my opinion, *Lieut. Commander Bolus was seriously to blame* for not having transferred about 44 of his passengers from *Thetis* to *Grebecock* before the trial dive commenced'. (My italics)

Here was culpability. Here was responsibility. Here too, in a personal minute from Winston Spencer Churchill, was a classic example of the Navy and the Government protecting their own, protecting themselves and the officer class from taking responsibility for a calamity that claimed 99 lives; 'I should be glad if Lieut. Woods' mind could be set at rest'.

In other words with one hand the respective Sea Lords acknowledged areas of fault and at the same time with the other hand recommend the publication of an 'Official' report of the Enquiry that apportions no fault. Given the rush to war and the 'bad press' that any other conclusion would bring in its wake clearly Churchill and everyone else in 'the establishment' wanted the whole '*Thetis* affair' to stay exactly where it was: 'submerged by the war'! Out of sight and out of mind. Similarly Churchill, all of the Admiralty

Sea Lords and many very high ranking Naval Officers and officials **KNEW**, by virtue of their involvement with the Internal Navy Report, that mistakes had been made by Naval Officers. These same people then decided to gloss the whole business over with the 'official line' of 'no fault.'

Here was another example of 'the Navy Way', looking after their own and anyone outside of the circle became 'incidental'. Frankly when I read it, I was, and continue to be, both shocked and angry at the world, and the way of the world, of 1939.

In August 1940 Lieut.Woods was awarded the Distinguished Service Cross for wartime service that he had undertaken after escaping from *Thetis*.

Lieut. Frederick Woods DSC died in a car crash outside of Marseilles in May 1946 and was buried at sea with full ceremonial honours on Saturday 25th May 1946.

After making contact with the Woods family they confirmed the almost incredible twist of fate that eventually befell 'Freddy' Woods, one of the men who escaped the steel coffin that was *Thetis*.

As a result of the motoring accident Lieut. Frederick Woods had drowned in just three inches of water ![33]

- Aftermath of a disaster

Between May 1998 and January 1999 I interviewed Howard Woods, the son of Lieut. Frederick Woods on two occasions. Howard is an honest and decent man whose father died when he was just three years old and he knew little of 'Freddy' except that he 'knew he was a hero'.[34] A loving stepfather came into his life quite soon after his father's death with whom he had a very happy childhood.

My choice at this point was to either publish the material without the knowledge of the Woods family and let the information come as a shock to them or to try and act in a more honourable manner and inform the family of what I had learned. I decided upon the latter course and it wasn't an easy thing to do, but during our second meeting I steeled myself and provided Howard with copies of the relevant documents. Naturally, he was surprised and disappointed.

REPORT ON THE FUNERAL OF LIEUT. COMMDR F.C.WOODS D.S.C. R.N.

At 1800 on Saturday the 25th. May the body of the late Lieut. Commdr. Woods D.S.C. R.N. was embarked in H.M.S. "Venus" at Villefranche for burial at sea. This took place the following morning at 1000, some two hundred miles off the French coast with full military honours. The service was conducted by the Reverend J.T.Cummin R.N.V.R.. During the service" Colours" were half-masted and H.M.S."Saumarez" and H.M.S."Volage", closed to two cables on either quarter to pay their last tribute to a gallant officer.

The official Royal Navy report of the funeral of Lieut. Commdr. F.G. Woods D.S.C. (His intials are given incorrectly as F.C.)

Lieut. Frederick Woods   Howard Woods

Howard Woods. Son of Lieut. Frederick Woods.

My parents weren't even married at the time of the disaster. So I wasn't even a thought in their mind! I'm not sure that they were even dating. There is an awful lot I don't know about. They got married in 1942 I think. She worked at Biggin Hill as a WRAF, Fighter Command. I don't know how they met or how long their courtship was. How long they were engaged or anything like that.

Freddie was a torpedo officer, a Lieutenant in charge of torpedoes. Everything I know about comes from the book...*Thetis - The Admiralty Regrets* ...so everything I have is second hand. So I know nothing for myself. Only what I've read in the book, and you'd be testing my memory if you asked me too many questions ...Which is not good...I just have a few things in a scrapbook.

At the time the book came out first, I was in my teens...we'd received a copy from Warren and Benson...I'd read a bit of it...they came to talk to mother ...I was away at boarding school, so, it probably happened while I was away. I have never met them myself. I'd read the book and not understood as a lot of it passed over my head at the time. I read the bit where my father opened the tubes and so on, I read it up to that point, and then if I remember rightly I sort of lost interest. I think it wasn't exactly to my family's liking, the book. I think also at the same time there was some sort of television programme going on at roughly the same time…anyway, what ever it is I didn't read it.

After he got out of *Thetis* I think he was just attached to HMS Dolphin at Gosport …a stone frigate…at least he was on 30 August 1939.. Then 12 January 1940 attached as a Lieutenant to HMS Norfolk... he never went back to serve on submarines. I was three years old and living in Malta. And my father was attached in some way to Mediterranean Fleet Command, I think. As a wireless officer /expert I think. I think he ended the War that way. The only details I have about his death was that he died in a car accident somewhere near Marseilles. And he was then buried at sea - in the scrapbook there's a note of exactly where - with a full naval ceremony.

I can remember it happening. I don't know whether my mother actually told me, but I can remember in Malta, I was playing with a large wooden train, shows what a different scale we moved in, I had a train with several wooden carriages and I remember it as being immense. I was playing with it and I can remember my mother coming in and crying and that was the moment I knew my father was dead. I don't know whether she said anything, but I just knew. She must have told me I suppose, but I don't really remember how I felt. I think I just took things as they come... I don't think I grieved as such... Selfishly orientated. ..resilient...unaware of the effect it had on me. I have memories, vaguely, as seen from my pram. He wasn't a big presence in my life. I can't remember how I felt about my mother feeling sad - it was too young really to think about it.

My son, Ian, said that he thought it was very strange how father had died... that he had drowned in three inches of water…I don't know where it comes from and Ian doesn't know where it comes from. He thinks I told him that. I don't remember that. All I can remember - I had the strongest impression not from any reason, but I had the impression that he drove off into a lake. But that conflicts with what my son Ian heard...neither of us really know the details... we do know he drowned as a result of a car accident …. I don't remember being very curious. ......I don't remember asking. The story of the car crash... maybe I heard it from Gran. I never was really aware of who he was and the connection to the *Thetis*…I knew he was a hero...I never really thought when I knew about his *Thetis* connection…haven't a clue. I've not the vaguest idea. I should imagine it was when Warren and Benson started doing this work.

No. I knew he was a hero and so I must have known that when I was about seven, because that is when I went to school. So I'm pretty sure I knew he was a hero at that stage. I knew he had a DSC because I'd seen the medal...I can remember always thinking that the medal was something to do with *Thetis,* but it wasn't, it was nothing to do with *Thetis.* He got that at Dunkirk but again I don't know how exactly. Early on I was fairly muddled about what had happened.

Freddy Woods' grandson, Howard's son Ian Woods was present at the time and contributed to the interview.....

Ian Woods: As far as I'm aware the only reason I became interested in it was when I finally actually met your (Howard's) mum - then started hearing about why Den wasn't your real father and stepbrothers and such.

Howard Woods: Mum married again in 1947...I was 4 or 5 years old...He was a very good step father - very good father in fact. A great chap. We were living in Selsey when she told me about Den...I think shortly before she got married she told me and I thought this is alright, I don't remember feeling at all unhappy about it anyway.

Remember there was rationing at the time, the first day I met him he took me down to the sweet shop and bought me ice cream...my mother always held that sweets were bad for the teeth and she had always held my sweet ration back ..so for the first time I actually tasted ice cream, so this gave me a very good impression of my new father...I liked him straight away.

But there was something I knew I had to do sometime or other. Get round to it and organise it. Just that other things got in the way. They are still in the way to some extent. Still I've no difficulty with what happened and so on. I want to learn about that. But it's getting the effort to get things together.

Ian Woods :I think my impression or the idea I've got is that I haven't got any interest in it but simply because Den wasn't my proper Grandfather. I wanted to know why there was this disparity in who these extra relations were. So a bit of curiosity about that. But then again I've only got the recent interest because of the book. Other than that all I've been telling since I was about seven when I must have got this story about the three inches of water thing, and it's been just something to tell my friends and that Grandad survived a submarine accident and drowned after the war. I've not had any other information other than that to go on till this book came out, till I saw the book in a book shop when I was at University in Bangor in 1997 and bought a copy for Dad.

Howard Woods: I've never even heard of the Disaster Fund... Not a peep. Never even knew it existed. Never heard about it at all. Never even thought about it. I assumed the Navy would look after dependants. Just assumed they would. But obviously not.

I think the accident happened because there is nobody in place to make a decision how to go about things. There is no organisation there really to get things together and make things happen. And that is history the fact that they didn't have it. A number of people on the ground made mistakes but you can't hold them individually to blame, I'm talking about after the accident.

You think it is stupid - why weren't these people whisked from here to there, why weren't they. Everybody felt somehow responsible but if they weren't aware that anybody else could take responsibility for them, and I suspect that all of this just as an organisational mess...headless chicken... If there was a man right at the top, and there was a point where one man right at the top could have made some decisions, that would have made a difference, then I think that he is to blame.

In the book there is a point where a very high official in the Admiralty has a chance to make a difference to get people to a site quickly, or what have you, and he didn't make that decision, so I think that is a crucial decision. But I think basically it is just a comedy of errors and with a number of people making the wrong decisions which cumulatively sort of made a real catastrophe.

You can see how such things happen. In my own line - computers - they are used in all sorts of complicated situations, like in the ambulance service in London where a new system was installed and it couldn't cope and all the way along there were people who could have made decisions about well it isn't coping with this situation or we know we've got this real situation to cope with and how are we going to test it, but it didn't happen, because nobody had that sort of responsibility. No understanding of the sort of situation that the whole system would have to cope with.

I've got a feeling that there is a parallel between that. I can see that I write programmes and I test them, that I can build in mistakes that no one can be aware of. That chap who painted the bitumastic on the tap, that my dad opened, and it didn't let the water out, I can see how I might have been him and actually done it and no one would have been aware of it because there is just no way that the system behind him could have picked it up. Because it wasn't sufficiently dense. He didn't have the multiple checks, the depth of checking that you need to do in order to make a system like that. So much more expensive to face up to a complex situation like that you've got to invest a hell of a lot more. We take risks when building ships.

I don't believe that the submarine was considered more valuable than the men...no I really don't believe that. There is no precedent in the Navy I don't think for that. I can see a policy situation like in the *Lusitania* whereby politicians make decisions but as regards this thing which is a sort of detail problem quite a low level in the organisation of things...No I don't think so. If you look at the cost after the event, how much it cost...It must be enormously expensive to let the thing sink. It must be cheaper to get the people out and let the boat sink...look at the people who were in that boat. Look who was in there. Head of submarines, whole load of experts, Cammell Laird people of great value, a whole load of experienced submariners, a complete crew in fact which cost quite a lot of money to produce, which you know they didn't have, they paid more to submarine crews to get people to be on a submarine.

I don't know what the financial sums are but I would have thought that on a cold equated method it is not possible to say that it would be cheaper to not damage the craft and not get the people out. Anyway I don't believe that anyone on the ground could actually make a decision like that. I don't think they thought that way.

- Aftermath of a disaster

Lieut. Frederick Woods , his wife Joyce and baby son Howard

Lieut. Frederick Woods on his way to the London Law Courts.

CERTIFICATE FOR WOUNDS AND HURTS

These are to Certify *the Right Honourable*
the Lords Commissioners of the Admiralty, that

(Name in full)   (Rank or Rating)   (Port Division and Official or Register, No.)

Frederick Greville WOODS. Lieutenant. R.N.

belonging to His Majesty's Ship "Thetis"

being then actually upon His Majesty's Service in that

Here describe the particular duty.

he was a member of the crew of the above Submarine

'Injured' or 'Wounded'
Date

~~was~~ injured ~~on~~ 2nd June 1939 by

Here describe minutely the nature of the injury sustained and the manner in which it occurred as required by Article 829 of the King's Regulations.

sustaining slight abrasions of back and right hand
together with nervous shock, as the result of escaping
in a "Davis Escape" apparatus from H.M.Submarine "Thetis".

Personal Description

Age about 25 years   Born at or near Simla.   Height 5 ft. 11. ins
Hair Brown.   Eyes Brown.   Complexion Fresh.

Particular Marks or Scars.

Scar right knee.

Date 3rd June 19 39.

Signature of Commanding Officer of Ship or Marine Division. HA Shears.

Rank Commander

Signature of Person who witnessed the accident CP Mills

Rank Lieutenant.

Signature of Medical Officer GS Cockram

Rank Surgeon Comdr

NOTE:—The grant of a Hurt Certificate to a Petty Officer or Man is to be noted on his Service Certificate.

Royal Navy form M183. Certificate of wounds and hurts sustained by Lieut. Frederick Woods following his escape from *Thetis*.

- Aftermath of a disaster

What 'Freddy' Woods did was make a mistake, this does not however make him a coward. Woods was awarded the Distinguished Service Cross for his wartime service. Who can ever know his motives for doing what he did on *Thetis*? Who has not made a mistake and then 'overcompensated' in an effort to redeem themselves as Woods certainly did in volunteering, through either guilt or fear, to try and reverse the *Thetis'* predicament?

I have no wish to hurt the families of those left behind, I was looking for the truth for everyone concerned.

The difference between the truth and the lack of the truth is that had not Winston Churchill, the Admiralty, the Navy, the judiciary and the 'Officer Class' closed ranks and hidden the truth from the nation things could have been so different for those left behind.

Had the worthies who sat in judgement and drip fed minuscule amounts to relatives not considered themselves demigods and guardians of the social regimen of the time things could have been so different.

Had responsibility been apportioned upon either the shoulders of the Admiralty, Cammell Laird or individuals, the families' legal appeal for damages may not have failed and perhaps the dependants of the working class men from Cammell Laird may have had a better life after *Thetis* than the life that they ended up enduring, almost begging for assistance from those in positions of power.

Such were the secrets and scandals of the loss of HMS *Thetis* that hot summer day in June 1939.

The Case for Arnold

During all of my research in the Thetis affair the son of Leading Stoker Walter Charles Arnold, Derek Arnold, has not only been an invaluable source of material he has also provided me with sometimes much needed support to carry on with the book despite the difficulties and frustrations of obtaining information, which were all, in the end, overcome. We have had the odd few pints together and he has become a friend. Apart from, understandably, rejecting my coveting of the fabulous solid brass model of Thetis that Derek made when he was working 'on the tools', there is nothing that he has refused me. This final sector is my attempt to thank him and to put the record straight for Walter Charles Arnold.

I knew from our conversations that Derek felt aggrieved about his fathers treatment in the immediate aftermath of the sinking but also about the fact that his father was never given any recognition for his efforts. Then again, as Derek himself would tell anyone who cared to listen, nor did his father **seek** any such recognition, he was 'that kind of guy'.

It just didn't seem right to me either and while poring over the documents and records now available from the period I found, as an incidental to the main theme of the research, that perhaps Walter Arnold had not had the recognition he deserved because either the Navy had simply forgotten him or because they didn't agree that the *Thetis* survivor had done anything worthy of recognition.

Walter Charles Arnold was the only naval rating to survive the tragedy of the Thetis. After being heavily sedated aboard the destroyer *Brazen,* he was spirited away from the scene of the disaster. This was not the case with the other three survivors from the submarine who were transferred to the Liverpool & Glasgow Salvage vessel *Vigilant* which then disembarked them at Liverpool. Why was Arnold treated differently ? Why was he sedated? He himself was less than happy about the situation. When he did finally clear himself of the effects of the drugs *Brazen* was steaming past Holyhead well away from the scene of the sinking. He is on record as thinking at the time that there was something amiss as he was the lone survivor on *Brazen* and the only rating too! There was more than a hint of snobbery in the air as *Brazen* continued on her way south to Plymouth.

- Aftermath of a disaster

His arrival at Plymouth itself had all the trappings of a bizarre ritual even by Royal Navy standards. *Brazen* was met by an ambulance complete with a doctor and even a baggage party. One thing Arnold didn't have with him was any baggage! He was soon to be placed in a private isolation ward at the Stonehouse Naval Hospital and visited by none other the Surgeon Rear Admiral. The conversation did not revolve around medical matters as after a brief 'how are you?' to the stoker the doctors first words were ' Well, I really came to tell you not to talk to anyone about what happened in *Thetis* until you get permission from the Admiralty.'[1]

When he eventually got home to Birkenhead he was smuggled between home and Cammell Lairds' Yard and was then to spend many wearisome and probably heartbreaking days back in Anglesey helping the Royal Navy and the Police to try and identify the bodies of his one time shipmates. Testimony to his efforts and the reliance placed upon him are the gruesome notes kept on record at the Public Records Office in London. Samples of these are given here.[2] Many of the 'Unidentified Naval Ratings' have the notes 'Leading Stoker Arnold thought it might be either x or y or z' or 'Leading stoker Arnold suggests X'. Only Walter Arnold really knew the crew of *Thetis,* those officers who survived would not know the men nor would Frank Shaw, the Cammell Laird survivor, only Walter Arnold. Typical notes from his observations are below:-

NUMBER 162

Unidentified Naval Rating

HEIGHT.	Medium
APPEARANCE.	Dressed in the uniform of a Naval Rating. No distinctive mark or badges on tunic. No marks on body.
VALUABLES.	Small metal wrist watch, chromium plated band, on left wrist (No name or number) Cash 3/6 $^{1}/_{2}$
REMARKS.	Of those unidentified wrist watches worn by:- J.Costley, S.Crombleholme. Costley was tattooed therefore probably not him. Leading Stoker Arnold suggests S. Crombleholme.
	Mrs. Crombleholme asked to identify the watch from a sketch and wrote back an ambiguous letter. The watch is being sent to her for a positive answer.

NUMBER 117

Unidentified Naval Rating

HEIGHT.	5ft 7 ins
APPEARANCE.	Dressed in Naval uniform of a Ldg Sto.
	Underneath overalls with Ldg. Stokers badges.
	Black boots size 8. Sound top teeth, one missing at front. Fair bottom teeth, one tooth overlaps another on right side.
	Tattoo marks:- Bird in flight on right hand between thumb and index finger, letter in beak. The name Jean underneath. On both forearms a sailing ship. Beneath Tattoo on left forearm was sentence 'In the days of ommand'.
REMARKS.	Leading Stoker Arnold thought it might be Graham, Allen or Smith, probably the latter.

More than a year after the disaster, in July 1940, a formal Coroners inquest, with a jury, was held at Holyhead. The Admiralty appointed agents present at the inquiry were from the Liverpool Castle Street firm of Batesons & Co. who sent their reports to the Admiralty. Here too Walter Arnold's evidence was to be read out, but in the event the Coroner, after hearing Woods' evidence read out, felt that ' it was fairly clear that all the evidence had been called' … he then summed up to the Jury who without retiring brought in a verdict of 'Accidental death' with no blame attached to anyone'[3]. Thus a perfect mirror image of the findings of the 'Official' Enquiry held the previous year in London.

However what is more revealing yet is a minute attached to the same report from Batesons drawing the Secretary of the Admiralty's attention specifically to the anti- penultimate and penultimate paragraphs'.[4] These two paragraphs are reproduced below:-

'The Coroner then publicly drew attention to the very valuable services rendered by Stoker Arnold both to himself and to the Police in connection with the Inquest and in particular with the identification of the bodies. He said that a great debt was owed to Stoker Arnold for these services rendered in what must have been to him harrowing circumstances and that his help in this respect was invaluable. We were specifically asked to pass these remarks on to the proper quarters.

- Aftermath of a disaster

Informally the Coroner told us that he understood that although some promises had been made to Stoker Arnold that something would be done for him specifically in recognition of his services nothing had apparently been done at all. We do not of course know what the facts may be but there seems to be some degree of feeling on this subject in Holyhead and we overheard some members of the Jury speaking to the same effect'.

The internal naval responses to the 'promises' made to Stoker Arnold and the groundswell of opinion that he was 'a hero' are reproduced below:- 'Nothing is known of any such promises, by whom they were made or to what services they refer.' it continues... 'Naval Branch has no knowledge of any such promise. It is possible, however, that the service which is referred to is the action of Arnold in going into the escape chamber with a civilian after four others had been killed through getting in a panic in the chamber and ripping off their gear. It is believed that Arnold forced his companion to keep his gear on after the water in the escape chamber had risen above their heads... The people speaking on behalf of Arnold may have in mind the case of petty Officer Willis, who was awarded the Albert Medal for his service when *HMS Poseidon* was lost, he being responsible, through his behaviour, for many members of the crew getting safely away through the escape apparatus. It is recalled that the press made rather a lot of Arnold's escape, and the fact that he was 'in the news' is illustrated by an anonymous letter contained in N.5646/39, now attached'.

Then: 'Apart from letters of appreciation to various persons who rendered assistance after *Thetis* sank, no action appears to have been taken with regard to Naval survivors except an appreciation to Lieut.Woods for his conduct subsequent to the disaster.... there is no doubt that Leading Stoker Arnold conducted himself in accordance with the highest traditions of the Service and that his action during the escape phase saved the life of Mr. Frank Shaw. He appears to have given clear and straightforward evidence at the Public Enquiry and rendered valuable assistance during the identification of the bodies recovered from *Thetis*.
In view of (the above) remarks it is proposed to submit for consideration that some form of recognition of his services be accorded to Arnold'.[5]

Incredibly, more than a year after the disaster the Heads of various Naval Branches say that *'nothing is known ...of such promises, by whom they were made or **to what services they referred'**.* Comparisons are even made with the award of a medal to a Petty Officer following a completely different submarine incident.

Continuing with ' *it is recalled that the press made rather a lot of Arnold's escape*' (the anonymous letter referred to was not attached to the file), the 'brass' at the Admiralty had either forgotten or chosen to forget the bravery of this rating as well as his conduct and his essential personal knowledge of the crew of *Thetis* during the aftermath of the sinking, …after all the press had 'made rather a lot of it.'

Yet on the same document one Naval Head of Branch, that of Naval Equipment, refers to the matter of 'promises' and Stoker Arnold is precisely credited with saving Frank Shaw's life having acted '*in the highest traditions of the service'*… and that '*it is proposed to submit for consideration that some form of recognition for his services be accorded to Arnold'*.

I apologise for the increasing use of the word incredible here, but that is the only word for these staggering revelations. The same Head of Naval Branch who appears supportive of some form of recognition for Arnold notes that '*an appreciation to Lieut. Woods*' had been recorded.

Leading Stoker Walter Charles Arnold never received any form of recognition whatsoever for his part in the *Thetis* affair. Nor did he even get his pay! He couldn't even get his wages out of the Navy for some six months!! It is testimony to his wife May that she was able to struggle through this time and care for the infant Derek Arnold.

What then **did** Leading Stoker Walter Arnold get for his pains ? What the Leading Stoker **did** get was an opportunity, an opportunity to fight a war! In his gripping foreword to the Warren & Benson Book- '*Thetis -The Admiralty Regrets*' Derek recounts his father's war record. In brief, his father, not surprisingly, after his next posting to the submarine HMS *Spearfish* found he was no longer able to serve in submarines, feeling claustrophobic. He went on to serve on numerous famous vessels in the Atlantic, North Sea, Mediterranean and Pacific campaigns. His brothers lost their lives to the submarine service and his brothers-in-law also suffered enormously during their submarine service. During the 1960's the Arnold family as a whole were honoured and one of five new accommodation blocks for senior ratings at HMS *Dolphin* (Fort Blockhouse) Gosport was named **ARNOLD.**

Walter Arnold himself had survived *Thetis*, saving a man's life into the bargain...torpedoes, bombing, machine gun attacks and a ramming. He had also kept his mouth shut, as ordered. He continued to serve many months after the end of the second World War and thus missed the 'singing and dancing' that overcame the nation at the time. At the end of his war service he ended up in a fairly menial occupation working at the local soap works to provide for his family.

He gave, and risked, for the British Royal Navy twenty-two years of his life and they gave him nothing in return but his standard navy pension.

Should 'the brass' read this... look to your laurels...remember Stoker Walter Arnold.

Walter Arnold enjoys a smoke in the works canteen. He is central to the picture, on the second table from the front with a cigarette in his mouth.
Photograph courtesy of Derek Arnold.

I should like to add one final poignant note on the story of *Thetis*. A note upon good fortune once more. Perhaps not completely relevant to this particular perspective on the *Thetis* disaster it is a story about those left behind; about love and losing one's love.

One of my radio broadcasts was passed on to a woman from Sussex (well out of range of BBC Radio Merseyside) Maureen Miller, who contacted me. Maureen had no direct connection with *Thetis* and had just lost her mother, whose maiden name was Edith Lawton, in the spring of 1998. Her father had died some ten years earlier.

Maureen knew that her mother had a fiancee before her father came along. The fiancee who never became her father had been lost aboard a submarine called *Thetis*. His name was Tommy Mortimer and he hailed from Craghead, County Durham. Edith was from Washington, on Tyneside and worked as a nurse in Hartlepool. Tommy had been a Royal Navy Telegraphist; that was all she knew.

Upon clearing her mother's things Maureen found a photograph of Tommy and a love letter to her mother from him, written the day before *Thetis* sailed.

Edith and Tommy had planned to be married in the autumn of 1939. Maureen's mother had secretly held onto this last love letter from Tommy for almost sixty years. Every time I read Tommy Mortimer's letter to Edith it brings a lump to my throat and a tear to my eyes.

Maureen has given me permission to include Tommy's words to her mother in the concluding pages of this book. Perhaps it may not be the last page on the *Thetis* disaster in Liverpool Bay, in June 1939.

191 Borough Road

Birkenhead

Cheshire

31st May 1939

My Darling,

I hope that you had an enjoyable weekend and that the weather did not prove too warm for you, and also that you had a weekend off for the holidays. As I told you in my last letter I was working practically all the time and I have had a few more extra hours in and now we go to sea tomorrow for our diving trials so I think myself that I shall be pretty glad when this week is over.

Now I've got all my moans off my chest I hope you excuse me in having to take them on your shoulders again. If all goes well and we have no further mishaps with the boat we shall all leave here on June 14th . We had a very good evening last night. A crowd of us from the boat went and played a crowd darts and finished up with a good sing song and all the people there said it was the best evening they had had for years. On Tuesday coming we are having another farewell dance and this time all the proceeds are going to the aid of charity so someone will benefit about £25, it is a pity we have to leave so soon or else we would be having another farewell dance.

I have heard nothing more about the marriage allowance age been dropped but I suppose soon we shall be getting full particulars and then we shall be able to arrange for our wedding which I hope will take place about October, but please do not give your notice in until we can actually get together and make final preparations darling.

Have just had a knock on the door and off to work I go so I shall drop you a line very soon so for the present Au Revoir with all my love, lots of kisses and best wishes

Always Your Own Ever - loving

Tommy XXXXXXXX

Royal Navy Telegraphist Tommy Mortimer, a Craghead, Co. Durham lad,
sweetheart of Edith Lawton and making plans to marry her....in 1939.

- Aftermath of a disaster

Epilogue

It is my earnest hope that this book has been well received. I can hardly hope that you have 'enjoyed' it given the dreadful and often harrowing experiences and injustices that it exposes. All that can be offered in mitigation was a search for the truth.

This search had many friends, some opponents and a great deal of good fortune, hard work and amazing coincidence. The threads of the story of *Thetis* are entangled and diverse and I found myself travelling along them and often finding a crossover that those involved were unaware of. I thought that this was very sad for those still left.

The only father that Peter Wells ever knew was, in fact, his grandfather.

Howard Woods and Edie Smithers live within a 20 minute bus ride of each other but have never met.

Howard Woods simply wrote to me asking for a copy of the book after his son had bought a copy when a student in Bangor, North Wales... after I received his request I rang him and asked 'are you who I think you are ?'.... and he was.

I only discovered Lieut. Woods' real cause of death by accident when talking to his grandson Ian.

The unpublished Internal Navy Report might still be gathering dust in Gosport had not fortune stepped in.

Bill Allen only heard about the new book from a fare in his Cardiff taxi. He only got in touch with me over a spelling mistake and would probably never have seen his mother on film had he not done so.

Bill and Cynthia Allen live just a few miles from Roy Batten and his mother, a *Thetis* widow, in Pontypridd... they have never met each other.

John Glenn and Derek Arnold had never met.

Harry Dillon-Shallard has lived all of his life in the Portsmouth area, the home of HM Submarines... he has never been contacted by the museum or anyone else for his testimony.

Shirley Grimsdale and her fathers photographs came my way through Anglesey connections. We had never met each other until another amazing coincidence, in March 1999, on Anglesey!

Perhaps most regrettable of all is the lack of contact between the

Birkenhead relatives of the Summers, Cravens, Beatties, Wattersons, Kiplings, Robinsons and Homers.

Regrettable that is... to me. I did not lose anybody close to me but sincerely feel their loss and also their by now, often diluted anger. That is why I wrote this book. Sixty years is almost a lifetime, times and people change and move on...perhaps 60 years on from the millennium more 'modern' disasters such as Hillsborough and the *Herald of Free Enterprise* may be compared to my views by other writers with their own observations. I suspect I shall not be here, but I did what I could.

As this book goes to press in the spring of 1999 I have learned that the number of living widows of naval ratings is now only two. I feel privileged to have talked to one of them, Edie Smithers, and the son of the other, Gladys Batten. I was also proud to have spoken with May Levelle, a 90 year old *Thetis* widow who had remarried and been widowed for a second time.

In 2000 the name of Cammell Laird lives on, used by a new and completely different company as they repair and convert various vessels with great success on part of the site of this once great shipyard. Since the republication of '*The Admiralty Regrets*' the local council of the town of Birkenhead, Wirral, is, upon the 60th anniversary of the tragedy, to dedicate a new memorial at the old Birkenhead Priory, overlooking the shipyard, to those lost on *Thetis*. Would they have done it without the '*Admiralty Regrets*' book, Fred Lawless' radio play and the resulting publicity? Sixty years on perhaps the kindest view would be 'better late than never'...such is politics.

In my view, paramount to the politics, most of the above mentioned people have never met each other and I consider myself fortunate to have met with them all. It has been an intriguing, absorbing and very demanding two and a half years.

I shall also be pleased, in more than some small way, if I have managed to give them a voice for the first time in sixty years, and perhaps to have helped them find a way out of the darkness and injustice that *Thetis,* and their loved ones, were shrouded in.

If I have... that'll do.

William David Roberts - 1999

The 'Ripple Effect' - 2009
- Upon the 70th Anniversary of the loss of HMS *Thetis*

This book is now on its fifth print run. It has been staggeringly successful, which perhaps speaks volumes for the *Thetis* story and those people in this book that were left behind. During the years since the first publication some quite amazing things have happened.

Since the first printing of this book the younger sister of Ldg. Seaman John Turner contacted me.

Mrs Joyce Bentley of Ashton-under-Lyne was **extremely** angry when she discovered, in this book, that there had been some deceit in her own family after losing John....in so much that what scant payments WERE made to Johns family from the memorial fund had been 'incorrectly' claimed.

Joyce went on the become the driving force and the focal point behind the TFA.....the Thetis Families Association....in an effort to organise those that were left to try and make some sense of it all as a pressure group. I know from my own endeavours that this is no easy task.....the relatives of such a disparate group of people are all different, as were their loved ones, and can be very demanding.

Then in the year 2000, on August 12th, the Kursk happened!

Here it was all over again. The Russian vessel was the biggest attack submarine ever built and was lost in the Barents Sea with all 118 hands. Some 20 sailors had survived in a tiny pocket of air after the initial catastrophic explosion ...only for the same indecision, political posturing and bad leadership to rob them of their lives too.

The world, all governments, and especially Joyce Bentley, were horrified. How on earth could such a thing still happen in the year 2000? The TFA wanted to try and make sure that it could not happen again.

Joyce, as the chairperson of the TFA, travelled up and down the country meeting surviving family members of those lost on Thetis, lobbied MPs at the Houses of Parliament, was invited to Westminster Abbey for the Royal Navy submarine centenary service, being introduced to Queen Elizabeth II and the Duke of Edinburgh, taught herself how to use computers and e-mail and sent out regular newsletters. All this as a single mother who was only 7 years old when her older brother John was lost on *Thetis*.

After all of her superhuman efforts Joyce has succeeded in getting submarine safety very much higher on the agenda of the international maritime community. She is as I write, still busy helping to organise a 70th anniversary memorial service at Birkenhead.

Joyce Bentley has done her brother John and all of those lost on *Thetis* a great service. She has made the world a safer place for their brothers who work beneath the waves.

In late 1999 a well-known Merseyside playwright, Marc Gee, who wanted to adapt this book into a stage play, approached me. We talked about it and I was happy to give Marc advise on details, technicalities and the likelihood of certain words and expression being used by either Cammell Laird or Naval personnel, but the actual 'creative force' behind the play would be his domain. I heard a first read through of the play only a month later in his girlfriend Angela's front room and was moved to tears. As the play grew closer to it's preview at the Liverpool Bluecoat Arts centre, my regular tears at every rehearsal become something the cast would predict saying 'there he goes again'…such is the powerful, dramatic and moving adaptation entitled simply **HMS THETIS**, that was to be a great success. So much so that many local people in Birkenhead called for the production to be staged in the town where *Thetis* was born and where many of her victims came from.

The result was the first ever theatre production in February 2000 at the brand new Pacific Road Theatre in Birkenhead which was also a great success.

During the dying months of the millennium I received a very excited e-mail from Phillp Price in Australia. His mother is Margaret Broad, a daughter of Cammell Laird Electrician Samuel Broad, who was lost on the submarine. Her Aunty Joan, who still lived on the Wirral, had told Margaret and her younger sister Mary about this book. These two Birkenhead born women were very excited about the book and even more excited when we spoke on the phone about the forthcoming play. So excited that they decided to travel from their home to come to Birkenhead to see the production. Margaret (Maggie) lives near Sydney and Mary (Bunty) in Tasmania!!

That's a long way to come and see a play and we spent many hours together during their visit.

This is the story of a *Thetis* family from the other side of the world…

- Aftermath of a disaster

[above] Margaret (left) and Mary Broad in 1946 at Holt Hill Convent, Birkenhead.
[above right] At Aunty Joans in Bromborough, Wirral. circa 2000, from left Aunty Joan, Mary, Maggie.

Margaret Anne Broad DoB 24.11.37 and Mary Eileen Broad DoB 9.12.38

Maggie: I was born in Birkenhead, in Birkenhead Hospital actually and we lived at 39 Bankville Road Birkenhead. My father was Samuel Broad, an electrician working at Cammell Laird. I was only 18 months old when he was lost on HMS *Thetis,* the submarine.

My earliest memories of what happened were much later, I remember that we used to sit around the fireplace and have cries for a dad I never knew existed anyway. So that was around when I was 7 or 8…I'd started to go to school and heard other children talking about their dad and realised that I didn't have one.

All we knew was that dad died on a submarine in Liverpool Bay in 1939 but we were never really given any great details of that at all…just snippets of what relatives told us and things like that. I don't know whether our relatives believed that ignorant was innocent – if you were ignorant of the facts and details then it wouldn't hurt you. That is what it was all about. That's why I wouldn't get any great detail. Only that he was a great guy and that is end of story, just about, for me anyway.

We didn't really get the whole story until we read your book to be honest.
The Admiralty Regrets gave us nothing, only technical knowledge and that was something above me that I didn't understand anyway. So really it was to get at

all the facts and all the details was your book… and here we are now 62 years old.

Later on our step dad came along and apparently he cut up all the photographs of our dad… I thought that was a pretty lousy trick. Although when we had the opportunity, when mum got married, to take his name, we refused to take his name. Absolutely point blank.

I think it was prior to going to Tasmania in 1955, so we were 16 and 17. And we refused to take his name, and kept the Broad name, dad's name.

By then we were sort of reconciled to it and accepted it and really it didn't even come in great conversations 'Oh my dad died on the *Thetis*' you know. Or sometimes it rang a bell to some people and other times it didn't. Even some of the older Australian's remembered it; that's for sure. Of course as soon as you mention 1939 they immediately think it was lost in the war of course. .

Mary: I was a year younger than my sister…. Just a babe in arms…I knew nothing at all. I think I figured out that I didn't have a dad more or less the same as Maggie, going to school,… when other kids around have got a dad and we didn't. Some of the nuns at our school, Holt Hill Convent, realised that we didn't have a dad and they were the ones that shunned it off …that it was just not mentioned to us too much at all. They gave a little bit more consideration to the fact that we didn't have a dad and I know that changed when my mother remarried because she married a divorcee, and attitudes changed completely towards us unfortunately…. they weren't in favour of divorce and remarriage… and mum got married in a Registry Office and not a church.

We really felt it too, believe it or not…. I don't know about Maggie, but I really did feel it at school. There was a difference in the attitude towards us from the nuns…It flipped to perhaps even antagonism….all bar for one nun that I really got on with. She was Mother Pauline, the cookery nun. She had more understanding than any of them. Then the head nun changed and we had Mother Mary Monica. She was a wonderful nun. She had understanding. But the others didn't have any at all.

I knew no more than my sister until we came back to England 21 years ago, and uncle Les and auntie Nora took us to Holyhead and showed us that's where the submarine went down and the memorial grave there. And dad's name was on it. That was all.

We knew that he was buried in Town Lane cemetery in Bebington because we lived in Briardale Road and quite often we would go and see his grave and stand there and talk to him in our own little way. We would just say we miss you dad, sort of thing, in your own way…. I remember the song, even when I was on the ship going to Australia, I'd get on the deck and think and sing 'Oh my Papa'.

Mum didn't talk about it much though….but then your book came out. Your book opened my eyes too! I didn't really know much at all till we read the book. Being in Tasmania, Australia I would have been 16 and Maggie 17. That is the time when we would have been curious to know about it, but it was a no-no because Joe, our step dad, was on the scene.

Had we have been in England perhaps we could have gone to nana and grandpa Corker, or Auntie Joan or Pattie and they might have talked about it, but because we were so many miles away it was just never, ever talked about… we were a hell of a long way away you know and it was just never talked about and if you are on the phone you never ever brought anything like that up.

Then again I do understand now why I am very protective with my children and that they do and always have done a lot with their father. It was always 'Dad will be home in a minute' and he was number one and they'd run out to him. I'd get tears in my eyes when I saw them walking with their hands behind their backs like dad, very straight and erect.

Maggie: I have to say too that I encouraged that relationship even to the detriment of my own relationship with my children. I brought out the relationship between their father and my children I did that and was my primary concern. I think it was good to see it as Mary said a lot of the things that we didn't receive ourselves it was nice to see that my children were able to, and that is very satisfying and very rewarding and helps heal…because you can see it in the generation you've created yourself.

I can remember mum getting about £1 a week. I used to collect the envelope out of the letterbox for mum…..we knew that there was something coming and it was connected to dad somehow…It was a distant thing it wasn't really talked about. But I knew that it was some money in an envelope that was coming through for mum and she picked it up and every week.

Mary: I do remember two occasions going to the judge with mum to try and get some money…they are really vivid in my mind. One time was because we both joined the Girl Guides. We were due to go on a camping trip, and we were to ask for special uniform and a sleeping bag to go away camping with. It was instilled in us then, that we had to be on our best behaviour, we would be dressed as smart as mum could possible do, and she always said to ask for more money than we want, so then you might get the amount that you really wanted. And the other time was when we wanted a coat, we both wanted camel coats and I remember going for that.

Maggie : Mum used some of the money to pay for our assisted package. To get us out to Australia...I just imagine that the Judge was in his robes, wig and behind this huge desk, in Birkenhead...It was extremely awesome. All the hype prior to going, don't misbehave, don't speak until you are spoken to. I hated it. I absolutely hated it. Often my mother would do it, but not for the reasons she had put on the paper... So to me it was a dishonest act... So I hated the whole bloody thing.

Mary: It was to pay the bloody bills.

Maggie: So I hated it. Absolutely hated it for that reason...We didn't challenge it. At that early stage of our lives we didn't... but I know that I hated it.

Mary: If we could do anything about it now, if the money from the disaster fund could ever be distributed properly...it would probably come and I'd go out with the children and the grandchildren, but as I said to you from what everybody was saying we wouldn't mind making it into a movie. Because really speaking, to me, it is too late, I'm on my feet, I don't really need it. You can't say no to money but I'm not desperate for it... I know that some of those relatives still alive could do with some help.

Maggie: If I had a chance to do something with it, I would definitely see that the widows remaining have the rest of their lives in absolute bloody comfort. I could do with it but I'd prefer it goes to making a movie, to let people sit back and have a look and see the absolute cover ups that go on in this country and how all this secrecy covers up people's mistakes...and what length people go to, to do that... to not tell the truth and things like that... I find people prefer the truth. If you made a mistake then just sort of be honest about it.

The whole thing was absolutely abhorrent and was done wrong and took away the rights of women in 1939... I absolutely against anything like that. In those days people weren't talking about rights of women but they weren't allowed to make decisions about money... It was taken out of their hands completely. I think that is so unjust.

If I were to fight for anything, it would be for that reason. I could probably do with the money but I don't want it. I'll just go on with my simple life as I am. I'd prefer it to go into a movie so everyone can pay attention, and everyone can say that shouldn't bloody well have happened.

These two Birkenhead born Australian women are a formidable pair of individuals. I suspect that the British authorities should count themselves fortunate that the women were unaware of the full tragic story of their fathers death until quite late in their lives. If they and Joyce Bentley and I had got together thirty years earlier they would probably have made quite a nuisance of themselves to the authorities.

*   *   *   *   *

The Northern Echo, based in Darlington, carried the *Thetis* story when this book was first published, with, naturally, a particular focus on the north eastern boys lost on *Thetis*.

Mrs. Edna Rankin from Newcastle contacted me. She had missed the *Northern Echo* article but someone had told her about it afterwards and she had to go to the local library to see it. She told me that when she saw a large photo of Tommy Mortimer she 'just cried and cried'. She had not seen her older brother since she was 15 years old. Edna told me that she '*had not cried as much in sixty years as she had the last few weeks.*'

She shows copies of the newspaper article to friends but insists that they read it after she has left them, as it upsets her still. I apologise Edna, I didn't mean to upset anyone, just to get to the truth at last... as I hope the book conveys.

Edna also told me what she thought of the events of sixty years ago...she said '*it was a very very upsetting time... it was all the Navy's fault...the Navy just stood by and did nothing... and we missed him so much because he was such a fine young man*'. She remembers too Edith and Tommy coming to the family home in Craghead, Co. Durham to 'show off' their engagement ring...and that was the last time I saw our Tommy'.

*   *   *   *   *

The young Lancashire lad lost on *Thetis*, Stan Crombleholme is remembered earlier in this book by his sister Edith as *'a Troop Leader with the Scouts, did everybody a good turn if he could...popular with the girls too.'*

Much later, Miriam Wardell from Accrington, six miles from Stan's home town of Blackburn came to my notice. Miriam was born in September 1938 , her mother was Lizzie Booth. Lizzie had never married, bringing up Miriam alone. Miriam never knew her father or anything about him, though, as children are wont to do, she would often go 'rooting around' at home and find photographs of a man in uniform.....Miriam says she just **KNEW** instinctively it was her father....but never ever asked about him.

Miriam lived her own life, marrying and having 3 children of her own...until the middle 1970's shortly before her mother died. Lizzie finally asked Miriam if she ' wanted to know more about her father.' Miriam remembers that as Lizzie told her story, she just cried and cried all the way through it.

In 1938 Lizzie had a sweetheart. Young Stan Crombleholme, who was indeed *'popular with the girls'*. They were together on the eve of Miriam's birth but had an argument... so Stan left..

Lizzie had her baby shrouded in secrecy but her parents forced her to tell them who the father was. Somehow they found Stan and made him visit his new born baby. As far as we know this was the only time Stan saw his daughter and he returned to the Royal Navy. Nine months later Stan was lost on *Thetis*.

Stan's sister Edith Bleakly knew nothing of her niece Miriam.

Stan had in fact left a wonderful present behind for his little sister Edith...but Edith never got it....until this book brought them together after 60 years living within just six miles of each other.

I recall clearly telling Edith to sit down and take a deep breath before I told her about Stan's' child. Her first response was to say *'Well. I thought I'd heard everything'*.

Miriam says that she always knew that she had an Aunt but did not know where. She had to think long and hard before making contact with her 'Aunt Edith' for fear of rejection, feeling somehow that she had been rejected before.

When they did meet Edith accepted Miriam immediately...it was quite an emotional time.

Edith told Miriam that ' *she saved everything of Stan's his letters, photographs, even his hairbrushes and tobacco tin.....and she often wondered why on earth she always saved all those things.....now she knew.'* Today all of these things of Stan's are kept by his daughter Miriam.

After that Edith and Miriam spent a great deal of time together until Edith's death some two years later. Miriam still says today that those two years were the most wonderful years of her life, she felt as though they had known each other forever.

Stan's last letter to his mother before he died says that he *'has something to tell her'*.

Was Stan going to tell all about Lizzie and Miriam?

Better late than never, Miriam gained an Aunt Edith and a cousin in Edith's daughter Pat who lives in Lytham-St-Annes, Lancashire.

I wish all of them all the happiness they can find in the world.

W. David Roberts 2009

References: Introduction

[1] David Roberts., 'Cammell Laird - The Golden Years' (Manchester, Printwise Publications, 1991.[Reprinted Edition, Merseyside, Avid Publications, 1998]).

[2] David Roberts, *Life at Lairds - memories of working shipyard men* (Merseyside, Avid Publications, 1993).

[3] *Cammell Laird - Old Ships and Hardships - the story of a shipyard* (Merseyside, Avid Publications, 1994). Duration approx. 50 minutes. Produced, Directed & Narrated by David Roberts.

[4] C. Warren & J. Benson, *The Admiralty Regrets* (London, Harrop, 1956).

[5] C. Warren & J. Benson, *Thetis - The Admiralty Regrets - the disaster in Liverpool Bay* edited by David Roberts, Foreword by Derek Arnold, Postscript by David Roberts (Merseyside, Avid Publications, 1997).

[6] Fred Lawless, Scriptwriter, 'Close enough to touch ' (Radio 4 Drama, 10.10.1997).

[7] Interview with Agnes Gaul, daughter of George Summers, Electrician on *Thetis.*

[8] Warren & Benson, *Thetis,* Appendix 1.

[9] Warren & Benson, *Thetis,* p 29.

[10] Godfrey Winn, *Home from the sea - life on the Lower Deck* (London. Hutchinson, 1944), pp 13 - 14.

[11] P. J. Waller, *Democracy and Sectarianism - a political and social history of Liverpool 1868 - 1939* (Liverpool, Liverpool University Press, 1981), p 343.

[12] Warren & Benson, *Thetis,* p 135.

[13] Warren & Benson, *Thetis,* e.g. The treatment of survivor Ldg. Stoker Walter Arnold after the disaster and interview with Derek Arnold.

[14] Warren & Benson, *Thetis,* p 32.

[15] Letter from Patrick Strevens to BBC Radio Drama Dept. Patrick was the son of the Captain of the Trinity House Vessel *Beacon* which was equipped with heavy lifting gear. The Royal Navy never asked for any assistance from this vessel.

[16] Letter offering assistance from Utility Airways of Hooton, Cheshire, to Secretary of The Admiralty 1st July 1939. Rejected by Admiralty reply of 10th July 1939/ PRO ADM116/6885.

[17] Unpublished confidential document from Internal Navy Enquiry Board, 'Finding of the Board of Enquiry into the loss of HMS *Thetis*', RN Submarine Museum, Gosport / Fort Blockhouse Archives, 29.6.39. Also held in PRO.

[18] *Liverpool Echo,* June 6th 1939.

[19] *Daily Express,* 2nd June 1939 .

[20] Oral evidence from interviews and letters; e.g. Agnes Gaul, and Brenda Gore - Brown, daughter of R. D. Glenn, RN Commissioning Engineer aboard *Thetis,* letter to D.Roberts of 14.12.98.

[21] David Zeni, *The Forgotten Empress - The Empress of Ireland Story* (Avid Publications 2000)

[22] Zeni, *The Forgotten Empress,* p 7.

References : Class: Officers, Men & Civilians

[1] E.J.Hobsbawm, *Industry and Empire - from 1750 to the present day* (Middlesex, Pelican Books, 1968), p 16 .

[2] R. Dahrendorf, *On Britain* (London, British Broadcasting Corporation Books , 1982).

[3] Dahrendorf, *On Britain* p 55.

[4] Interview with Commander Jeff Tall R.N (Rt.), 20.1.98.

[5] Tall interview, 20.1.98.

[6] D. Mathew, *British Seamen* (London, William Collins, 1943).

[7] Mathew, *British Seamen* p 48.

[8] Oral History Recordings, Lower Deck 1910 - 1922, Imperial War Museum, (henceforth cited as IWM), No. 000660/24, Reel 23, Adshead, Gilbert, 3rd Class Engine Room Artificer RN, 1909 - 1923.

[9] Certificate of the Service of John Ifor Roberts in the Royal Navy, Official No. KX 155185. In the possession of W.D.Roberts.

[10] A. Ereira, *The Invergordon Mutiny* (London, Routledge & Kegan Paul, 1981).

[11] A. Carew, *The Lower Deck of the Royal Navy 1900 -1939 - Invergordon in Perspective* (Manchester, Manchester University Press, 1981).

[12] Barry Duncan, *Invergordon 31 - How the men of the RN struck and won* (Southampton, published by the author, 1976).

[13] Duncan, *Invergordon 31,* p 5.

[14] L.F. Guttridge, *MUTINY - A History of Naval Insurrection* (Shepperton, Ian Allan Publishing, 1992).

[15] Paul Thompson, *The Voice of the Past - Oral History* (Oxford, Oxford University Press, 1978).

[16] *The Invergordon Mutiny 1931* and *Lower Deck 1910 - 1922* (London, IWM Publications, 1987).

[17] IWM, Oral History Recordings, Lower Deck 1910-1922, Ref. No.000679/48, Reel 25, Clarkson, George Michael, Joiner 1st Class. RN 1905-1937.

[18] IWM, Oral History Recordings, Lower Deck 1910-1922, Ref. No 000670/02, Reel 02, Clarke, Allan Arthur, Signalman. RN 1917-1923.

[19] E. Smithies & C.J. Bruce, *War at Sea 1939 - 1945* (London, Constable, 1992).

[20] Smithies & Bruce, *War at Sea,* p2.

[21] IWM, Clarkson, George Michael, Joiner 1st Class, R27.

[22] IWM, Clarkson, George Michael, Joiner 1st Class, R27.

[23] IWM, Oral History Recordings, The Invergordon Mutiny 1931, Ref.No. 6672/3, Len Wincott, Able Seaman, RN, R2.

[24] IWM Oral History Recordings, The Invergordon Mutiny 1931, Ref.No. 5835, Charles Edward Wild, Stoker 2nd Class, RN .

[25] IWM, Oral History Recordings, The Invergordon Mutiny 1931, Ref.No. 5852/2, William Patrick Wood, Boy Seaman, RN, R2.

[26] IWM, William Patrick Wood.

[27] Ereira, *The Invergordon Mutiny,* p 156.

[28] Guttridge, *MUTINY,* p198.
[29] Guttridge, *MUTINY,* all of Chapter 14.
[30] Guttridge, *MUTINY,* p2.
[31] Guttridge, *MUTINY,* p3.
[32] Evidence from interview, Marjorie Beattie (nee Watterson).

[33] Beattie interview.

References: The *Thetis* Disaster

[1] Warren & Benson, *Thetis,* p14.
[2] H. J. Tabb and S. A. T. Warren, 'Quality Control applied to Nuclear Submarine Construction', *Quarterly Transactions,* Royal Institute of Naval Architects, 1966, Vol.108.
[3] Warren & Benson, *Thetis,* p160.
[4] Warren & Benson, *Thetis,* p160.
[5] Warren & Benson, *Thetis,* p16.
[6] Warren & Benson, *Thetis,* p17.
[7] Evidence from interview, John Glenn, son of Roy Glenn.
[8] Evidence from interview, Derek Arnold, son of Walter Arnold.
[9] Warren & Benson, *Thetis,* p16.
[10] Glenn Interview.
[11] Glenn Interview.
[12] Warren & Benson, *Thetis,* p36.
[13] Warren & Benson, *Thetis,* p41.
[14] Further details of times, tonnage, speeds etc. can be obtained from Warren & Benson, *Thetis,* pp 118-122.
[15] Once again the minute by minute detailed treatment can be found in Warren & Benson, *Thetis,* pp 101-102.
[16] *Daily Express,* June 6th 1939, p6.
[17] Public Records Office Record Ref. ADM/116
[18] As note 17

References: The *Thetis* Disaster Narrated

[1] Interview with Jean Newton (nee Beattie), daughter of William Beattie, Cammell Laird Caulker, lost on *Thetis.*
[2] BBC News Bulletin Transcript for 2.6.1939 10.45pm (BBC Manchester Radio Archives).
[3] BBC News Bulletin Transcript for 3.6.1939 10.30am (BBC Manchester Radio Archives).
[4] BBC News Bulletin Transcript for 3.6.1939 9.00pm (BBC Manchester Radio Archives).
[5] Public Records Office Record Ref. ADM/116, correspondence between Liverpool and Glasgow Salvage Co. and Messers, Cammell Laird and Company.
[6] Granada Television News, 1st June 1989.
[7] *Daily Express,* June 6th 1939, p 6.
[8] *The Sporting Mail and Morning News,* June 2nd 1939.

[9] Newspaper clipping from the collection of Derek Arnold, Origin Unknown, probable date 2nd June 1939.

[10] *Daily Herald,* June 3rd 1939, p 2.

[11] *Daily Herald,* June 3rd 1939, p 2.

[12] *Daily Herald,* June 3rd 1939, p 2.

[13] *Daily Herald,* June 3rd 1939, p 2.

[14] *Daily Herald,* June 3rd 1939, p 2.

[15] *Daily Herald,* June 3rd 1939, p 2.

[16] H.P.K. Oram, edited by Wendy Harris, *The Rogue's Yarn - The Sea Going Life of Captain 'Joe' Oram* (London, Leo Cooper, 1993), p 184.

[17] *The London Evening Standard,* July 5th 1939.

[18] *The London Evening Standard,* July 5th 1939.

[19] H.P.K.Oram, edited by Wendy Harris, *'The Rogue's Yarn'* .

[20] H.P.K.Oram, *'The Rogue's Yarn'* p167.

[21] H.P.K.Oram, *'The Rogue's Yarn'* p174.

[22] Report of the Tribunal of Enquiry into the loss of HMS *Thetis* (London, HMSO, April 1940).

[23] *The London Evening News,* June 6th 1939, p unknown.

[24] Granada Television News, 1st June 1989.

[25] Newspaper clipping from the collection of Derek Arnold, origin unknown, probable date 2nd June 1939.

[26] Interview with anonymous newspaper Advertising Executive. September 1997.

[27] *Daily Herald,* June 6th 1939.

[28] Telephone enquiry, the Charities Commission, Queens Dock, Liverpool.1.10.97.

[29] Warren & Benson, *Thetis,* p 137.

References: Aftermath and Today

[1] Interview with Victoria 'May' Levelle, formerly Summers, widow of George Summers, Electrician, lost on *Thetis.*

[2] Evidence from interview, not to be identified.

[3] Gaul interview.

[4] Gaul Interview.

[5] Levelle Interview.

[6] Newton Interview.

[7] Interviews with Peter Wells, son of Stoker Petty Officer J.W. Wells, lost on *Thetis.*

[8] Correspondence to Mrs.Dorothy Wells, 'unmarried wife' of Stoker Petty Officer J.W. Wells, lost on *Thetis,* from The Secretary of the Admiralty, London SW1, various dates between 1951 and 1952.

[9] Correspondence from Commander D.P.B. 'Paddy' Ryan OBE, RN, Rt., 20th March 1998.

[10] Interview with Edith Bleakley (nee Crombleholme), sister of Able Seaman Stanley Crombleholme, lost on *Thetis.*

[11] Warren & Benson, *Thetis*, p 137.
[12] Warren & Benson, *Thetis*, p 137.
[13] Letter from David Roberts to Frank Field MP, Nov.4th 1998.
[14] Correspondence from Mr.Frank Field MP, Nov.11th 1997.
[15] Correspondence from Barclays Bank Press Office, Asmita Kapadia, Jan.12th 1998.
[16] Barclays Bank, Jan.12th 1998.
[17] Correspondence from D. Roberts to Royal Naval Benevolent Trust, (henceforth RNBT), 19th December 1997.
[18] Correspondence from RNBT, D.C. Gallamore, Grants Secretary, 23.12.97.
[19] Correspondence from RNBT, Commander Jeremy Owens RN, Chief Executive of the RNBT, 5th April 1998.
[20] The £1000 increase is taken from an enclosure to the **same letter** from the RNBT, whilst the £250,000 figure is a speculative one from the son of a victim, Commander D.P.B. 'Paddy' Ryan OBE RN (Rt.).
[21] Letter from H.C.B. Myers to Rt. Hon. Montague Collet - Norman P.C., D.S.O. 28th June 1940. Bank of England Archives.
[22] Correspondence from RNBT, 5th April 1998.
[23] Letter from Royal Naval Museum Portsmouth. Matthew Sheldon- Curator of Manuscripts. 1.6.98
[24] Letter from Mr.D.Hosken. Clerk to the Council, Penwith District Council, Penzance, Cornwall. 3rd March 1999. Penwith D.C launched and managed the Penlee Disaster Fund.
[25] Interview, Mrs. Joan Traynor, Treasurer, Hillsborough Family Support Group.
[26] Letter from Bank of England, Mr. H.G. Gillett, 29.4.98.
[27] E.g. Writ issued in the High Court of Justice, King's Bench Division on Behalf on Victoria Summers against Cammell Laird, Lieut. Frederick Woods, Sybil Bolus and Matilda Ann Hambrook, 28th November 1939, PRO. ADM 116 TS32/115.
[28] See copies of damages claims e.g. Victoria 'May' Summers, PRO. ADM 116.
[29] Personal Minute from First Sea Lord Winston Spencer Churchill. No.194, PRO. ADM116/4115, Case 5469.
[30] Reply from Second Sea Lord to personal minute no 194, PRO. ADM116/4115, Case 5469.
[31] Reply from Second Sea Lord, see ref. 30.
[32] Unpublished confidential document from Internal Navy Enquiry Board.
[33] Interview with Howard Woods, son of Lieut. Frederick Woods, escaped from *Thetis*.
[34] Woods interview.

References: The Case for Arnold

[1] Warren & Benson, *Thetis* - The Admiralty Regrets p131
[2] PRO. ADM 116/6885
[3] PRO ADM 116/4115 case 5469. Report from Admiralty agents Batesons of 14 Castle Street, Liverpool, to the Admiralty 4th July 1940.
[4] As note 3
[5] As note 3

Bibliography and Sources

Public Record Office, Kew, London
Reference Numbers / Files pertaining to the loss of HMS *Thetis* in 1939.
ADM1/ 14365
ADM116/ 4115
ADM116/4311
ADM116/4429
ADM116/4460
ADM 116 / 3819 Case 5488 vol. 3
ADM116 / 3820 Case 5488 vol. 4
ADM116 / 3821 Case 5488 vol. 5
ADM116 / 3822 Case 5488 vol. 6

Imperial War Museum Dept. of Sound Archives, Lambeth, London.
Reference Numbers of archive interviews consulted (R= Reel Number).
Carr, Nicholas Smiles. 5809/1 R1
Cloake C . 5804/1 R1
Day, George 6667/2 R2
Wild , Charles Edward 5835/1 R1
Wincott, Len 6672/3 R2 & R3
Wood, William Patrick. 5852/2 R2
Adshead, Gilbert 000660/24 R24
Basford, Walter Nicholson 000669/19 R17
Bevis, Cyril Charles 000756/06 R06
Clarke, Allan Arthur 000670/05 R01
Clarkson, George Michael 000679/48 R25
Fox, Ernest George 000735/15 R09
Parsons, William Allen 000736/09 R07
Willis, Reginald 000758/15 R13
Wood, William Patrick 5852/2 R2

Royal Naval Submarine Museum, Gosport / Fort Blockhouse.
Unpublished confidential document from Internal Navy Enquiry Board. Finding of
the Board of Enquiry into the loss of HMS *Thetis*. 29.6.39. RN Submarine Museum.
Gosport/ Fort Blockhouse Archives. Also in PRO.

BBC Radio Archives.
News Bulletins Transcripts for first week in June 1939. Copies consulted courtesy of
Mr. Fred Lawless.

Newspapers

Daily Express, 2nd June 1939.
Daily Express, June 6th 1939.
Daily Herald, June 3rd 1939.
Daily Herald, June 6th 1939.
Liverpool Echo, June 6th 1939.
The London Evening News, June 6th 1939.
The London Evening Standard, July 5th 1939.
The Sporting Mail and Morning News, June 2nd 1939.

Other Records

Report of the Tribunal of Enquiry into the loss of HMS *Thetis* (London. HMSO. April 1940).

Interviews (both Audio and Video).

Allen, Bill, son of Ldg. Telegraphist William Earnest Allen, lost on *Thetis.*

Arnold, Derek, son of Ldg. Stoker Walter Arnold, escaped from *Thetis.*

Beattie (nee Watterson), Marjorie, daughter of William Watterson, Cammell Laird Ships Fitter, lost on *Thetis.*

Bleakley (nee Crombleholme), Edith, sister of Able Seaman Stanley Crombleholme, lost on *Thetis.*

Craven, John, son of Archie Craven, Cammell Laird Ships Fitter, lost on *Thetis.*

Daly (nee Allen) Cynthia, daughter of Ldg. Telegraphist William Earnest Allen, lost on *Thetis.*

Dillon - Shallard, Harry, son of Harrry Dillon-Shallard, Chief Stoker, lost on *Thetis.*

Gaul (nee Summers), Agnes, daughter of George Summers, Cammell Laird Electrician, lost on *Thetis.*

Glenn, John, son of RN Commissioned Engineer Roy Glenn, lost on *Thetis.*

Homer, Hanley, son of Richard Homer, Cammell Laird Engine Fitter, lost on *Thetis.*

Kipling, Robert, son of Robert Kipling, Cammell Laird Foreman Caulker, lost on *Thetis.*

Levelle, (formerly Summers), Victoria 'May', widow of George Summers, Cammell Laird Electrician, lost on *Thetis.* .

Moore (nee Robinson) Barbara, daughter of Cammell Laird Chief Engineer Arthur Robinson, lost on *Thetis.*

Newton (nee Beattie), Jean, daughter of William Beattie, Cammell Laird Caulker, lost on *Thetis.*

Ryan, Paddy, son of Lieut. Patrick Edward James Ryan, lost on *Thetis.*

Smithers, Edith G., of Woking Surrey, widow of Petty Officer C.E.Smithers, lost on *Thetis.*

Wells, Peter, son of Stoker Petty Officer J.W.Wells lost on *Thetis*.

Woods, Howard, son of Lieut. Frederick Woods, escaped from *Thetis*. Elder brother of Norman Douglas Willcox, Mersey Pilot, lost on *Thetis*.

Books & Journals

Carew, A. *The Lower Deck of the Royal Navy 1900-1939 - Invergordon in Perspective,* (Manchester, Manchester University Press, 1981).

Dahrendorf, R., *On Britain,* (London, British Broadcasting Corporation Books, 1982).

Duncan, Barry, *Invergordon 31- How the men of the RN struck and won,* (Southampton, published by the author, 1976).

Ereira, A., *The Invergordon Mutiny,* (London, Routledge & Kegan Paul, 1981).

Guttridge, L. F., *MUTINY - A History of Naval Insurrection,* (Shepperton, Ian Allan Publishing, 1992).

Hobsbawm, E. J., *Industry and Empire - from 1750 to the present day,* (Middlesex, Pelican Books, 1968).

The Invergordon Mutiny 1931, (Imperial War Museum Publications, London, 1987).

Lower Deck 1910 - 1922, (Imperial War Museum Publications, London, 1987).

Mathew, D., *British Seamen,* (London, William Collins, 1943).

Oram, H. P. K., edited by Wendy Harris, *The Rogue's Yarn –The Sea Going Life of Captain 'Joe' Oram,* (London, Leo Cooper, 1993).

Roberts, David, *Cammell Laird - the golden years,* (Manchester, Printwise Publications, 1991. [Reprinted edition, Merseyside, Avid Publications, 1998]).

Roberts, David., *Life at Lairds - memories of working shipyard men,* (Merseyside, Avid Publications, 1993).

Simpson, Colin. *Lusitania,* (Merseyside, Avid Publications, 1997).

Smithies E. & Bruce C. J., *War at Sea 1939-1945,* (London, Constable, 1992).

Tabb, H. J. & Warren, S. A. T., 'Quality Control applied to Nuclear Submarine Construction', *Quarterly Transactions,* Royal Institute of Naval Architects, 1966 Vol. 108.

Thompson, Paul, *The voice of the Past - Oral History,* (Oxford, Oxford University Press, 1978).

Waller, P.J., *Democracy and Sectarianism - a political and social history of Liverpool 1868 - 1939,* (Liverpool, Liverpool University Press, 1981).

Warren C. & Benson J., *The Admiralty Regrets,* (London, Harrop, 1956).

Warren C. & Benson J., *Thetis - The Admiralty Regrets - the disaster in Liverpool Bay,* edited by David Roberts, Foreword by Derek Arnold, Postscript by David Roberts, (Merseyside, Avid Publications, 1997).

Winn, Godfrey., *Home from the sea- Life on the Lower Deck,* (London, Hutchinson, 1944).
Zeni, David., *The Forgotten Empress - The Empress of Ireland Story,* (Tiverton, Devon, Halsgrove, 1998).

Other Sources

Granada Television News. 1st June 1989. Private collection of Derek Arnold.
Roberts, W. David. *Cammell Laird - Old Ships and Hardships - the story of a shipyard,* (Merseyside, Avid Publications, 1994). Film. Duration 56 minutes, Produced, Directed & Narrated by David Roberts .
The authors own experiences growing up in Birkenhead from a shipbuilding family and serving his own five year engineering apprenticeship as a mechanical fitter in the Birkenhead shipyard of Cammell Laird & Co. Ltd. (Shipbuilders & Engineers) during the 1960's.

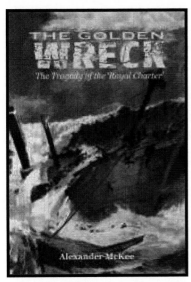

THE GOLDEN WRECK

Alexander McKee

The effects of the hurricane of October 1849 were to shock the nation. 133 ships were sunk, 90 were badly damaged and almost 800 people lost their lives.

More than half of those that perished were on one ship - The *Royal Charter*.

After two months at sea voyaging more than 12,000 miles from the Australian goldfields, disaster struck off Anglesey when she was just hours away from her home port of Liverpool.

Many of her passengers were returning home with the fruits of their labours

-GOLD!

The worst shipwreck in Welsh history, this is the story of the *Royal Charter*...and her gold.

ISBN 978 1 902964 02 7 £14.50

JUST NUISANCE AB - His full story

by Terence Sisson

The amazing but true story of the only dog that was officially enlisted into the British Royal Navy, a Great Dane whose name was Nuisance, his official rank and name was AB Just Nuisance. Famed for his preference for the company of navy ratings (he wasn't too keen on Officers) in and around the famous World War II naval base of Simonstown, South Africa, Nuisance helped many a sailor rejoin his ship after a night on the town.

Today his own statue overlooking the bay off the Cape of Good Hope commemorates AB Just Nuisance.

£10.00

- Aftermath of a disaster

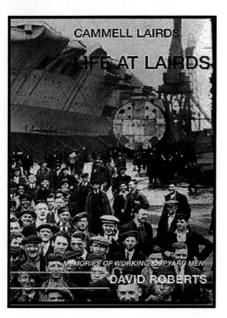

Life at Lairds - 'Memories of Working Shipyard Men'
by David Roberts

'The time may not be far off when young people will ask, What did they do there, what were they like? This book answers the questions......'

Sea Breezes

'A book full of anecdotes and rich in humanity...a piece of social history.....'

Liverpool Echo

ISBN 0 9521020 1 3   £9.00

CAMMELL LAIRD - THE GOLDEN YEARS
by David Roberts.
With a foreword by Frank Field MP.

'Captures life in the prosperous years at the historic Birkenhead shipyard......'
Liverpool Echo

'Puts into perspective ... the strikes... the Polaris contract... and those who worked at the yard...' Sea Breezes

ISBN 0 9521020 2 1   £9.00.

FORGOTTEN EMPRESS
- The Tragedy of the Empress of Ireland
- by David Zeni

Tells the fascinating story of the Canadian Pacific Passenger liner RMS *Empress of Ireland*. On her way home to Liverpool from Canada, she was sunk in a collision on the St. Lawrence River. Two years after the *Titanic*, it was, in terms of passenger fatalities, an even greater tragedy. These two ships, along with the *Lusitania*, form a triumvirate of maritime tragedies, all within a three-year period, that sent shock waves around the world.

Yet whilst *Titanic* and *Lusitania* seem to be almost household names, the disaster that befell the Empress of Ireland has until now always been shrouded in the cloak of history, as impenetrable as the fog that brought about her total loss, along with 1,012 lives, on 29th May 1914. With a chilling connection to the 'Crippen Murders' and containing never-before-published material.

Forgotten Empress grips the reader in such a way it is hard to put aside... a thoroughly excellent book.

'...dubbed 'The 'Forgotten Empress'...the second in a shocking trio of tragedies at sea...sandwiched in between the disasters of the Titanic and the Lusitania, ...it was a sudden death... that sent Liverpool into mourning...' Liverpool Echo

' Zeni brings a fresh, moment by moment urgency to this real life tragic drama' Winnipeg Free Press

ISBN   978-1-902964-15-7   £14.50

- Aftermath of a disaster

CHILDREN OF THE BENARES
- by RALPH BARKER

Foreword by Beth Williams (nee Cummings) - the only Liverpool Survivor.

The Ellerman and City passenger liner City of Benares left Liverpool on Friday 13th September 1940 carrying a precious cargo - 90 children from the bombed cities of Britain bound for safe haven away from the war - to Canada.

Four days later, without warning, she was torpedoed and sunk by a German U-boat in mid - Atlantic. 256 people were lost including, at first count, 83 of the evacuee children.

An event that shocked the world in its brutality, much use of the atrocity was made by the British authorities in an attempt to persuade the United States into joining the conflict.

However it was not long before the parents of the lost children, who had entrusted their loved ones to the evacuation scheme, began to suspect those same authorities of neglect, when they learned that the promised naval escort for the convoy had abandoned the unarmed ships twenty-one hours before the U-boat struck!

There were allegations of crew rushing the lifeboats, poor equipment and even racial prejudice in the ensuing clamour for an explanation. Yet somehow a formal investigation was avoided and the scandal covered up.

Children of the Benares is a gripping story of the disaster itself and exposes at last what went on behind the scenes at the Ministry of Shipping and the British Admiralty. It is a chilling tale of fallibility and human survival.

ISBN 978-1-902964-07-2   £15.50

BLUE FUNNEL
- VOYAGE EAST
by Award winning author
Richard Woodman

What was life like aboard a British vessel in the last great days of the Merchant Navy?
Blue Funnel - Voyage East takes us in one of the Holt Line's 'China Boats' on a typical trip out of the Mersey, to the Far East and back again by way of Suez. The time is the 1960s and it is a style of seafaring now totally lost among today's container ships and roll on - roll off ferries.
We keep the long watches of the night; observe officers and men, sea and weather, in every mood. We learn about the transvestites of Singapore and the almond-eyed whores of Hong Kong, as well as the intricacies of derricks and cargo stowage - human hair and hog bristle from China, liquid latex and palm oil from Malaya. We can puzzle over the mysteries of navigation, what motivates the First Mate and why any sane man should go to sea, far from home and the love of good women.
The author draws on his many years service in Blue Funnel cargo liners to capture the sights, smells, enormous satisfactions and aching sadness that attended the 'carriage of general cargo in open stows'.

'This is life at sea, warts and all, and a better book because of it.'
..........Sea Breezes

'...describes an ordinary voyage, on an ordinary cargo ship through the eyes of an ordinary officer. He describes it exactly. Not for women and children.' ………….. Fairplay

'Richard Woodman has managed to capture the very essence of seagoing of the period... For those who never went to sea VOYAGE EAST will be an
illuminating read, for those who did, it will bring a wry smile to their face and perhaps a wistful look over their shoulder.' Seascape

ISBN 978-1-902964-04-1 £15.50

- Aftermath of a disaster

RUNCORN - A TOWN NOT SO NEW

by H.F. STARKEY

To many people Runcorn is a New Town but it is also an ancient one.
Its history goes back to a third century Roman settlement on Halton Brow and
it was mentioned in the Anglo-Saxon Chronicle for 914.
However this book concerns the town's recent history. It is a pictorial record of
a town which has undergone profound change. The archive photographs recall
forgotten vistas as well as traditional customs and practices of times past
together with vanished industries, rural landscapes and buildings which may now
be beyond the memories of even the oldest Runcornians.
H.F. (Bert) Starkey has written numerous books on the towns history and his
latest book aims to present different aspects of life by using photographs which
have never been seen before. It is hoped that this book will bring back
memories for old Runcornians and that it will introduce younger Runcorn folk
and newcomers to the town's interesting story.

ISBN 978-1-902964-08-9 £15.00

DVD

'Cammell Laird, Old Ships and Hardships'
- The Story of a Shipyard.

After an extensive search for moving footage of this world famous shipyard at work a video of the history of this shipyard has at last been compiled. How Cammell Laird served the nation through two World Wars, building world famous vessels like the Rodney, Hood, Mauritania, Ark Royal, Windsor Castle and many more, up to the tragic day in 1993 when Lairds was shut down.

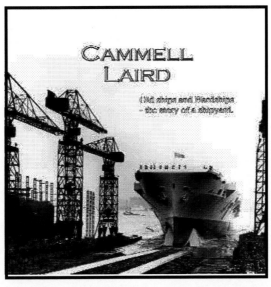

The story of the yard is also told through the voices of the men who worked at Lairds; Welders, Cranedrivers, Electricians and Plumbers, they tell of the hardships of building ships in all weathers and the lighter moments that came from some of the 'characters' of the yard.

'contains rare archive film & photographs that anyone connected with the world famous shipyard will remember and enjoy.'....... Birkenhead News

Running time approx: 56.00 mins -. £17.95

- Aftermath of a disaster

Blue Funnel - Voyages and Voices
Compiled with the help of never before published film taken all over the world by some of those men who actually sailed with 'Blueys' on many of their well-known vessels.
Contains some of the sights and sounds of typical Blue Funnel voyages; leaving the home shores of the UK, sailing through both the Suez and Panama canals, the legendary gilly gilly man, Hong Kong, Singapore, Kobe, Tokyo, and other 'exotic' ports.
We also see and hear the thoughts and memories of some of those who actually sailed with 'Blueys' over their working lives, from Able Seaman to Captain, Steward to Engineer.

'*...The film is a must for anyone who sailed with 'Blueys' or who sailed in the merchant navy of old...*' Sea Breezes
Running time approx.: 56.00 mins -. £17.95

Blue Funnel - Voyages and Voices
-Take Two

After the success of the first Blue Funnel DVD, here is the next one...Voyages and Voices - Take 2.
Since the first film ex - Alfred Holt men have popped up all over the world with their amazing old cine footage and photographs. These coupled with more memories of those who actually sailed with Blue Funnel, provide us with another glimpse of what the heydays of the British merchant navy, and in particular Holt's, was like.
This time we also include some moving film of the other arm of Holts, the Glen Line or Red Funnel ships, just as important, remembered and revered as their 'blue sisters'.

'*...an outstanding DVD....*' - Shipping Today & Yesterday

'*...an excellent film....packed to the gunwhales....an hour of sheer pleasure*'
- Sea Breezes
Running time approx: 60.00 mins -. £17.95